THE

GRACE OF CHRIST,

OR

SINNERS SAVED

BY

UNMERITED KINDNESS.

BY WM. S. PLUMER, D.D.

"We believe that through the grace of our Lord Jesus Christ we shall be saved even as they."—Acts xv. 11.

PHILADELPHIA:
PRESBYTERIAN BOARD OF PUBLICATION,
No. 821 CHESTNUT STREET.

Stereotyped by Slote & Mooney, Philadelphia.

Wm. S. Martien, Printer.

CONTENTS.

CHAPTER XII.

CHAPTER XIII.

CHAPTER XIV.

CHAPTER XV.

CHAPTER XVI.

CHAPTER XVII.

CHAPTER XVIII.

CHAPTER XIX.

CHAPTER XX.

CHAPTER XXI.

CHAPTER XXII.

CHAPTER XXIII.

CHAPTER XXIV.

CHAPTER XXV.

CHAPTER XXVI.

CHAPTER XXVII.

CHAPTER XXVIII.

CHAPTER XXIX.

CHAPTER XXX.

CHAPTER XXXI.

CHAPTER XXXII.

CHAPTER XXXIII.

CHAPTER XXXIV.

CHAPTER XXXV.

CHAPTER XXXVI.

CHAPTER XXXVII.

CHAPTER XXXVIII.

THE

GRACE OF CHRIST.

CHAPTER I.

INTRODUCTION.

Is salvation by grace, or is it of debt? Did God owe it to man to provide for him a Saviour? Do men deserve all the wrath revealed from heaven against ungodliness? Is the sentence of condemnation just? Cannot human merits avail something towards eternal happiness? Is man able to turn himself to God and subdue his own sins? Is the ruin of the soul by sin partial, or total? Are men very far gone from righteousness before divine grace renews them? When Christ came, what did he do and suffer for us? How does his mediation avail for the lost? Is there mercy for all, who come to God through Jesus Christ? Are the provisions of the gospel suited to the wants of men? Is salvation necessary? Is it infinitely important? Is it possible?

These and many similar questions are continually undergoing discussion. In fact they are themes well worthy of the closest and most solemn inquiry. They are of paramount and universal interest. He, who seeks not the truth in these matters, must be found guilty of criminal recklessness. Whatever else may claim his attention, here are matters of still higher importance. These things pertain to the well-being of man and the honour of God. They lay hold of eternity. No man ever gave up his mind with too much candour, with undue love of truth, or with excessive earnestness to the investigation of the Scriptures on themes of so vast moment.

It ought not to be denied that there are difficulties in the way of every inquirer. The prejudices of men are strong and their passions violent. These mightily hinder our reception of the truth. The world also is full of error. Men love darkness rather than light. The friends of sound doctrine are often both timid and supine. The propagators of false notions are lively and confident. It is easy to embrace error. To know the right way demands patience, inquiry, humility. The great things of God are not to be learned by those who restrain prayer. How few men are found crying, "Open thou mine eyes, that I may behold wondrous things out of thy law!"

Yet it is possible by the aid of God's word and Spirit to learn the truth on all these matters. Thousands have made that great attainment. They have lived long lives and died in the possession and profession of the truth as it is in Jesus. When God bids us search the Scriptures, he sends us not on a fool's errand, nor commands an impossible task. Indeed it is a part of God's plan concerning his people that "we all come in the unity of the faith, and of the knowledge of the Son of God, unto a perfect man, unto the stature of the fulness of Christ: that we henceforth be no more children, tossed to and fro, and carried about with every wind of doctrine, by the sleight of men, and cunning craftiness, whereby they lie in wait to deceive." Eph. iv. 13, 14. And so it has happened that from the first founding of the Church of God, those, who gave the best evidence of being taught of God, have remarkably agreed in the great truths of religion. The matters on which they have fully harmonized have been like the continents and larger islands of our globe, while those, on which they have doubted or differed, may be compared to the lesser islands of the sea, many of which are but barren rocks or beds of sand. This has been demonstrably true since the founding of the Christian Church. The abundant outpouring of the Holy Spirit was the first glorious event succeeding the ascension of Christ. The second was the calling of the Gentiles, and the opening of a wide and effectual door to their conversion. This was hailed with joy by the truly pious portion of the Jewish nation. When Peter gave them an account of the commencement of this work, "they glorified God, saying, Then hath God also to the Gentiles granted repentance unto life." Acts xi. 18. This is what we should naturally expect. If a man loves God, whom he has not seen, he is sure to love his brother, whom he has seen. He, who in his heart glorifies Christ, will desire that all men should do the same. A converted man, who had no joy at seeing sinners coming to Christ, would be a monster, such as has never yet appeared. The bringing in of the Gentiles gave rise to questions, the settlement of which required the calling of a Synod, consisting of apostles, elders and brethren. The chief matter before the council respected the relation of the converts from paganism to the ceremonial law of Moses. But in his address Peter gave a summary of the faith of himself and ot his brethren. These are his words: "We believe that through the grace of our Lord Jesus Christ, we shall be saved even as they." Concerning the method and Author of salvation there was among them no disagreement. He therefore speaks for all, "We believe;" and he says there is but one scheme of mercy for Jew and Gentile. "We" and "they" relate to the Israelites and the pagans. Christ broke down the middle wall of partition between them, abolishing their old mutual enmity by his cross, and making them one in him. His church is not provincial or national, but catholic or universal. It is not confined to any one people, but was intended for the whole race, and embraces all true believers.

Thus Simon Peter expressed the faith of the church of Christ nineteen years after our Lord's ascension to glory. Whatever reluctance some have had to publishing their creed, the apostles had none. Their great object was to let men know what and why they believed. There is no solid argument against the use of doctrinal formulas, long or short, if they are sound, scriptural, and well-understood. They should express the truth in clear terms, and be honestly held before they are professed. "Prove all things; hold fast that which is good." 1 Thess. v. 21. "Hold fast the form of sound words, which thou hast heard of me, in faith and love which is in Christ Jesus." 2 Tim. i. 13. The salvation of the gospel is common to all, who are "sanctified by God the Father, preserved in Jesus Christ, and called." Jude 3. In this first Synod we have the Christian faith in epitome.

From that age to the present, the true faith has often been obscured, marred and corrupted by many, yet it has always won the love and confidence of persons and communities, just in proportion as they loved our Lord Jesus Christ, and abounded in the knowledge of his salvation. At times it has seemed as if all the world would soon be drunken with the sorcery of fatal error. But when the enemy has come in like a flood, the Spirit of the Lord has lifted up a standard against him; and the cause of truth and righteousness has revived.

As the character of this work is not polemic but practical, the references to books and pages are entirely omitted in the margin. The form of the work is popular, not scientific. It is designed not for the few, but for the masses. The chief object aimed at is to lead men to the foot of the cross, to encourage them to make Christ all and in all, to seek no other way of mercy but by the Redeemer, to satisfy all, who revere God's word, of the perfect safety of a soul resting on the grace of Christ, and on that alone for all it needs for its complete deliverance from sin and misery, and so to comfort all that mourn for sin, give courage to the timid but real disciple of Christ, and ultimately to give all the glory to him, to whom it belongs.

If men are saved by grace, it is because they need mercy; and if men are sinners they require a Saviour. The first subject therefore in this treatise is the extent of the wants of men. The second is the supply of those wants in the grace of our Lord Jesus Christ.

The remainder of the work is taken up in considering some things growing out of the preceding discussions.

May He, to whom we owe all that is pleasant in our history, and all that is animating in our prospects, graciously own this book, and bless its pages to the enlightening, comforting, edifying and saving of many souls.

CHAPTER II.

ALL MEN ARE SINNERS.

JEWS and Gentiles, Greeks and Barbarians, bond and free, are sinners. If they are not, they need not mercy but mere justice. Yet inspired men never preached the doctrine of human innocence. They all knew and taught just the reverse. In the first chapter of his epistle to the Romans, Paul clearly proves that the Gentiles are sinners: "When they knew God, they glorified him not as God, neither were thankful, but became vain in their imaginations, and their foolish heart was darkened. Professing themselves to be wise, they became fools; and changed the glory of the incorruptible God into an image made like to corruptible man, and to birds, and four-footed beasts, and creeping things. Wherefore God also gave them up to uncleanness through the lusts of their own hearts, to dishonour their own bodies between themselves; who changed the truth of God into a lie, and worshipped and served the creature more than the Creator, who is blessed for ever. Amen. For this cause God gave them up to vile affections. * * * And even as they did not like to retain God in their knowledge, God gave them up to a reprobate mind to do those things which are not convenient; being filled with all unrighteousness, fornication, wickedness, covetousness, maliciousness; full of envy, murder, debate, deceit, malignity,

2

whisperers, backbiters, haters of God, despiteful, proud, boasters, inventors of evil things, disobedient to parents, without understanding, covenant-breakers, without natural affection, implacable, unmerciful; who knowing the judgment of God, that they which commit such things are worthy of death, not only do the same, but have pleasure in them that do them." Could reasoning be more sound and conclusive? There is no way of escaping its force. Beyond a question the Gentiles are sinners.

In the third chapter of the same epistle Paul shows that all men, not excepting the Jews, are sinners: "What then? are we [Jews] better than they [Gentiles]? No, in no wise: for we have before proved both Jews and Gentiles, that they are all under sin; as it is written, There is none righteous, no, not one. There is none that understandeth, there is none that seeketh after God. They are all gone out of the way; they are together become unprofitable; there is none that doeth good, no, not one. Their throat is an open sepulchre; with their tongues they have used deceit; the poison of asps is under their lips; whose mouth is full of cursing and bitterness. Their feet are swift to shed blood. Destruction and misery are in their ways; and the way of peace have they not known. There is no fear of God before their eyes." More direct or cogent reasoning is no where found. It covers all cases. As a fair inference from it the apostle says, every mouth must be stopped, and all the world stand guilty before God, and that by the deeds of the law there shall no flesh be justified in his sight.

No man will deny that our views of human guilt or innocence, human merit or demerit, will materially modify all our views in religion. This doctrine of the sinfulness of man is therefore, if true, very important, and so it may be well to look further at the arguments by which it is maintained. If men are enemies of God, it is high time they should know it. What then is the testimony of the Holy Ghost in other parts of Scripture? It is peculiarly clear: "There is no man that sinneth not." 1 Kings viii. 46. "If (God) will contend with (man), he cannot answer one of a thousand." Job ix. 3. "Enter not into judgment with thy servant, for in thy sight shall no man living be justified." Psa. cxliii. 2. "There is not a just man upon earth that doeth good and sinneth not." Ecc. vii. 20. "If we say that we have no sin, we deceive ourselves and the truth is not in us." "If we say that we have not sinned, we make him a liar, and his word is not in us." 1 John i. 8, 10. In all the range of sober writings on serious matters, where can you find more pointed and explicit declarations? Who dare take up the challenge of the wise man, when he says: "Who can say, I have made my heart clean, I am pure from my sin?" Prov. xx. 9. "The heart of the sons of men is full of evil, and madness is in their heart while they live; and after that they go to the dead." Ecc. ix. 3. "The whole world lieth in wickedness." 1 John v. 19. "In many things we offend all." James iii. 2.

The Scriptures speak a language no less distinct respecting our sins of omission. "All have sinned and come short of the glory of God." Rom. iii. 23. In Christ's account of the final judgment in Matt. xxv. 42—46, the only sins charged upon the wicked are sins of omission. "I was a hungered and ye gave me no meat; I was thirsty and ye gave me no drink," &c

In that solemn scene on the last night of Belshazzar's life, when Daniel was called in as it were to pronounce sentence on the royal offender, one of his charges, and one that has a fearful significance was, "Thou hast not humbled thyself." Another still more comprehensive was, "The God in whose hand thy breath is, and whose are all thy ways, hast thou not glorified." Dan. v. 22, 23. If in reviewing the guilt of such a monster of depravity as Belshazzar, such prominence was due to the neglect of duty, it is easy to see what must be the vast amount of sin of omission among men generally. The law is, "Thou shalt love the Lord thy God with all thy heart, and with all thy soul, and with all thy strength, and with all thy mind; and thy neighbour as thyself." This law is infinitely holy, just and good. Where is the living man that ever met these righteous demands even for an hour? Men must all be sinners, or they could not be so deficient in obedience to this fundamental law of God's empire. Never was a complaint more just, or a rebuke more timely than when God says: "If I be a father, where is my honour? and if I be a master, where is my fear?" Mal. i. 6. "Man, if his heart were not depraved, might have had a disposition to *gratitude to God for his goodness*, in proportion to his disposition to *anger towards men for their injuries*." Who will say that any such proportion is observed?

Such was the corruption of the entire race of man that the Judge of all the earth destroyed the world, one family alone excepted, with a deluge. The reason assigned by God himself for this terrific judgment was the wickedness of men: "My Spirit shall not always strive with men." "And God saw that the wickedness of man was great in the earth, and that every imagination of the thoughts of his heart was only evil continually. And it repented the Lord that he had made man on the earth, and it grieved him at his heart." "And God looked upon the earth, and behold, it was corrupt; for all flesh had corrupted his way on the earth." Gen. vi. 3, 5, 6, 12. If man naturally loved holiness and goodness, one would have said that the length of life in the ante-diluvian ages would have been very favourable to the establishment of individuals and communities in all virtues and moral excellencies. Instead of this, "the earth was corrupt before God, and the earth was filled with violence." Gen. vi. 11. Longevity wrought misery to man and dishonour to God. The destruction of the old world was either just or unjust. If any say it was unjust, they blasphemously impeach God's character. If they admit that it was just, then they say it was deserved, and so admit that human wickedness is dreadful.

There is no candid reader of the Scriptures, who will deny that one of the duties urged in God's word upon all men is that of repentance. But can that duty be incumbent on the pure and holy? Is it not worse than mere folly to call on those to repent, who have nothing to repent of, to require men to be sorry for having committed no sin, to change their mind and behaviour concerning their unfaltering obedience to God? To ask a holy being to repent is to call on him to apostatize from God. In like manner the Scriptures call on men to confess their sins and to forsake them, promising mercy to such. But have sinless angels ever been called to such work? Is it not absurd to require such things of the innocent? For a man to confess a fault which he never committed is a gratuitous falsehood, an insult to God. So also in prayer we are taught to say, "Forgive us our debts." How idle to plead for mercy, when we need nothing but sheer justice; to beg for forgiveness, when we are chargeable with no offence!

Jesus Christ and his apostles often speak of men as condemned, as under wrath, as liable to death. How can this be so, unless men deserve these things? But if they deserve them, they are sinners. In short, no such book of contradictions and extravagancies can be found as the Bible, unless man is a sinner. Bloody sacrifices are wholly unfit to be offered for the sinless. If men are all innocent, Jesus Christ redeemed no one by his blood, for the reason that no one needed redemption. If men are not sinners, the Holy Ghost never could convict them of sin, nor convert them from sin; and so the entire gospel would be glad tidings to no one. If men are not sinners, the preaching of Peter on the day of Pentecost, of Paul on Mars Hill, and of all others, who have held forth the truths of the Gospel was a cruel aggravation of human miseries, which nothing could justify. If men are innocent, all urgency, yea all concern about salvation is fanaticism. But it should not be forgotten that whenever men's interests clash, when controversies arise, when litigations commence, they always regard each other as sinful. Nor is this all. Every good man, whom the world has ever seen, has pronounced on his own case that he was not innocent. David said, "I have sinned against the Lord." Isaiah said, "Woe is me, for I am a man of unclean lips." Job said, "Behold I am vile." Peter said, "I am a sinful man." Paul said, "I am the chief of sinners." Surely if converted and inspired men so judged of their case, in a word, if the best men the world ever saw were sinners, all men must be alienated from God. One reason for admitting this doctrine is that *it is true.* This is the grand reason for admitting any doctrine and should end all controversy about it. But we may well remember that whatever humbles us, and causes us to take our place in the dust before God is good for us and is probably true. The right place for sinners is one of deep self-abasement. It is also important to us never to forget that in denying our lost and miserable condition we do thereby refuse Christ and all his mercies. "Till our necessities be understood, redemption cannot be well understood." "That is the reason we are no better, because our disease is not perfectly known: that is the reason we are no better, because we know not how bad we are." If there is no sin, there can be no salvation. If we are not great sinners, Christ is not a great Saviour.

CHAPTER III.

SIN IS A GREAT EVIL.

TELL me what you think of sin, and I will tell you what you think of God, of Christ, of the Spirit, of the divine law, of the blessed Gospel, and of all necessary truth. He, who looks upon sin merely as a fiction, as a misfortune, or as a trifle, sees no necessity either for deep repentance or a great atonement. He, who sees no sin in himself, will feel no need of a Saviour. He, who is conscious of no evil at work in his heart, will desire no change of nature. He, who regards sin as a slight affair, will think a few tears, or an outward reformation ample satisfaction. The truth is, no man ever thought himself a greater sinner before God than he really was. Nor was any man ever more distressed at his sins than he had just cause to be. He, who never felt it to be "an evil and a bitter thing to depart from God," is to this hour an enemy of his Maker, a rebel against his rightful and righteous Sovereign.

When God speaks of the evil of sin it is in such language as this: "Be astonished, O ye heavens, at this, and be horribly afraid; be ye very desolate, saith the LORD. For my people have committed two evils:

they have forsaken me the fountain of living waters, and hewed them out cisterns, broken cisterns, which can hold no water." Jer. ii. 12, 13. God is a God of truth, and would never speak thus about anything that was not atrocious and enormous in its very nature. Yet it should be observed that he mentions only such sins as are chargeable to all men, even the most moral and decent. In this estimate of the evil of sin the righteous do well agree with God. The most piteous and bitter cries, that ever ascended from earth to heaven, were uttered under the sting of sin, or were for deliverance from its power. In doctrine there can be no worse tendency than that which diminishes men's abhorrence of iniquity. Nor is there a darker sign in religious experience than the slightness of the impressions some have concerning the heinous nature of all sin. It is worse than poverty, sickness, reproach. It is worse than all sufferings. The reason is because it is "exceeding sinful." The worst thing that can be said of any thought, word, or deed is that it is wicked. It may be foolish, but if it is sinful, that is infinitely worse. It may be vulgar, and as such should be avoided; but if it is sinful, it should be avoided, were it ever so polite. An act may offend man, and yet be very praiseworthy; but if it displeases God, nothing can excuse its commission.

Some have proposed curious and unprofitable questions respecting the *infinitude* of the evil of sin. An answer to them would probably give rise to a host of others like them, and so there would be no end of folly. Besides, men do not propose or discuss idle questions, when they are anxious to know how they may be saved from sin. Then they cry: "Men and brethren, what must we do? Is there mercy, is there help, is there hope for such perishing sinners as we are? if so, where can we find salvation?" Questions, that are merely curious and not practical in religion, are unworthy of study and consideration. Yet it may be proper to say that anything is to us infinite, the dimensions of which we cannot gauge, the greatness of which we cannot understand. In this sense sin is an infinite evil. We cannot set bounds to it. We cannot say, Thus far it comes and no further. "Sin, when it is finished, bringeth forth death." And who but God can tell all that is included in that fearful word, *death?* Moreover, sin is committed against an infinite God. The ill-desert of any evil deed is to be determined in part by the dignity of the person, against whom it is directed. To strike a brother is wrong; to strike a parent is worse. To strike a fellow-soldier is punishable with chains; to strike a commanding officer is punishable with death. On this principle the Bible reasons: "If any man sin against another, the judge shall judge him; but if a man sin against the LORD, who shall entreat for him?" 1 Sam. ii. 25. God is our Maker, Father, Governor, and Judge. He is glorious in holiness, fearful in praises, doing wonders. He is the best of all friends, the greatest of all beings, the most bountiful of all benefactors. By ties stronger than death and more lasting than the sun, we are bound to love, fear, honour and obey him. To sin against him is so impudent, ungrateful and wicked, that no created mind can ever adequately estimate its atrocity; and so it is an infinite evil. If sin had its own way, it would dethrone the Almighty. All rebellion tends to the utter subversion of the government against which it is committed; and all sin is rebellion against the government of God. If men saw their sins aright, they would more highly prize divine mercy; and if they had more worthy conceptions of God's grace, they would have more abasing views of themselves.

We may learn much of the evil nature of sin by the names which the Bible gives to it, and to those who practise it. It is called disobedience, transgression, iniquity, foolishness, madness, rebellion, evil, evil fruit, uncleanness, filthiness, pollution, perverseness, frowardness, stubbornness, revolt, an abomination, an accursed thing. In like manner deeds of wickedness are called evil works, works of darkness, dead works, works of the flesh, works of the devil. And wicked men are called sinners, unjust, unholy, unrighteous, filthy, evil men, evil doers, seducers, despisers, children of darkness, children of the devil, children of hell, corrupters, idolators, enemies of God, enemies of all righteousness, adversaries of God and man, liars, deceivers.

From low, meagre apprehensions of the divine nature and law flow a slight estimate of the evil of sin, spiritual pride, self-conceit, and a disesteem of the most precious righteousness of Jesus Christ. He, who can go to Gethsemane and Calvary, and come away with slight views of the evil nature of sin, must be blind indeed. There God speaks in accents not to be misunderstood but by the wilful. Yet such is the perverseness of men that they often refuse to learn even at the cross of Christ. Beveridge says: "Man's understanding is so darkened that he can see nothing of God in God, nothing of holiness in holiness, nothing of good in good, nothing of evil in evil, nor anything of sinfulness in sin. Nay, it is so darkened that he fancies himself to see good in evil, and evil in good, happiness in sin, and misery in holiness." We all naturally belong to the generation of "the blind people that have eyes, and the deaf that have ears." In coincidence with these general views Brookes says: "No sin can be little, because there is no little God to sin against."

Bunyan near death said: "No sin against God can be little; because it is against the great God of heaven and earth; but if the sinner can find out a little God, it may be easy to find out little sins."

John Owen says: "He that hath slight thoughts of sin, never had great thoughts of God."

Luther said: "From the error of not knowing or understanding what sin is, there necessarily arises another error, that people cannot know or understand what grace is."

The Westminster Assembly says: "Every sin, even the least, being against the sovereignty, goodness, and holiness of God, and against his righteous law, deserveth his wrath and curse, both in this life, and that which is to come, and cannot be expiated but by the blood of Christ."

Paul says: "The wages of sin is death."

Chrysostom says: "There is in human affairs nothing that is truly terrific but sin. In all things else, in poverty, in sickness, in disgrace, and in death, (which is held to be the greatest of all evils) there is nothing that is really dreadful. With the wise man they are all empty names. But to offend God, to do what he disapproves, this is real evil."

Truly every wise man will say that he has cause to cry, Show me my sin, my lost condition; show me thy love, thy mercy. Show me the extent, the holiness, the spirituality of thy commandments. Reveal thy Son in me. Let him be the cure of sin, both of its horrible pollution and its horrible guilt.

CHAPTER IV.

HOW THE PIOUS REGARD SIN IN THEMSELVES AND IN OTHERS.

"I ABHOR myself, and repent in dust and ashes;" "O wretched man that I am, who shall deliver me from the body of this death?" "O my God, I am ashamed and blush to lift up my face to thee;" "Cast me not away from thy presence and take not thy Holy Spirit from me." These are but specimens of the deep humiliation, self-loathing, bitterness of soul, and painful apprehension which the righteous of every age feel for their own sins. There is a sense, in which every good man regards himself as the chief of sinners. That is, every one, who really knows his own heart, and has seen the sad work, which sin has made in his moral character, is able as before God to say more evil of himself than of any other being. The souls of such are filled with a godly sorrow, which worketh repentance to salvation, not to be repented of. Nor is this sorrow a solitary sentiment. What carefulness it works in all the regenerate, yea, what clearing of themselves, yea, what indignation, yea, what fear, yea, what vehement desire, yea, what zeal, yea, what revenge! In fine it is certain that no sentiment is more powerful in its effects on men's hearts, than this self-abasement for personal vileness in the sight of God.

Sin in the heart of the believer is to him exceedingly odious.

Some may say that Christians are chiefly distressed at their own sins, because they fear that they will prove their ruin at last. Those, who bring this charge, should know that the righteous seldom endure greater anguish of mind than that produced by the sins of others. This grief is not confined to any one class of good men. The young convert, the strong man in Christ, and the aged servant of the Lord alike show their sadness when others are known to offend against God. It is therefore illogical and unfair to impute this distress to weakness of mind, to nervous debility, or to personal apprehension of coming wrath. It is a part of genuine Christian feeling. He, who cares not that others offend God, has never wept aright over his own sins. So certainly as the heart is savingly changed, will men hate and be made sad by all sin, even though it be in a stranger. Was not the soul of righteous Lot vexed from day to day by the wickedness of his neighbours? Did not David cry, "I beheld the transgressors and was grieved, because they kept not thy word?" Again he says: "Horror hath taken hold of me because of the wicked that forsake thy law;" and "rivers of water run down mine eyes, because they keep not thy law." Jeremiah felt just so: "Oh that my head were waters, and mine eyes a fountain of tears, that I might weep day and night for the slain of the daughter of my people." Ezekiel tells us how God, by an angel of mercy, "set a mark upon the foreheads of the men, that did sigh and cry for all the abominations" done in the land. Jesus himself was often grieved at the wickedness of men. He wept over the very city, which was about to shed his blood. There must be something very heinous in the nature of sin thus to awaken grief and abhorrence in every virtuous mind. To be indifferent to the moral character of those around us, if such a state of mind be possible, is proof of a sad benumbing of all virtuous sensibilities. To take pleasure in those, who make a trade of sin, and do abominable wickedness, is full proof of one's loving iniquity for its own sake.

But why does the Christian weep for the sins of others? He may do it as a man. Some sins bring shame, and poverty, and punishment on those, who commit them; and all, who are connected with them, are to some extent involved in suffering. In this way the pious and the ungodly members of a family often weep together over the intemperance, or other ruinous and disgraceful vice of one of their number. But the good man stops not here. He weeps as a Christian. He is greatly grieved that God is dishonoured. This is the main cause of all his grief. And as he is benevolent, he is sorry that men will expose themselves to Jehovah's curse. It makes him tremble to see men pulling down wrath on themselves. He is also grieved at the probable ill effects of a bad example, in seducing others from the right way. He is specially afflicted at the blindness and wantonness of sinners, in despising mercy, rejecting Christ and vexing the Holy Spirit. Self-love commonly steps not in to shut the eyes of a Christian to the hatefulness of sin, when he sees it in others.

When others sin, good men see what they themselves were before conversion, or what they would have been but for the restraints of providence. An eminent servant of Christ seeing a culprit led to execution said, "There goes John Bradford by nature." Can any man thus see himself mirrored forth in the life of another, and not be humbled and grieved? Should he, who thus transgresses, be a professor of Christ's religion, and eminent in gifts or station, the anguish felt is the more keen, because God is thus greatly dishonoured, Christ is wounded in the house of his frinds, the enemy takes occasion to utter new and bitter reproaches against religion, and the wicked are greatly emboldened in wrong-doing. Such a lapse commonly shakes all those secure thoughts, which men have of their own spiritual state, and awakens jealousies, over one's self, which are like coals of juniper. If David fell, much more may a weak believer. If the tempest tears up cedars by the roots, what shall become of the tender plants? If a giant may be overcome, how much more a child? So that the open sins of professors, in proportion to their eminence, lead God's people to great heart-searchings and strong fears lest hidden iniquity should at last be their ruin. Let it be so; for "if the sins of others be not our fear, they may be our practice. What the best have done, the weakest *may* imitate. There is scarcely any notorious sin, into which self-confidence may not plunge us. There is hardly any sin, from which a holy and watchful fear may not happily preserve us." O that men would remember that, "Blessed is he that feareth always." Preservation from sin is better than recovery from its snares. A man may escape death by a malignant pestilence, though it attack him, but it will probably leave him weak and liable to other diseases. How surely will a wise man profit by the errors of others! "In vain is the net spread in the sight of any bird." When the land is full of enemies, no wise man says, "There is no danger."

Of all unamiable and unchristian tempers none is more dangerous to its possessor than harshness to a fallen brother, founded on confidence in our own strength. "Brethren, if a man be overtaken in a fault, ye which are spiritual restore such an one, in the spirit of meekness, considering thyself, lest thou also be tempted." We cannot pity erring men too much, but in the abhorrence of sin there is no danger of excess, nor can we pray too fervently, nor watch too closely against falling into the evil practices, which we lament or reprehend in others. Sin is the worst of evils. So greatly do good men hate it, that they have long preferred anything else rather than its defilement. Joseph said: "How can I do this great wickedness and sin against God?" and cheerfully went to prison rather than yield to temptation. Moses also chose "rather to suffer affliction with the people of God, than to enjoy the pleasures of sin for a season; esteeming the reproach of Christ greater riches than the treasures of Egypt: for he had respect unto the recompense of the reward." Anselm said: "If sin were on one side, and hell on the other, I would sooner leap into hell than willingly sin against my God." Good old David Rice, the apostle of Kentucky, alluding to the irreligion of his day, said: "As I see a propriety in it, so I feel an inclination to go mourning to my grave."

How base and cruel it is in unconverted persons by their wickedness to afflict all their pious friends, and then upbraid them for not being happy! How can one be joyful, when he sees those, whom he loves most, rejecting God, and "digging into hell?" Esther said, "How can I endure to see the destruction of my kindred?" And Paul said: "I say the truth in Christ, I lie not, my conscience also bearing me witness in the Holy Ghost, that I have great heaviness, and continual sorrow in my heart. For I could wish that myself were accursed from Christ, for my brethren, my kinsmen according to the flesh." What anguish wrings the heart of a pious wife, or child, who lives for years with the growing conviction that he, for whom they have so long wept and prayed, will yet pretty certainly die without hope! And who can describe the fearful tumult, or crushing sorrow, when the eyes of such an one are closed in death, and pious survivors have no reason to believe that the separation which then takes place is other than eternal!

CHAPTER V.

THE HEART OF MAN IS ALL WRONG.

LET us look at our own hearts. There is a mystery in all iniquity. In Scripture it is often called a lie, guile, deceit. The heart of man is full of all treachery; so that "there is no faithfulness in their mouth; their inward part is very wickedness; their throat is an open sepulchre; they flatter with their tongue." "His mouth is full of cursing, and deceit, and fraud." "They speak vanity every one with his neighbour: with flattering lips and with a double heart do they speak." "The counsels of the wicked are deceit." "They hold fast deceit; they refuse to return." "The heart is deceitful above all things." It deceives every being but one. It would deceive Him, if he were not omniscient. None but God knows all the depths of iniquity and duplicity within us. Genuine conviction is attended with a sense of the divine knowledge and hatred of our sins. What unconverted man can without terror dwell on the words, "Thou God seest me?" To the regenerate it is for a joy that God knows all their hearts, and will search and cleanse them. When the wicked sin greedily, and have no checks in their consciences, you may know that it is because God is not in all their thoughts. "Do you think that I believe there is a God, when I do such things?" said Nero to Seneca, who was reproving him for his vices.

Though the language of the Bible is strong, it is just. God declares, and every Christian knows by sad experience that his heart is deceitful *above all things.* Among beasts, the fox and serpent are deceitful. But their arts are few and can soon be learned. The currents of the sea are deceitful, yet you may soon acquire a knowledge of the dangers thence arising. There is a law in their variations. Even the magnetic needle is not always true to the pole. Yet its variations can be precisely calculated. But no mortal knows how much his heart varies from the law of God. "Who can understand his errors?" Ps. xix. 12. A broken tooth or foot out of joint can never be safely trusted. Men know this and never wittingly rely upon them. But all men put more or less confidence in their own hearts.

Man is the only creature on earth that seems to practise self-deception. The fox deceives his pursuers, not himself. But man "feedeth on ashes: a deceived heart hath turned him aside, that he cannot deliver his soul, nor say, Is there not a lie in my right hand?" Isa. xliv. 20. Who has not often seen that "there is a way that seemeth right unto a man, but the end thereof are the ways of death?" Prov. xvi. 25. How timely is that exhortation of Paul, "Let no man deceive himself!" 1 Cor. iii. 18. How strange and yet how common that he, whose heart has deceived him a thousand times, should yet confide in it as if it had always been honest!

Education is sometimes so conducted as to make us blind to our real characters. One trained at a Jesuit's school complained: "I have been so long in the habit of concealing my real sentiments from others, that I hardly know what they are." Few men have been such adepts in the arts of a corrupt court as Talleyrand; but many still live, who think with him that "language was designed to conceal thought." In such cases "deceiving and being deceived" are commonly united. That we should sometimes deceive others is proof of our depravity; but that we should spend our lives in self-deception is truly marvellous. Men of the fewest virtues commonly have the best conceit of themselves. Peter solemnly averred his adhesion to Christ, though all others should forsake him; yet in the trying hour his conduct was worse than that of any but the traitor. When forewarned of his wickedness Hazael felt insulted, and cried. "But what! is thy servant a dog, that he should do this great thing?" Yet he very soon perpetrated all the horrible crimes, which had been foretold. Above most men Ahab sold himself to do iniquity, and thus brought dire curses on his person and kingdom; yet, as soon as he saw Elijah, he said, "Art *thou* he that troubleth Israel?" A perfect knowledge of the treachery of our hearts is possessed by none but God; a just knowledge of them belongs to no portion of mankind, but those who are enlightened by the Holy Ghost.

The heart is also vile. It is "desperately wicked." It loves vanity, and folly, and sin. It hates holiness, and truth, and divine restraints. It is a sink of iniquity, a pool of pestilential waters, a cage of unclean birds, a sepulchre full of dead men's bones. It is torn by wild, fierce, unhallowed passions. It rejects good and chooses evil. It is wholly corrupt. There is no soundness in it. It is full of evil. "Out of the heart proceed evil thoughts, murders, adulteries, fornications, thefts, false witness, blasphemies." Matt. xv. 19.

Men may rail at the vices, principles, and prejudices of others, and be worse themselves. "He, that trusteth in his own heart is a fool." Prov. xxviii. 26. If the word, *fool*, here as in some other cases designates a wicked man, it is well applied. None but *bad* men lean upon their own hearts, their own wisdom and counsels, their own strength and sufficiency, their own merit and righteousness. If the word, *fool*, points out one, who is destitute of wisdom, then who lacks that quality so much as he, who believes his heart upright and honest, when all his life it has been leading him away from God, and practising on him the grossest deceptions? Surely human nature is a poor thing. Man at his best estate is altogether vanity. "Before conversion, his heart is the worst part about him." Every wise man will say with Paul: "I know that in me, that is, in my flesh, there dwelleth no good thing." Rom. vii. 18.

Sometimes the word, *heart*, is in Scripture used to designate the conscience, as where it is said, "if our heart condemn us, God is greater than our heart, and knoweth all things." We all have by nature "an evil conscience." The state of the world judged by the entire state of men's consciences, presents one of the most appalling subjects of contemplation. "He that hath a *blind* conscience, which sees nothing; a *dead* conscience, which feels nothing; and a *dumb* conscience, which says nothing, is in as miserable a condition as a man can be in on this side hell."

CHAPTER VI.

WICKED MEN ARE LIKE WICKED ANGELS.

SUCH is the sad state of man by nature that he bears a fearful resemblance to fallen angels. This truth is very abasing to human pride. To declare it is a high offence in the judgment of many men of uncircumcised ears and hearts. They wait not to ask what is meant by it, nor what are the evidences of its truth. They instantly repel the charge with indignation. This truth, like any other, may be announced in an offensive manner; but it is a truth, which must never be given up.

No one asserts that unrenewed men now on earth are as wicked as they possibly can be. If they live a day longer in sin, they will be worse. And if they go to eternity without a change of heart, they will be far, far worse. Continuance in sin hardens the heart, and makes men more and more reckless and desperate. "Evil men and seducers shall wax worse and worse." Satan himself is more hardened and more malignant than when he first revolted. No man all of a sudden sinks to the lowest depths of debasement.

Of course it is not asserted that men are now positively as bad as the angels who kept not their first estate. Man has not time on earth to work out such completeness of evil as his elder brethren, who fell into sin, have attained. Moreover, most men have some degree of conscience, some natural affection, some regard to the proprieties of life, and some hope of future repentance, which restrain their evil natures. And yet wicked men are like wicked angels in the sense in which a child is like a man, or a whelp like a lion. Let us see:

All admit that wicked angels have no holiness. In this wicked men are precisely like them. They do not love God's law, or nature, or government. They are alienated from him, and opposed to all his attributes and authority. They do not glorify him, do not delight in him, do not find pleasure in thinking on his name. They choose sin and death, rather than holiness and life. "The carnal mind is enmity against God: for it is not subject to the law of God, neither indeed can be. So then they that are in the flesh cannot please God." Wicked angels do not please God, neither do wicked men. Neither class intends nor desires to please him. Fallen angels are without God in their prison-house; and wicked men are without God in the world. Neither fallen angels nor fallen men feel towards God, as loyal subjects towards a prince, as faithful servants to a master, as dutiful children to a father.

The want of truth is a great sin among fallen angels and fallen men. Satàn is a deceiver, a slanderer, an accuser of the brethren, a liar and the father of lies. Men also are deceivers. They lay snares privily. They use cunning craftiness. They practise intrigue, imposture, and equivocation. They love and make a lie. They are a lie. "They delight in lies." The wicked are estranged from the womb: they go astray as soon as they be born, speaking lies. All the hopes of wicked men are but "refuges of lies," and the last day will show it.

Satan is cruel, unrelenting, and a murderer from the beginning. He delights in scenes of blood. His trade is to murder souls. Wicked men are murderers. They hate one another. They hate the just. They shed innocent blood. They murder souls. They have no compassion for the perishing: "He that hateth his brother is a murderer, and ye know that no murderer hath eternal life abiding in him." More than twice the whole number of inhabitants of the United States in 1852, that is, more than fifty millions of people have been murderously put to death in the last eighteen hundred years, simply because they professed to love the truth of God and the Saviour of sinners. Laws, public opinion, and God's providence now restrain many, but the heart of unrenewed man is as wicked as it ever was. It hates holiness, wherever seen. Those men who go about murdering souls by teaching false doctrine, are peculiarly like the great destroyer.

Satan is a robber. He would rob men of their salvation, Christ of his crown, and God of his glory. He plotted and instigated the robbery, which the Sabeans perpetrated upon Job. He is the great patron of pirates, footpads, burglars and thieves, and wicked men do his bidding. They oppress, defraud, and rob one another. They do more. They defraud the Almighty. "Will a man rob God? yet ye have robbed me * * * in tithes and offerings."

Fallen angels are greedy of sin and delight in wickedness. Wicked men are just so. "They sleep not except they have done some mischief." "They draw iniquity with a cart-rope." "They are mad upon their idols." They have pleasure in those that do iniquity. They delight themselves in a thing of naught. They are bent on backsliding.

Satan is a tempter and so are wicked men. He would have Job curse God and die; so his wife invites him to the horrid deed. He gives the text, "Thou shalt not surely die," and the Universalist takes it up and goes through the land, promising life to the wicked, salvation to the impenitent, heaven to the unbelieving.

In some things wicked men do what fallen angels never did. They reject mercy and grace, kindly offered to them by the Lord. Devils never did that. You say, They never had the opportunity. True, but they never did it. Neither did they ever laugh at eternity, judgment and damnation. They have too fearful a sense of the wrath of God to be able to mock and jest at the most terrible things. If these things be so, then we understand something of the import of our Saviour's words to the wicked of his day: "Ye are of your father the devil, and his works will ye do." How dreadful is sin! It converts angels into devils and men into fiends. There is no unfitness in the arrangement which God has made for having one great prison-house for all his incorrigible foes. The very place prepared for the devil and his angels, will be the abode of finally impenitent men. How dreadful will hell be, filled up with outlaws, robbers, murderers, liars, hypocrites, ingrates, enemies of God and of all righteousness, from among angels and men. And how startling is the thought that devils have stronger emotions pertaining to religion than some wicked men. "The devils believe and tremble." How many sinners neither believe nor tremble! And how many others who seem to believe, laugh at things which lay hold on eternity!

CHAPTER VII.

MAN IS UTTERLY HELPLESS.

As a sinner, man can neither commend nor convert himself to God. He cannot atone for his sins, he cannot satisfy divine justice, he cannot subdue his own iniquities, he cannot perform any holy action. In our day there are but few Protestants, who maintain that man can make any atonement for his sins against God; or redeem himself, by paying any ransom for his soul. "Christ hath redeemed us from the curse of the law;" "He is the propitiation for our sins;" "Behold the Lamb of God that taketh away the sin of the world." These and many similar passages of Scripture have brought all but outrageous errorists to acknowledge, that in the work of salvation we are wholly and absolutely indebted to the Lord Jesus Christ for reconciliation with God. He is our peace.

But some are not so ready to confess their indebtedness to the Holy Spirit for all right perceptions of truth, for all really good desires and proper motives, for all spiritual strength and power to do good. It is with extreme reluctance that men admit their utter helplessness in this respect. And yet the Scriptures speak a language as decisive, as unmistakable about our inability to purify our hearts as to make an atonement for transgression. Therefore when God promises aid it is on this wise: "He giveth power to the *faint;* and to them *that have no might* he increaseth strength." Isa. xl. 29. "Not by *might*, nor by *power*, but by my Spirit, saith the Lord of hosts." Zech. iv. 6. Even converted persons stand by borrowed strength. "Be strong *in the Lord*, and *in the power of his might.*" Eph. vi. 10. "As the branch cannot bear fruit of itself, except it abide in the vine, no more can ye except *ye abide in me.*" John xv. 4. "Be strong *in the grace that is in Christ Jesus.*" 2 Tim. ii. 1. Indeed the righteous have always delighted to acknowledge that all their strength is in God.

Of the helplessness of unregenerate man the Bible speaks in the clearest terms and in many ways. *First*, it teaches that he cannot see and know the truth. "The natural man receiveth not the things of the Spirit; for they are foolishness to him; neither can he know them, because they are spiritually discerned." 1 Cor. ii. 14. Left to themselves men are "always learning, but never able to come to the knowledge of the truth." 2 Tim. iii. 7. Accordingly unregenerate men are often spoken of as *blind;* and God very graciously promises to "bring the blind by a way that they knew not." Isa. xlii. 16. *Secondly*, without God's Holy Spirit men cannot believe, cannot receive Christ: "No man can come unto me, except the Father, which hath sent me, draw him." "No man can come unto me except it were given him of my Father." John vi. 44, 65. "How can ye believe, who receive honour one of another, and seek not the honour which cometh from God?" John v. 44. Even a disposition to hear God's word belongs to no man without God's Spirit. "Why do ye not understand my speech? Because ye cannot hear my word." John viii. 43. Lydia never attended to the preached gospel till the Lord opened her heart. Acts xvi. 14. *Thirdly,* without God's Spirit man cannot obey a single law of God. "The carnal mind is enmity against God; for it is not subject to the law of God, neither indeed can be." Rom. viii. 7.

The Church of God has always held this doctrine. Augustine, than whom the truth has perhaps never had an abler uninspired defender, says: "Neither doth a man begin to be converted, or changed from evil tc good by the beginnings of faith, unless the free and undeserved mercy of God work it in him." "So therefore let the grace of God be accounted of, that from the beginning of his good conversion to the end of his perfection, he that glorieth let him glory in the Lord. Because as none can begin a good work without the Lord, so none can perfect it without the Lord." "The Lord, that he might answer Pelagius to come, doth not say, 'Without me ye can hardly do any thing;' but he saith, 'Without me ye can do nothing.' And that he might also answer these men that were to come, in the very same sentence of the Gospel, he doth not say, 'Without me ye cannot *perfect,*' but 'Without me ye cannot *do* anything.' For if he had said, Ye cannot perfect, then these men might say, We have need of the help of God, not to begin to do good, for we have that of ourselves, but to perfect it." He subsequently quotes and remarks on those notable texts, "Not that we are sufficient of ourselves to think anything as of ourselves;" and "Who maketh thee to differ?" He also says that "unless God do help, we can have no piety or righteousness either in word or in will." "It is certain that we do will when we will, but it is he that makes us that we will that, which is good." "It is certain that we act when we act, but it is he that makes us to act, by affording most efficacious strength to our will."

Ambrose says: "Although it be in man to will that, which is evil, yet he hath no power to will that, which is good, except it be given him." In like manner Maxentius says: "We believe that natural free-will is able to do no more than to discern and desire carnal, or worldly things; which may seem glorious with men, but not with God. But those things that belong to eternal life, it can neither think, nor will, nor desire, nor perform, but only by the infusion and inward working of the Holy Ghost, who is also the Spirit of Christ." Fulgentius says: "We have not received the Spirit of God because we do believe, but that we may believe." "In the heart of man, faith can neither be conceived, nor increased unless the Holy Spirit does infuse it, and nourish it." "He delivers us not by finding faith in any man, but by giving it." Bernard says: "If human nature, when it was perfect, could not stand; how much less is it able of itself to rise up again, being now corrupt."

The Council of Orange, which met A. D. 529 holds: "If any man say that mercy is divinely conferred upon us believing, willing, desiring, endeavouring, labouring, watching, studying, asking, seeking, knocking without the grace of God, but doth not confess that it is only by the infusion and inspiration of the Holy Ghost into us that we believe, will, and are able to do all these things as we ought to do, and makes the help of grace to follow after either humility or obedience, nor will grant that it is the gift of grace itself that we are obedient and humble, he resisteth the apostle, who says, "What hast thou that thou hast not received?" and "By the grace of God I am what I am." So the African Council affirms the sentence of exclusion against Pelagius and Cœlestius "until they acknowledge, by open confession, that the grace of God by Jesus Christ our Lord doth help us by single acts, not only to know, but also to do righteousness; so that without it we can neither have, think, speak, nor do anything of the nature of true and holy piety."

The Latter Confession of Helvetia says that since the fall, the understanding and will "are so altered in man, that they are not able to do that now, which they could do before his fall." Again: "Man, not as yet regenerate, hath no free-will to good, no strength to perform that, which is good." In proof of this doctrine it presently quotes several texts of Scripture, of which the following are two: "Unto you it is given in the behalf of Christ, not only to believe on him, but also to suffer for his sake;" and, "It is God, which worketh in you both to will and to do of his good pleasure." Phil. i. 29 and ii. 13. The Confession of Basle says: "Our nature is defiled, and become so prone unto sin, that, except it be renewed by the Holy Ghost, man of himself can neither do nor will any good." John iii. 3. The Confession of Bohemia says: "That will of man, which before [the fall] was free, is now so corrupted, troubled and weakened, that henceforth of itself and without the grace of God, it cannot choose, judge or wish fully; nay it hath no desire, nor inclination, much less any ability to choose that good, wherewith God is pleased. For albeit it fell willingly, and of its own accord, yet, by itself, and by its own strength, it could not rise again, nor recover that fall; neither to this day, without the merciful help of God, is it able to do anything at all." Rom. vii. 19—23. Again: "No man by his own strength, or by the power of his own will, or of flesh and blood, can attain unto or have this saving or justifying faith, except God of his grace, by the Holy Ghost, and by the ministry of the Gospel preached, do plant it in the heart of whom he list, and when he list." John i. 13.

The Confession of England says, "that the law of God is perfect, and requireth of us perfect and full obedience;" and "that we are able by no means to fulfil that law in this worldly life." In one edition the Augsburg Confession speaks thus: "Man's will hath no power to perform a spiritual righteousness without the Holy Spirit;" and quotes in proof 1 Cor. ii. 14 and John xv. 5. The Confession of Saxony says: "Man by his natural strength is not able to free himself from sin and eternal death." The Confession of Wirtemburg says: "As a man corporally dead is not able by his own strength to prepare or convert himself to receive corporal life; so he, who is spiritually dead, is not able by his own power to convert himself to receive spiritual life." The churches of England and Ireland both teach that "the condition of man after the fall of Adam is such that he cannot turn and prepare himself, by his own natural strength and good works to faith and calling upon God." The Synod of Dort says that all men are "untoward to all good tending to salvation, forward to evil; dead in sins, slaves of sin, and neither will nor can (without the grace of the Holy Ghost, regenerating them) set straight their own crooked nature, no, nor so much as dispose themselves to the amending of it." The Westminster Confession says that by our "original corruption, we are utterly indisposed, disabled, and made opposite to all good, and wholly inclined to all evil." Alas! in what a sad condition we are by nature! Ambrose says: "Though bound with the chains of my sins, I am held fast hand and foot, and buried in dead works, on thy call, O God, I come forth free." Beveridge says: "I cannot pray, but I sin: I cannot hear or preach a sermon, but I sin: I cannot give an alms, or receive the sacrament, but I sin: nay, I cannot so much as confess my sins, but my confessions are still aggravations of them. My repentance needs to be repented of, my tears want washing, and the very washing of my tears needs still to be washed over again with the blood of my Redeemer." Truly all our hope is in free grace alone. If we are not still in the graves of death, it is because we are "risen with Christ."

Our helplessness, when left to ourselves, is as manifest in small as in great things, on little as on great occasions. It has long been observed that men are as apt to err from the right way upon a slight as upon a great provocation. Jonah said he did well to be angry, even unto death, about a gourd. A damsel put Peter to cursing and swearing. Job bore all his losses without one sinful word; but when falsely accused by his brethren, he entirely lost his temper. A bee has killed a man, who had survived the perils and grievous wounds of battle. Many will weigh every word and speak the whole truth in solemn judicature, and yet forfeit veracity in talking with a child, or in telling an amusing anecdote. I have seen a man bear with composure the burning of his house, and yet lose proper control of himself, when charged too much for a quire of paper. John Newton says: "The grace of God is as necessary to create a right temper in Christians on the breaking of a china plate as on the death of an only son." We as truly need help from God to enable us in a right spirit to bear the tooth-ache as to suffer martyrdom in the cause of truth. In all things, at all times we need the grace of Christ. By it alone can we be or do anything pleasing to God, or salutary to our own souls.

Many persons, who profess to be Arminians are as wide of holding the doctrines of Arminius, as those of Paul. The Leyden Professor says expressly: "It is impossible for free will without grace to begin or perfect any true or spiritual good. I say, the grace of Christ, which pertains to regeneration, is simply and absolutely necessary for the illumination of the mind, the ordering of the affections, and the inclination of the will to that, which is good. It is that which operates on the mind, the affections, and the will; which infuses good thoughts into the mind, inspires good desires into the affections, and leads the will to execute good thoughts and good desires. It goes before, accompanies, and follows. It excites, assists, works in us to will, and works with us that we may not will in vain. It averts temptations, stands by and aids us in temptations, supports us against the flesh, the world, and Satan; and, in the conflict, it grants us to enjoy the victory. It raises up again those, who are conquered and fallen, it establishes them, and endues them with new strength, and renders them more cautious. It begins, promotes, perfects, and consummates salvation. I confess, that the mind of the natural and carnal man is darkened, his affections are depraved, his will is refractory, and that the man is *dead in sin.*"

Richard Watson fully admits that "the sin of Adam introduced into his nature such a radical impotence and depravity, that it is impossible for his descendants to make any voluntary effort [of themselves] towards piety and virtue." He also quotes with entire approbation this celebrated sentence from Calvin: "Man is so totally overwhelmed, as with a deluge, that no part is free from sin, and therefore whatever proceeds from him is accounted sin." Would that many, who have subscribed the most orthodox formulas on this subject were really as sound as James Arminius and Richard Watson.

Do not all these Scriptures and reasonings from Scripture make it clear that the victory over sin will never be gained by an arm of flesh? Nature is too weak. She is broken, and crippled, and helpless. In this work, all men, if left to themselves, are stark naught. They have no might to do good, though they are mighty to do evil. One of the most instructive portions of personal history is the record of various attempts made by several great men to reform their hearts by a self-invented discipline, without the aid of God's Holy Spirit. They have reflected, have made resolutions, have drawn up schedules of their vices to be corrected, have examined their hearts, have found fault with their own efforts, and have formed new plans; but with the exception that now and then a decent exterior has been attained, all has been a sad failure. Their history was long ago given by Prosper: "Though there have been some, who by their natural understanding have endeavoured to resist vices, yet they have barrenly adorned only the life of this time; but they could not attain to true virtues and everlasting happiness." Bernard addresses such in these words: "What have you philosophers to do with virtues, who are ignorant of Christ, the virtue of God?" Fuller's soap and much water will not take out the scarlet dye and crimson hue. Leviathan is not thus taken. The core of depravity is not thus extracted. "Old Adam is always too strong for young Melancthon." Prodigality may wage war on covetousness, pride on the love of popularity, the love of ease on the love of show, but one evil passion cannot so expel another as to purify the heart. "Restrained sensuality often takes a miser's cap, or struts in pharisaic pride." It is easy to pass from one sin to another, but to become holy is never possible but by the power of God's efficacious grace. "Nature can no more cast out nature, than Satan can cast out Satan."

These views are strengthened by the fact that we not only have sinful natures, but have also formed sinful habits, whose power is terrific. "Can the Ethiopian change his skin? or the leopard his spots? then may ye also do good, that are accustomed to do evil." Jer. xiii. 23. "If Adam, when he had committed but one sin, and that in a moment, did not seek to regain his lost integrity, how can any other man, who by a multitude of sinful acts hath made his habits of a giant-like stature, completed many parts of wickedness, and scoffed at the rebukes of conscience?" The power of habit is such that even in the wanness and agony of death, its influence is often manifest in the whole manner of a dying man. But enough of this.

In full accordance with all that has been said, these things are noticeable in Scripture. *First*, God has mercifully promised the needed strength and grace: "My grace is sufficient for thee, for my strength is made perfect in weakness." 2 Cor. xii. 9. "The Lord will give strength unto his people." Psa. xxix. 11. "Thy people shall be willing in the day of thy power." Psa. cx. 3. See also Deut. xxx. 6—8; Ezek. xi. 19, 20 and many other places. *Secondly*, pious men do uniformly ascribe all their ability to God. "God is our refuge and strength, a very present help in trouble." Psa. xlvi. 1. "In the day when I cried thou answeredst me, and strengthenedst me with strength in my soul." Psa. cxxxviii. 3. "Sing aloud unto God our strength." Psa. lxxxi. 1. "Our sufficiency is of God." 2 Cor. iii. 5. "I laboured more abundantly than they all; yet not I, but the grace of God, which was with me." 1 Cor. xv. 10. *Thirdly*, wise and good men always have looked to God alone and not at all to themselves or other men for ability to do right. "O Lord God of Abraham, Isaac, and of Israel, our fathers, keep this for ever in the imagination of the thoughts of the heart of thy people, and prepare their heart unto thee." 1 Chron. xxix. 18. "O that my ways were directed to keep thy statutes." "Incline my heart unto thy testimonies." "Quicken me, so shall I keep the testimonies of thy mouth." Psa. cxix. 5, 36, 88. See also Heb. xiii. 20 and 21 and parallel passages. Let it, however, not be forgotten that our helplessness does not at all proceed from any defect in the original constitution of our minds as they came from the hands of God. He made man upright. It is sin, which has done all the mischief. This very helplessness is part and proof of our wickedness. Our very weakness is our crime. It is very wicked to have no right views of God, to have our minds full of ignorance and prejudices against him, to have no heart to fear, love, or obey him, or to fail to do these things perfectly. Thus the Scriptures abundantly teach. Paul says neither in the way of boasting, nor of excuse, but in confession and humiliation: "I know that in me (that is, in my flesh) dwelleth no good thing: for to will is present with me, but how to perform that which is good I find not." Rom. vii. 18 and context. "The flesh lusteth against the Spirit, and the Spirit against the flesh: and these are contrary the one to the other; so that ye cannot do the things that ye would." Gal. v. 17. He is not expressing approbation but reproof in so speaking to the Galatians. So when Peter describes a class of men, "having eyes full of adultery, and that cannot cease from sin;" 2 Pet. ii. 14, no man will so far pervert his meaning as to say that he is freeing these people from blame. It was in reproof that Christ said, "How can ye believe, who receive honour one of another?" &c. In fact there is no deeper guilt in man, than that contracted by having no heart to do right. The very essence of filial impiety consists in having no heart to love and honour one's parents. The very ground of impiety to God is to have no heart to know, or love, or obey him. To have eyes and not see, to have ears and not hear, to have a heart and not understand is the very sin Isaiah charged on degenerate Israel, the very sin of apostate angels. If the helplessness induced by sin were any excuse or palliation of sin, fallen angels would be quite innocent, at least excusable; for no sober man will say that they can by any possibility turn to God and live.

CHAPTER VIII.

WITHOUT DIVINE GRACE MEN DO NOTHING BUT SIN.

THOSE, who live in sin, sin all the time. It is their trade, and they work hard at it. They love it, and are greedy of iniquity. They "love death." They "dig up evil." They "fill up their sin ALWAYS." They "do ALWAYS resist the Holy Ghost." Never for an hour do they love God supremely. They sin without cessation.

Two things are required to make an action right. One is that it be lawful in itself. The other is that it be done with a right motive. If the thing done be itself wrong, no motives can make it right. To steal, or curse, or murder, or despise the poor, or hate the just, can never under any circumstances be right. To do evil that good may come is the doctrine of none but devils, and the worst of men. On the other hand the thing done may be right in itself, but the motive, which governs us, may be wrong, and so the act may be sinful because the motive is sinful. Bad motives in good actions are like dead flies in sweet ointments. They corrupt the whole. The heart is everything. Most men of the world in Christian countries do many things, which are very proper, but not from love to God. No man, who has not been born again, ever does anything with holy motives. His life is better than his heart. Indeed his heart is the worst part of him. It is all wrong. It is hard, and proud, and selfish, and unbelieving, and without any love to God. So far from pleasing God, all the unregenerate are continually offending him. Their very best works are but "splendid sins."

There are reasons found in human nature, which render it certain that unrenewed men will do nothing but sin. They are blind and see no beauty in holiness. They have no spiritual discernment. "They have eyes but they see not." "They know not what they do." If they do not see the beauty of holiness, how can they love it? No being can love that, which does not seem to him good or comely.

The man, who is without the grace of God, never fully approves the law of God, as holy, just and good, nor adopts it as the rule of his life. He does some things which it requires, and abstains from some things which it forbids, not because he loves God or his law, but because it promotes his health, or wealth, or honour, or quiet, to do so. God is not in all his thoughts. He would live very much as he does if the law of God were not known to him. Ask him, and he will tell you that he does not aim with a single eye to honour God in everything. He does not frame his doings to that end at all. All the lines of his conduct meet and end in himself. He is without God in the world. He serves the creature more than the Creator. Nor is his heart without objects of love. He loves the world and the things of the world. When he prospers in the things that perish, he counts himself happy. He is greatly pleased with gold and silver, and objects of sense, and works of art. These are his gods, because he sets his heart on them. He thinks of them ten times as much and a thousand times as eagerly as he thinks of God.

What makes his case worse is that he is commonly much at ease. He is well pleased with himself. He is not sighing over his failures, and lamenting his sins. He thinks he is nearly good enough. Rivers of water never run down his eyes for his own sins or the sins of others. He seldom cries, "God, be merciful to me a sinner," and when he does, it is rather a form than a hearty prayer. His real belief is that God could not righteously and for ever condemn him; at least he says, "If I am lost, I know not what will become of many others." Would it not be strange that one, who cares not to serve God, should do it? that he, who tries to please himself and wicked men, should as by accident please God? that he, who seeks the honour that comes from man, should find the honour that comes from God only? Surely there is no such confusion where God reigns. He does not put darkness for light, bitter for sweet, sin for holiness, and vice for virtue.

Nor should men be offended at this doctrine. It is not new. It is not of human invention. It is not the doctrine held by a few only. It is not a mere theory. It is very practical, very important. No truth concerns any man more than this. It is the very doctrine of the Bible in many places. Paul says: "They that are after the flesh [who are unrenewed by God's Spirit] do mind the things of the flesh. * * To be carnally-minded is death. * * The carnal [or unregenerate] mind is enmity against God; for it is not subject to the law of God, neither indeed can be. So then they that are in the flesh cannot please God."

Rom. viii. 5—8. Could words be plainer or stronger? Until God shall be pleased with a heart that is *enmity* against him, and with a mind that "*cannot be subject*" to his law, until he shall cease to be a holy God, he cannot be pleased with anything done by a man who has not the Spirit of God, and whose heart has not been mightily changed.

Ploughing is itself a lawful act. If there be no ploughing, there can be no bread. Yet God says: "The ploughing of the wicked is sin." Yea, he puts it down with other sins, that greatly offend him. The whole verse reads thus: "An high look, and a proud heart, and the ploughing of the wicked is sin." Prov. xxi. 4. If God had intended to teach that everything, even the most common and necessary thing done by wicked men, was sinful, could he have chosen more fit words?

But, here is a passage, which shows that all the religious services of sinners are defiled with sin. "The sacrifice of the wicked is an abomination to the Lord: but the prayer of the upright is his delight." There are but two classes of men known in the Bible. They are called saints and sinners, the just and the unjust, the righteous and the wicked, men of the way and men of the world. Their end will be different, because their characters are different.

From the earliest ages of the Christian church this has been the uniform doctrine, held and insisted on by God's people. Basil in his treatise on baptism says expressly that it is not possible, nor a thing pleasing and acceptable to God, for one that is the servant of sin to perform righteousness, according to the rule of the saints' piety. In proof he urges these words of our Saviour: "Let us first make the tree good, and then the fruit will be good;" and let us "first make clean the inside of the cup and platter," and then the outside will be wholly clean. He also refers to 2 Cor. vii. 1. Jerome says: "Let us pronounce our sentence against those that do not believe in Christ, and yet think themselves valiant, and wise, and temperate, and just, that they may know that none can live without Christ, without whom all virtue is in vice," or vicious. Augustine says: "Be it far from us to think that true virtue should be in any one, unless he be a righteous man. And let it be as far from us to think that any one is truly righteous, unless he live by faith." "All the life of unbelievers is sin, and there is nothing good without the chief good: for where the knowledge of the eternal and unchange able truth is wanting, there is but false virtue in the best manners." Again: "The man is first to be changed, that his works may be changed; for if a man remain in that state that he is evil, he cannot have good works."

Gregory says: "If faith be not first begotten in our hearts, all the other things cannot be good, though they may seem good."

The Church of England and the Protestant Episcopal Church in the United States of America do both say of works done before the grace of Christ and the inspiration of his Spirit, because "they are not done as God hath willed and commanded them to be done, we doubt not but they have the nature of sin."

The 5th article of the Church of Ireland contains the same words without alteration. It holds also this language: "We have no power to do good works, pleasing and acceptable unto God, without the grace of God preventing [going before] us, that we may have a good will, and working with us when we have that good will." It also incorporates these words from the Lambeth Articles: "The condition of man after the fall of Adam is such, that he cannot turn, and prepare himself, by his own natural strength and good works, to faith, and calling upon God."

The Reformed Churches generally fully agree with the above testimonies.

The Synod of Dort says: "There is indeed remaining in man, since the fall, some light of nature, by the help of which, he retains certain notions concerning God and natural things; concerning the difference of things honourable and shameful, and manifests some desire after virtue and external discipline: but so far from his being able, by this light of nature, to attain to the saving knowledge of God, or to turn himself to him, he does not use it rightly in natural and civil things: nay, indeed, whatever thing it may at length be, he contaminates it all in various ways, and holds it in unrighteousness, which when he does, he is rendered inexcusable before God."

The French Confession says: "Although man can somewhat discern between good and evil, yet we affirm, that whatsoever light he hath, it straightway becometh darkness, when the question is of seeking God, so that by his understanding and reason he can never come to God. Also, although he be endued with will, whereby he is moved to this or that, yet in as much as it is altogether captivated under sin, it hath no liberty at all to desire good, but such as it hath received by grace and of the gift of God."

The Augsburg Confession, which is the standard of the Lutheran churches in Germany and America, says: "We condemn the Pelagians and all such as they are, who teach that by the only powers of nature, without the Holy Spirit, we may love God above all, and fulfil the law of God, as touching the substance of our actions. We do freely and necessarily mislike these dreams; for they do obscure the benefits of Christ. For therefore is Christ the Mediator set forth, and mercy promised in the gospel, because that the law cannot be satisfied by man's nature, as Paul witnesseth when he saith, (Rom. viii.) 'The wisdom of the flesh is enmity against God; for it is not subject to the law of God, neither indeed can be.' For albeit that man's nature by itself can after some sort perform external works (for it can contain the hands from theft and murder) yet can it not make those inward motions, as true fear, true faith, patience, and chastity, unless the Holy Ghost do govern and help our hearts. And yet in this place also do we teach, that it is also the commandment of God, that the carnal motions should be restrained by the industry of reason and by civil discipline, as Paul saith, * * 'The law is given to the unjust.'" And again: "Albeit that men by their own strength be able to do outward honest deeds in some sort, and must also perform this civil obedience; yet so long as men are void of faith, they are in the power of the devil, who driveth them to shameful sins, occupieth their minds with wicked and blasphemous opinions, for that is the kingdom and tyranny of the devil. Moreover, nature is weak, and cannot without God's help strengthen itself to any spiritual works."

The Moravian Confession says: "And since through faith the Holy Spirit is given, thus also the heart is made fit to do good works. For before that, as long as it is without the Holy Spirit, it is too weak; and besides it is in the power of the devil, who impels the poor human nature to many sins. * * * Without faith and without Christ, human nature and ability is far too weak to do good works; as to call upon God, to show patience in suffering, to love one's neighbour, diligently to discharge offices entrusted to us, to be obedient, to avoid evil lusts. Such noble and truly good works cannot be done without the help of Christ, as he himself speaks—John xv. 'Without me ye can do nothing.'"

The Westminster Confession says: "Works done by unregenerate men, although for the matter of them they may be things which God commands, and of good use both to themselves and others; yet because they proceed not from a heart purified by faith; nor are done in a right manner, according to the word; nor to a right end, the glory of God; they are therefore sinful, and cannot please God, or make a man meet to receive grace from God. And yet their neglect of them is more sinful and displeasing unto God."

This article is found without alteration in the Confessions of all the Presbyterian bodies of Scotland, Ireland, and Canada, and of the Presbyterian Church in the United States of America. It was incorporated entire into the Savoy Confession, into the Saybrook Platform, into the London Baptist Confession, into the Philadelphia Baptist Confession, as well as into the Confession of numerous smaller bodies in this and other countries.

The eighth article of the Methodist Episcopal Church, of the Methodist Episcopal Church South, and of the Protestant Methodist Church in the United States, is in these words:

"The condition of man after the fall of Adam is such, that he cannot turn and prepare himself by his own natural strength and works to faith, and calling upon God: wherefore we have no power to do good works, pleasant and acceptable to God, without the grace of God by Christ preventing us, that we may have that good will, and working with us, when we have that good will."

The Confession of Sueveland says: "Good works (which are good indeed) do proceed from a lively faith, by the Holy Ghost, and are done of the faithful according to the will or rule of God's word."

The Confession of Basle says: "The Lord himself saith, 'Without me ye can do nothing;' John xv. 5; that is, nothing that may please God and be for your salvation. * * Faith and love are the fountain and square of all virtues and good works, according to the testimony of the Apostle: 'The end of the commandment is love, out of a pure heart, and a good conscience, and faith not feigned.' 1 Tim. i. 5. And again: 'Without faith it is impossible to please God.' Heb. xi. 6."

The Confession of Belgia says: "We are justified by faith in Christ, yea, even before such time as we could bring forth any good work: for our works before faith can no more be good, than the fruit of a tree can be good, before the tree itself be good."

The Confession of Saxony says: "External discipline, even where it is most honest, is not a fulfilling of the law. * * But all this discipline is an external government, such as it is; like unto the leaf of the fig-tree, wherewith our first parents, after their fall, did cover their nakedness: neither doth it any more take away sin, and the corruption of nature, and death, than those fig-leaves did."

The Confession of Wirtemberg says: "We confess and believe that to do and practise such righteousness as is acceptable to God, these virtues be necessary—faith, hope, and love: and that man cannot of himself conceive these virtues, but doth receive them of the favour and grace of God."

These extracts from the standards of different bodies of Christians might have been much more extended. They are, however, sufficient to show that the doctrine here set forth is not novel; is not the doctrine of a few extreme writers, but is the common doctrine of the purest and most zealous churches. The fair arguments used and the texts quoted in these Confessions do mightily strengthen the arguments and proofs before quoted. It is not too much to say that it has been fairly and scripturally proven, that unregenerate men do sin always, and that none of them do anything but sin against God.

Is not the misery of an unregenerate state indescribable and unfathomable? No wonder that pious Ezra, having some just sense of the evil of sin, and the vileness of men, "did eat no bread, nor drink water because of the transgression of them that had been carried away." No wonder that Jeremiah said of the wicked of his day: "If ye will not hear it, my soul shall weep in secret places." Even Daniel "was astonied for one hour and his thoughts troubled him," when he foresaw the ruin which the king of Babylon was about to bring on himself by his royal crimes. All the unregenerate do nothing but sin. If for a while they seem to reform, they soon return to their wickedness, as the dog to his vomit, or the sow that was washed to her wallowing in the mire. All their goodness is as the morning cloud; as the early dew it passeth away. They sometimes return from outward acts of sin; but they return not unto the Lord. When the unclean spirit is gone out of a man and returns again, "the last state of that man is worse than the first." Matt. xii. 45. Neither mercies, nor judgments, nor promises, nor threatenings, nor hopes, nor fears, without the grace and spirit of Christ, will or can ever cure the love, or arrest the practice, of sin.

CHAPTER IX.

THE CORRUPTION OF MAN IS HEREDITARY.

No mere man was ever born without a sinful nature. The Son of God miraculously derived his human nature from his mother alone, and escaped the taint of original sin. Mary herself however was a sinner and needed a Saviour, as she readily confessed. Luke i. 47. As Eusebius Emesenus said, "the mother of the Redeemer is not otherwise loosed from the bonds of ancient sin, than by redemption." All the Pope's letters on this subject about the middle of the nineteenth century are idle dreams. Every human being whose descent has been in the ordinary way has inherited a corrupt nature. The faith of the people of God on this subject has been as uniform as on any other truth of the Gospel. In Psa. li. 5, in the midst of the humblest and most penitent confessions, David says: "Behold, I was shapen in iniquity, and in sin did my mother conceive me." All attempts to set aside the clear teachings of this passage have been such as rather to shock by their profaneness, than to deceive by their plausibility. Sound commentators have been wonderfully agreed as to the teaching of this verse. Ambrose says: "All are born in sin, as David witnesseth," and then quotes these words. Luther says: "It is a great part of wisdom, for one to know, that there is nothing good in us, but vain sin, that we do not think and speak so triflingly of sin as those, who say that it is nothing else than the thoughts, words, and deeds, which are contrary to the law of God. But if thou wilt rightly point out according to this Psalm, what sin is, thou must say, that all is sin, which is born of father and mother, even before the time that man is of age to know what to do, speak, or think." Calvin says: "David does not confess himself guilty merely of some one or more sins, as formerly, but he rises higher, that from his mother's womb he has brought forth nothing but sin, and by nature is wholly corrupt, and, as it were, immersed in sin. And certainly we have no solid conviction of sin, unless we are led to accuse our whole nature of corruption." Perhaps in all his writings this great man has not made a remark more fully coincident with religious experience, and of more weight in personal piety than the last sentence quoted from him: "*Certainly we have no solid conviction of sin, unless we are led to accuse our whole nature of corruption.*" Bishop Patrick's paraphrase of the verse is: "It is true indeed, and thou, O Lord, knowest it better than I, that there is in me an innate proneness to evil; but I am so far from representing this as an excuse for what I have done, that I confess the consideration of it ought to have rendered me the more watchful and diligent to suppress those bad inclinations; which I knew to be so natural, that I brought them into the world with me."

Bishop Horne says: "The divine mercy is implored by the penitent, fourthly, because that alone can dry up the fountain of original corruption, from which the streams of actual transgression derive themselves; and which is here only lamented as their cause, not as their excuse; seeing that the greater our danger is of falling, the greater should be our care to stand. David was the offspring of the marriage-bed, which is declared to be 'honourable and undefiled.' No more, therefore, can be intended here, than that a creature begotten by a sinner, and formed in the womb of a sinner, cannot be without that taint, which is hereditary to every son and daughter of Adam and Eve."

Matthew Henry says: "He confesses his original corruption." * * "He elsewhere speaks of the piety of his mother, that she was God's handmaid, and he pleads his relation to her, (Psa. cxvi. 16, and lxxxvi. 16,) and yet he here says she conceived him in sin; for though she was, by grace, a child of God, she was by nature a daughter of Eve, and not excepted from the common character. Note, It is to be sadly lamented by every one of us that we brought into the world with us a corrupt nature, wretchedly degenerated from its primitive purity and rectitude."

Dr. Scott says that David, "having received from his parents Adam's fallen nature with all its evil propensities, confesses that he was conceived and shapen in iniquity."

Hengstenberg says that the doctrine of original sin is so plainly taught here, "that nothing but the most confused mind can deny it. For when David confesses, that even before the development of his consciousness, before the time of his distinguishing between good and evil, that even at his birth, nay at his very conception, sin dwelt in him, and had so poisoned his nature, that he was quite incapable of attaining to true righteousness and wisdom; he places himself in direct collision with those, who consider sin merely as a product of the abused freedom of each individual, and leaves room for no other derivation of sinfulness than this, that it goes down from parents to their children, according to the word, 'what is born of the flesh is flesh.'"

Dr. J. A. Alexander says: "Having just before confessed his actual transgressions, he now acknowledges the corruption of his nature."

Theologians no less than commentators have taken the same view of this text. Even John Taylor of Norwich admits that the first clause is correctly translated "I was born in sin." Whereupon Edwards well says, "If it is owned that man is *born in sin*, it is not worth the while to dispute, whether it is expressly asserted that he is conceived in sin." Bishop Beveridge says, "Sin was in his heart, whilst he was in his mother's womb; for seeing he was conceived in sin, sin must needs be conceived in him." Alexander Hill says: "The Scriptures not only declare that all have sinned, but they seem to refer the abounding of iniquity to a cause antecedent to education, example or the operation of particular circumstances; and in numberless places they represent the nature of man as corrupt. Of this kind are the following: 'The imagination of man's heart is evil from his youth.' 'Behold I was shapen in iniquity, and in sin did my mother conceive me.' 'The wicked are estranged from the womb, they go astray as soon as they be born, speaking lies.' 'Who can bring a clean thing out of an unclean? Not one.'" Dr. Leonard Woods of Andover says: "Is it not a plain matter of fact, that a depraved nature, a propensity to sin, is transmitted from parent to child, and has descended from the common ancestor of our race to all his posterity? Are we not 'degenerate plants of a strange vine?' And if depravity comes in this way, what impropriety is there in calling it *hereditary?*" These views have been presented chiefly in connection with one text of Scripture, rather than to call attention to many. If any prefer to examine others, they are easily found. The true spirit of David's confession in Psa. li. 5 is fully coincident with the sentiments of every deeply humble and penitent man that ever lived.

Different Christian Churches have spoken very strongly and harmoniously on the subject of native depravity. The Confession of Bohemia says: "A second kind of sin is original sin, naturally engendered in us, and hereditary; wherein we are all conceived and born into this world." The Confession of France says: "We believe that all the offspring of Adam is infected with this contagion, which we call original sin: that is a stain spreading itself by propagation, and not by imitation only as the Pelagians thought; all whose errors we do detest. Neither do we think it necessary to search how this sin may be derived from one unto another. For it is sufficient that those things which God gave unto Adam, were not given to him alone, but also to all his posterity; and therefore we, in his person, being deprived of all these good gifts are fallen into all this misery and curse."

The Confession of England holds this language: "We say also that every person is born in sin, and leadeth his life in sin: that nobody is able truly to say his heart is clean." The Confession of Scotland says that by the fall "the image of God was utterly defaced in man; and he, and his posterity of nature became enemies to God, slaves to Satan, and servants to sin." The Confession of Belgia teaches that, "Original sin is a corruption of the whole nature, and an hereditary evil; wherewith even the very infants in their mothers' womb are polluted; (Psa. li. 5,) the which also as a most noisome root doth branch out most abundantly all kind of sin in man." The Augsburg Confession says that "after the fall of Adam, all men descended one from another after a natural manner have original sin, even when they are born." The Confession of Saxony says: "As touching original sin, we do plainly affirm that we do retain the consent of the true Church of God, delivered to us from the first fathers, prophets, apostles, and the apostles' scholars, even unto Augustine, and after his time, and we do expressly condemn Pelagius, and all those, who have scattered in the Church like doting follies." The Confession of Wirtemberg says: "We believe and confess that in the beginning, man was created of God, just, wise, endued with free will, adorned with the Holy Ghost, and happy; but that afterwards for his disobedience, he was deprived of the Holy Ghost, and made the bondman of Satan, and subject both to corporal and eternal damnation; and that evil did not stay in one only Adam, but was derived into all the posterity." The Church of England, the Church of Ireland, and the Wesleyan Methodist Churches all hold this language: "Original sin standeth not in the following of Adam (as the Pelagians do vainly talk) but in the corruption of the nature of every man, that naturally is engendered of the offspring of Adam, whereby man is very far [Latin edition, *quàm longissimè*] gone from original righteousness, and of his own nature inclined to evil and that continually." The Synod of Dort says: "Such as man was after the fall, such children he begat; namely, a corrupt issue from a corrupt father; this corruption being by the just judgment of God derived from Adam to all his posterity (Christ only excepted) and that not by imitation (as of old the Pelagians would have it), but by the propagation of nature." The London and Philadelphia Baptist, the Savoy, Cambridge and Boston Congregational, and the Presbyterian Confessions in Great Britain and America, say that a "corrupted nature is conveyed to all the posterity of our first parents," and that thereby "we are utterly indisposed, disabled, and made opposite to all good, and wholly inclined to all evil."

The Heidelberg Catechism, speaking of the misery of man, says:

"3. Whence knowest thou thy misery?

Out of the law of God.

4. What doth the law of God require of us?

Christ teacheth us briefly, (Matt. xxii. 37—40,) "Thou shalt love the Lord thy God with all thy heart, with all thy soul, with all thy mind, and with all thy strength. This is the first and the great command; and the second is like to this: Thou shalt love thy neighbour as thyself. On these two commands hang the whole law and the prophets."

5. Canst thou keep all these things perfectly?

In no wise; for I am prone by nature to hate God and my neighbour.

6. Did God then create man so wicked and perverse?

By no means, but God created man good, and after his own image, in righteousness and true holiness, that he might rightly know God his Creator, heartily love him, and live with him in eternal happiness, to glorify him and praise him.

7. Whence, then, proceeds this depravity of human nature?

From the fall and disobedience of our first parents, Adam and Eve, in Paradise; hence our nature is become so corrupt, that we are all conceived and born in sin.

8. Are we then so corrupt that we are wholly incapable of doing any good, and inclined to all wickedness?

Indeed we are, except we are regenerated by the Spirit of God.

9. Doth not God then do injustice to man, by requiring of him, in his law, that which he cannot perform?

Not at all; for God made man capable of performing it; but man, by the instigation of the devil, and his own wilful disobedience, deprived himself and all his posterity of those divine gifts.

10. Will God suffer such disobedience and rebellion to go unpunished?

By no means, but he is terribly displeased with our original as well as actual sins; and will punish them in his just judgment temporally and eternally, as he hath declared, "Cursed is every one that continueth not in all things which are written in the book of the law, to do them."

11. Is not God then also merciful?

God is indeed merciful, but also just; therefore his justice requires that sin, which is committed against the most high majesty of God, be also punished with extreme, that is, with everlasting punishment, both of body and soul."

John Wesley says, "If, therefore, we take away this foundation, that man is by nature foolish and sinful, fallen short of the glorious image of God, *the Christian system falls at once;* nor will it deserve so honourable an appellation as that of a 'cunningly devised fable.'"

Richard Watson says: "The true Arminian, as fully as the Calvinist, admits the doctrine of the total depravity of human nature in consequence of the fall of our first parents." Arminius, speaking of *the first sin of the first man*, says: "The whole of this sin is not peculiar to our first parents, but is common to the whole race, and to all their posterity, who at the time when the first sin was committed, were in their loins, and who afterwards descended from them in the natural mode of propagation."

Richard Baxter says: "You cannot exempt infants themselves from sin and misery without exempting them from Christ the Redeemer, and the remedy." "If infants have no sin and misery, then they are none of the body, the church, which Christ loved and gave himself for, that he might cleanse it."

Beveridge says: "Adam begat Seth and all his posterity in his own likeness, (Gen. v. 3,) and, if in his own likeness, then sinners like himself. A wolf begets wolves, not lambs; so a sinner begat sinners, not saints."

Corrupt as is the Church of Rome, and false as is

her system of doctrine by reason of countless human inventions and idle traditions, yet she has never denied original sin. The Council of Trent did "decree, confess, and declare" that any man fatally errs, "whosoever shall affirm that Adam's prevarication injured himself only, and not his posterity, and that he lost the purity and righteousness, which he had received from God, for himself only, and not also for us; or that when he became polluted by disobedience he transmitted to all mankind corporal death and punishment only, but not sin also which is the death of the soul." The great champion of that Church, Bellarmine, in his commentary on the Psalms, remarking on these words, "*Behold I was shapen in iniquity, and in sin did my mother conceive me,*" says that David was speaking of our "first origin, and of the sin of the first man transfused into us by generation, from which we have become weak and prone to sin." And he brings in St. Augustine arguing for the same sense because David was the fruit of a lawful and "chaste marriage between his pious parents." In like manner Bossuet says: "David was descended from Jesse, a just man, and from his wife. Why therefore does he say that he had been conceived in sin, except that he had taken the person of human kind, had his mind turned to the fetters, which bind all, and had adverted to the stock or fountain of death, the origin of iniquity?"

Let the celebrated saying of Augustine not be forgotten: "Neither the guilty unbeliever, nor the justified believer begets innocent but guilty children; because the generation of both is from corrupted nature." Nor is the remark of Calvin less weighty: "Original sin is properly accounted sin in the sight of God, because there could be no guilt without crime."

As frequent allusion is made to the Pelagians it may be useful here to insert their opinions on the subject of the native corruption of man. Pelagius says: "In our birth we are equally destitute of virtue and vice; and previously to moral agency, there is nothing in man, but that which God created in him." His disciple Cœlestius held that "infants are born in that state in which Adam was before he sinned." Julian, another of the same school, held that "human nature in the time of our being born is rich in the gift of innocence;" and "nobody is born with sin." It is a very favourite idea with all Pelagians that sin consists only in acts, and is a voluntary transgression of known law and nothing else. Thus Pelagius himself says: "It is disputed concerning nature, whether it is debilitated or deteriorated by sin. And here, in my opinion, the first inquiry ought to be, what is sin? Is it a substance, or is it a mere name devoid of substance; not a thing, not an existence, not a body, nor anything else (which has a separate existence) but an act; and if this is its nature, as I believe it is, how could that which is devoid of substance debilitate or change human nature?" In reading such a clause one almost imagines himself listening to the lectures of an American heresiarch, labouring to prove that all sin consists in acts. As to the text of Scripture, on which such rely, it should be remembered that while we read "sin is the transgression of the law;" (1 John iii. 4,) the word rendered "transgression" is literally "want of conformity," and no one denies that sin is either a transgression of law, or a want of conformity to it. The same inspired apostle tells us that "all unrighteousness is sin," 1 John v. 17.

CHAPTER X.

MEN ARE GUILTY.—IMPUTATION OF ADAM'S SIN.—ACTUAL SINS.

In all inquiries it is important to understand the use of terms. This is quite true when we speak of *guilt* and of being *guilty*. The word *guilt* sometimes signifies a crime, an offence, a sin. In colloquial use this sense is common. So when we speak of *guilty* conduct, we mean it is sinful, or criminal conduct. Sometimes the word *guilt* is taken in the sense of *consciousness* of guilt. This is an improper but not an uncommon use of the word. Thus when a man is said to be borne down by his guilt, the meaning often is that he is oppressed by a sense of his sinfulness. Again, *guilt* is the state of a man justly charged with a crime. In this sense he, who has done the deed charged in an indictment, is said to be *guilty*. The charge is true of him. Again, *guilt* signifies exposure to forfeiture, or penalty, on account of some law violated. Thus Kent says, "A ship incurs guilt by the violation of a blockade." This was by far the most common sense of the word when our English translation of the Bible was made. Accordingly we there find the phrase "guilty of death," which evidently means justly liable to the penalty of death. Indeed our word, guilt, is derived from the Saxon, *gylt*, which signifies a fine or a debt. To pay a *gylt* was to pay a debt or fine.

This is also by far the most common sense of the word as used by theologians. Thus Edwards in his treatise on original sin says: "Universal guilt of sin might also be demonstrated from the appointment, and the declared use and end of the ancient sacrifices; and also from the ransom which every one that was numbered in Israel was directed to pay, to make atonement for his soul." So also Ridgley says: "Forgiveness of sin, without a right to eternal life, would render our justification incomplete; therefore, when any one is pardoned by an act of grace, he is put in possession of that which, by his rebellion, he had forfeited; he is considered, not only as released out of prison, but as one who has the privileges of a subject, such as those which he had before he committed the crime. Without this he would be like Absalom, when, upon Joab's intercession with David, the guilt of murder, which he had contracted, was remitted so far, as that he had liberty to return from Geshur, whither he was fled; nevertheless, he reckons himself not fully discharged from the guilt he had contracted, and concludes his return to Jerusalem, as it were, an insignificant privilege, unless, by being admitted to see the king's face, and enjoy the privileges, which he was possessed of before, he might be dealt with as one who was taken into favour, as well as forgiven." These are but specimens of the proof at hand that theologians use the term guilt in the sense of exposure to penal suffering. In this sense it is commonly used in this chapter. By saying that men are dreadfully guilty, it is taught that they are justly exposed and fairly liable to dreadful penal sufferings.

Man is not only vile and helpless, he is also guilty.

He is not only depraved and without strength, he is also condemned. The wicked not only have their consciences to clamour against them, but God is angry with them every day. Inspiration has settled it that we are "by nature the children of wrath even as others." Eph. ii. 3. Yes, *by nature* we are under wrath. To be a child of sorrow is to be subject to sorrow. To be a child of wrath is to be subject to wrath. This doctrine is taught in the most explicit terms. Paul says: "By one man sin entered into the world and death by sin;" "Through the offence of one many be dead;" "The judgment was by one to condemnation;" "By one man's offence death reigned by one;" "By the offence of one judgment came upon all men to condemnation;" "By one man's disobedience many were made sinners;" Rom. v. 12—19. "In Adam all die." 1 Cor. xv. 22. Clearer and more varied terms could not be required to teach us that we are *by nature* under a curse, liable to wrath, suffering a penalty. So the Church of Christ has always understood the sacred writers. This appears by many monuments of ancient and modern times.

Cyprian says: "There were before Christ also famous men, prophets and priests; but being conceived and born in sin, they wanted neither original nor personal guilt." Jerome says: "All men are held to be guilty, either in consequence of the sin of Adam, their ancient progenitor, or by their own personal act." So also the great weight of Augustine's arguments fell upon and crushed the favourite dogma of Pelagius, "that the consequences of Adam's sin were confined to his own person." He says: "We were all in that one man, when he, being one, corrupted us all." He also thus defended himself against the perversions of his views: "The opinion which I delivered, that sin injures no nature but that in which it is committed, the Pelagians apply to the support of their own doctrine, that little children cannot be hurt by the sin of another, but only by their own; but considering that, as they belong to human nature, which has contracted original sin, for human nature sinned in our first parents, it is true, therefore, that no sins can hurt human nature but its own." In fact a denial of the federal headship of Adam has commonly been followed by denying the federal headship of Christ. Although the enemies of truth are often rancorous in their opposition to the doctrine of our representation in Adam, yet the Church of God has never been ashamed of it. The Latter Confession of Helvetia having spoken of the fall of man into sin, death, and divers calamities, says: "By death we understand not only bodily death, which is once to be suffered of us all for sins, but also everlasting punishments due to our corruption and our sins." The Confession of Basle says that by the fall all mankind became "subject unto damnation." The Confession of Bohemia says that by the fall, man "cast headlong both himself and all his posterity into sin, death, and all kinds of miseries in this life, and into punishments eternal after this life." The Confession of France says: "We believe that this stain is indeed sin; because it maketh all and every man guilty of eternal death before God." The Confession of Belgia says that original sin "is so filthy and abominable in the sight of God that it alone is sufficient to the condemnation of all mankind." The Augsburg Confession begins its account of original sin by saying that it is "that guilt, whereby all that come into the world, are, through Adam's fall, subject to God's wrath and eternal death." The Churches of England and Ireland in their Articles say that "in every person born into the world original sin deserveth God's wrath and damnation." The Synod of Dort condemns the errors of those, who teach "that it cannot well be affirmed that original sin is sufficient for the condemning of all mankind, or for the deserving of temporal and eternal punishment." They declare that such go against the Apostle in Rom. v. 12—19, and vi. 23. The Westminster Confession, now so extensively adopted in Great Britain and America by orthodox churches, says: "Every sin, both original and actual, being a transgression of the righteous law of God, and contrary thereunto, doth, in its own nature, bring guilt upon the sinner; whereby he is bound over to the wrath of God, and curse of the law, and so made subject to death with all miseries, spiritual, temporal and eternal."

Should any be inclined to think these remarks needlessly protracted, let them remember, 1. that the doctrine of the guilt of Adam's first sin being imputed to his posterity has been opposed, vilified and maligned in an extraordinary way; and, 2. that the entire work of Christ as a Saviour will soon be deemed unnecessary by those, who are bold enough to deny original sin. The ablest writers the Church has ever had, have taken this view of this doctrine. Ridgley says: "The Apostle calls Adam *the figure of him that was to come.* Rom. v. 14. Now, in what was Adam a type of Christ? Not as he was a man, consisting of soul and body; for, in that respect, all that lived before

Christ might as justly be called types of him. Whenever we read of any person or thing being a type in Scripture, there are some peculiar circumstances, by which they may be distinguished from all other persons or things, that are not types. Now Adam was distinguished from all other persons, more especially as he was the federal head of all his posterity; and that he was so, appears from what the Apostle not only occasionally mentions, but largely insists on, and shows in what respect this was true; and he particularly observes, that as one conveyed death, the other was the head, or Prince of Life. These respective things, indeed, were directly opposite, therefore the analogy, or resemblance consisted only in the manner of conveying them; so that as death did not become due to us, in the first instance of our liableness to it, for our own actual sin, but the sin of Adam; that right we have to eternal life, by justification, is not the result of our own obedience, but Christ's. This is plainly the Apostle's method of reasoning."

The elder President Edwards says: "When the *doctrine* of original sin is spoken of, it is vulgarly understood in that latitude, which includes not only the *depravity of nature*, but the *imputation* of Adam's first sin; or, in other words, the liableness and exposedness of Adam's posterity, in the divine judgment, to partake of the punishment of that sin. So far as I know, most of those who have held one of these, have maintained the other; and most of those, who have opposed one, have opposed the other." He shows his estimate of the importance of this doctrine when he devotes an entire chapter to its separate consideration. He also says that "the rejection of the doctrine of original sin renders redemption unnecessary."

Thomas Boston in his discourse on Rom. v. 19 says: "There are only two ways how men might be made sinners by the disobedience of Adam; viz. either by imputation or imitation. The last is not meant; (1) Because some of those many who are made sinners are not capable of imitation or actual sin, viz. infants. (2) Because we are made righteous, not by the imitation, but imputation of Christ's righteousness; but as we are made righteous by the one, so we are made sinners by the other."

Owen says: Adam's "actual sin is imputed unto us, as that which becomes ours by that imputation, which before it was not."

Bishop Beveridge says: "We see the Apostle saying, 'All have sinned,' (Rom. v. 12,) before all were born, which could not be unless they had before sinned in him from whom they were born. And so, many render the words 'in whom all have sinned;' and therefore the same Apostle tells us, 'In Adam all died.' 1 Cor. xv. 22. Now how could all die in him, unless all sinned in him? For death is the wages of sin only, as well as the only wages of sin."

Richard Baxter says: "Infants are not made righteous by Christ, if they were not sinners; and sinners they cannot be by any but original sin."

The celebrated James Arminius of the University of Leyden, though erroneous in many things, yet closes a paragraph on original sin with these words: "From these things, the imputation of the sin of our first parents is necessarily inferred; for wherever there is the punishment of sin there is the imputation of the same." Again: "Whatever punishment was inflicted on our first parents, has also pervaded all their posterity, and still oppresses them; so that all are by nature children of wrath, (Eph. ii. 31,) obnoxious to condemnation, and to death temporal and eternal, (Rom. v. 12,) and are, lastly, devoid of that [primeval] righteousness and holiness; with which evils they would continue oppressed for ever, unless they were delivered from them by Jesus Christ; to whom be glory for ever and ever." (Rom. v. 18, 19.)

Richard Watson says: "In Romans v. Adam and Christ are contrasted in their public or federal character; and the hurt which mankind have derived from the one, and the healing they have received from the other, are also contrasted in various particulars, which are equally represented as the effects of the 'offence' of Adam, and of the 'obedience' of Christ. Adam, indeed, in verse 14, is called, with allusion to this public representative character, the figure, τυπος, type, or model of 'Him that was to come.' The same Apostle also adopts the phrases 'the first Adam,' and 'the second Adam,' which mode of speaking can only be explained on the ground, that as sin and death descended from one, so righteousness and life flow from the other; and that what Christ is to all his spiritual seed, that Adam is to all his natural descendants. On this, the parallel is founded, 'For as in Adam all die, so in Christ shall all be made alive;' (1 Cor. xv. 22,) words, which on any other hypothesis can have no natural signification."

Even Bellarmine says: "The sin of Adam is so imputed to all his posterity, as if they had all committed the same sin."

It ought constantly to be remembered that errorists have an almost uniform mode of attacking the truth. They would subvert the doctrine of universal depravity, and they begin by attacking native depravity. They would set aside the whole doctrine of original sin, and they commence by finding fault with the imputation of Adam's first sin. There is also a constant sinking down into lower error. Pelagius first propagated his errors by putting objections into the mouths of others, and by suggesting difficulties to the true doctrine. But his follower Julian unblushingly said: "The triune God should be adored as most just; and it has been made to appear most irrefragably, that the sin of another never can be imputed by him to little children." Again: "Hence that is evident, which we defend as most reasonable, that no one is born in sin, and that God never judges men to be guilty on account of their birth." "Children, inasmuch as they are children, never can be guilty, until they have done something by their own proper will." There is about as close an agreement between the enemies of truth in different ages as to the language they will adopt in opposing sound doctrine, as there is among its friends in the manner of maintaining it.

But as if this condemnation by nature, this death by the sin of our progenitor imputed to us, were not as fiery and terrible as men would have it, they rush into actual sins, and bring more wrath upon themselves by great wickedness and unrighteousness, by many acts of impiety and malice. They devise mischief upon their beds; they love vain thoughts; they rebel against God; break every precept of his law, and vex his Holy Spirit. In thought, word, and deed they are transgressors. They are as an unclean thing. Their consciences are defiled. Their wills are perverse. They have all done, and are all doing that which was forbidden. They have all failed and are daily failing to do what was commanded. The law, which they break, is holy, just and good. It is the only perfect law ever enacted. No sentence could be more just than this, "the soul that sinneth it shall die." Punishment is deserved by all transgressors. If there were no prohibitions to sin, men could not seem more eager after iniquity than at present. Not only so, the very prohibition provokes a longing for disobedience. "Sin, taking occasion by the commandment, wrought in me all manner of concupiscence." Rom. vii. 8. Thus "the whole world lieth in wickedness." Its guilt would instantly sink it to hell but for the patience and long-suffering of God. If the *precept* of the law is holy, just, and good, so is the *penalty*. God is the author of both. The human conscience whenever enlightened and aroused, pronounces damnation just. Psa. li. 4. The boldest sinners in the world will be speechless in the day of judgment. Guilt is a dreadful chain. It holds all its prisoners bound in affliction and iron. No man can give to God a ransom for himself, or for his brother; for "the redemption of the soul is precious," costly, infinitely costly. In the awards of the last day every conscience will acquiesce, and all cavilling at God's sovereign disposal of men will be for ever silenced. The sentence of exclusion from the presence of the Lord, and from the glory of his power, will be most righteous. Nothing could be more holy, more deserved. All heaven, all earth, all hell will see and feel how just it is. O man of the world, can thy hands be strong, or thy heart endure, when God shall call thee to account? "What wilt thou say when he shall punish thee?" Well did Augustine say, "Woe to the life of man, be it never so commendable, if thou examine it, setting mercy aside."

CHAPTER XI.

SELF-RIGHTEOUSNESS IS WORTHLESS.—MAN NEEDS A SAVIOUR.

OUR own merits are of no avail for salvation. Man never deserves the favourable regard of God. The more self-righteous any one is, the worse it is for him. He, who is found with a little counterfeit money on him, may be suspected, but he, who knowingly carries much of it, may be convicted. Self-righteousness is spurious coin. Whoever relies on his own goodness for salvation will surely perish. He puts darkness for light and bitter for sweet. He turns judgment into wormwood and righteousness into hemlock. Self-righteousness is a condemnation of God's law and an impeachment of his justice. There are but two ways in which man ever had solid peace. The first is by having a heart and life free from sin. When Adam was holy, his peace was unbroken. But we have all sinned, and this door is for ever closed against our race. Of all that have been born of woman, but one entered heaven by his own merits. That one was Jesus, the Son of God. The other way for us to have peace is to flee to Christ who is our peace, and hath made peace for all that believe on him. Those who receive him shall never come into condemnation. Their peace shall be like a river, which widens and deepens the farther it flows. The way, in which some secure a false peace and destroy themselves, is to shut their eyes on their offences, sear their own consciences, and persuade themselves that they are not verily and fearfully guilty, and have not grievously sinned against God. They spend their days in framing excuses, perhaps vindications of a life of rebellion and sin; or they boldly deny their guilt in every particular, as did the Jews in the days of Malachi, and of our Saviour. Self-righteousness seems to be born with sin, and to grow with its growth. A disposition to deny criminality is universal among men. Nothing but divine grace can effectually cure the habit of self-justification. One honest confession is a better sign of amendment, and promises more good than all excuses and denials. Indeed no saving mercy can come to him who will not confess his sins. The reason is that to him, who thinks he has no malady, all medicine is offensive. "The whole need not a physician." He who thinks he knows will not inquire. He, who says he sees, will not ask for a light. How can he wish to be better, who is already in his own esteem good enough? How can he who believes he has done no wrong, ask for pardon? Forgiveness to the innocent is impossible. To absolve the guiltless is an absurdity. The very offer of mercy to the sinless is an indignity.

Nothing in human nature seems to be more obstinate, or more difficult to eradicate than a self-righteous spirit. Without the grace of Christ going before, no man ever sought or desired a new heart, or a gracious pardon. Left to themselves, men will live in sin, die in sin, and lie down in eternal sorrow, rather than renounce their own goodness and abandon their self-righteous hopes.

It tends greatly to strengthen these delusions when men can plead natural amiability of temper, or a fair standing with the world for truth, justice and honour, or a decent and serious attention to the ordinances of religion. Christ said to the most exact observers of the Mosaic ritual, "the publicans and harlots go into the kingdom of God before you." "There are many who think they are safe, so long as they can find others worse than themselves. As if the fox should thank God that he is not a bear; or the wolf that he is not a lion; or the swine that he is not a wolf; whereas all this is nothing to the purpose, because God hath called his children to be sheep, neither shall any species of unclean beasts be tolerated in the Christian society, unless they become sensible of their disposition, and put it off as fast as they can by repentance and conversion." All observation goes to show that there is not among men a more hopeless class of offenders than those who trust in themselves that they are righteous and despise others. "All our righteousnesses are as filthy rags." "If I wash myself in snow-water, and make my hands never so clean, yet shalt thou plunge me in the ditch and mine own clothes shall abhor me. For he is not a man as I am, that I should answer him, and we should come together in judgment." Job ix. 30—32. "If thou, Lord, shouldst mark iniquities, O Lord, who shall stand?" Psa. cxxx. 3. See also Job iv. 17—20, and xv. 15, 16, and ix. 2, 3. How wisely did David plead, "Enter not into judgment with thy servant, for in thy sight shall no man living be justified." Psa. cxliii. 2. It is the part of wisdom for every mortal to say "If I justify myself, mine own mouth shall condemn me: if I say, I am perfect, it shall also prove me perverse." Job ix. 20. Let us confess, "all we like sheep have gone astray; we have turned every one to his own way," Peter (1 Pet. v. 5,) has forewarned us that "God resisteth the proud, and giveth grace to the humble." Here is the secret of the difference of the treatment received by the pharisee and the publican, the one with unhumbled heart pleading his own goodness, the other crying "God be merciful to me a sinner." Indeed it is the unvarying law of God's government that "whosoever shall exalt himself shall be abased, and he that humbleth himself shall be exalted." "Christ came not to call the righteous," he came to call "sinners to repentance." All this is well summed up in the Heidelberg Catechism. "62. But why cannot our good works be the whole or part of our righteousness before God?

Because that the righteousness which can be approved of before the tribunal of God, must be absolutely perfect, and in all respects conformable to the divine law; and also, that our best works in this life, are all imperfect and defiled with sin.

63. What! do our good works merit nothing, which yet God will reward in this and a future life?

This reward is not of merit, but of grace.

64. But doth not this doctrine make men careless and profane?

By no means; for it is impossible that those who are implanted into Christ by a true faith, should not bring forth the fruits of thankfulness."

The effect of all God's saving dealings with men's souls, is ultimately to bring them to remember their ways, and all their doings wherein they have been defiled; and to loathe themselves in their own sight for all their evils that they have committed, and to know that God is the LORD, when he has wrought with them for his name's sake, and not according to their wicked ways, nor according to their corrupt doings. Ezek. xx. 43, 44.

From all that has been said it follows that man needs the grace of Christ. Where evil exists a remedy is called for. He, who is sick, needs a physician. It would be better for the blind, if their eyes were opened; for the deaf, if their ears were unstopped; for the halt, if their lameness were taken away. The unclean need washing; the condemned, pardon. Those who are not holy should be renewed. To the diseased even painful remedies are a kindness. The perishing need mercy, the guilty need grace. The lost should be sought and found. The starving require bread; the thirsty, water; the wounded, oil and wine; the cold and naked, raiment and shelter. The truth is, we are dead in trespasses and sins, yea, *twice dead.* How strong this language, and yet how just! If any ma fight against it, his quarrel is with God, not with those, who by divine command preach the doctrine. The Bible is a sober book. It never mocks us. It never trifles with any man's feelings. It gives no idle alarms. It scatters all needless fears, and cuts up superstition by the roots; yet it says, we are dead, twice dead, dead by nature; dead by actual transgression; dead by the law; dead by a wilful, ungrateful, unbelieving rejection of Christ. What a death! Men are dead, like a very dry tree, which is ready to be plucked up by the roots. If a spark touches it, it is soon all in a blaze. There is in unconverted men, no spiritual life, no warmth of affection, towards God and

8*

holiness. They have no good hope through grace. The life and love of God are not in them. Separated from God, they cannot live. For as the branch severed from the vine, or the arm from the trunk, or the body from the soul is dead, being alone, so the spirit of man without God is dead also. Surely man in this state needs a Saviour. Never were necessities so extreme. If God intended to do something, "which angels would desire to look into," what would more surely gain his end, than to provide a Saviour for lost men? It is no insult to offer grace to such rebels as we are. A little humility, faith and love, would make us all adopt as our creed the words of Peter: "We believe that through the grace of our Lord Jesus Christ, we shall be saved even as they." At least we should say, that we never can be saved otherwise, and should greatly desire to be saved in this blessed way. If not thus saved we are for ever undone. Our true wisdom is to cry, "We do not present our supplications before thee for our righteousness, but for thy great mercies." Dan. ix. 18. This brings us naturally to the consideration of the amazing grace, actually shown to men in their salvation by Jesus Christ.

CHAPTER XII.

THE TRUE NOTION OF GRACE.

THE Synod of Dort says that "God oweth no man grace. For how can God become debtor to him, who hath nothing to give first, that it might be recompensed to him again? Nay, what can God owe him, who hath nought of his own but sin and untruth? Whosoever therefore is made partaker of this kind of grace, ever oweth and ever payeth thanks to God only." The term, *grace*, often occurs in Scripture. Sometimes it means beauty, as in Prov. i. 9 and iv. 9. But this is never the meaning of the word in the New Testament. There the generic idea of the term is favour, unmerited kindness, undeserved love, unbought pity, gift, mere gratuity. This grace is variously manifested. The gospel is itself called grace because it is the fruit and evidence of God's unmerited goodness. The privilege of preaching the gospel is for the same reason called grace And indeed it is a great favour to be allowed to publish the glad tidings of great joy. No man deserves such honour. Pardon of sin and acceptance with God are both often said to be by grace, by mercy undeserved. The work of purifying the hearts of his people and fitting them for glory is effected by the grace of God. God does it purely out of pity and love, and not at all out of regard to any merit of ours. Renewal and sanctification are rich fruits of mercy. Without God's grace salvation is absolutely impossible. A salvation, which failed to root out sin, and set up the reign of grace, would no doubt be pleasing to the carnal mind, and would delight a hypocrite; but could never satisfy the longings of a real child of God. Sin in its reigning power, no less than in its fearful guilt, must be destroyed, or it will destroy us. He, who fails to gain the victory over his lusts, fails of heaven. If they be not put down, we labour in vain and spend our strength for nought.

Hardly anything is more striking than the obstinate attachment of men to their own works, and their consequent aversion to the grace of God. The great mass of unrenewed men, even in Christian assemblies, have really no idea of ever being saved otherwise than by *becoming good*, and that in their own strength. They generally suspect that they are not now what they ought to be, but they intend to do better hereafter. They seem very ignorant of the extent, spirituality and holiness of the law; and thus while conscience does not flame out against them, they rest in the delusion that they are not very bad, and may easily improve. The very last thing which a sinner under conviction does, is to give up his self-confidence. He cleaves to it as if salvation depended upon his good opinion of himself. Indeed till God's Spirit enlightens his mind, he will not see that salvation can never be compassed by his own power or merit. So that the very process, by which a sinner is led to the Saviour, is usually one of extreme sadness. He has less and less, in his own esteem, worthy of honourable mention before God, until at last he finds out that he is nothing but a guilty, vile, lost, helpless, perishing sinner. To a Christian, who knows what is going on in the sinner's mind, these new views awaken lively hopes that a work of grace is begun in his heart. But often the sinner himself is almost in despair. He supposes that his convictions are forerunners of condemnation and rejection, not of conversion. And when he is led to Christ, and hope springs up in his mind, none is more surprised at the change in his views than himself. He did not expect deliverance in that way. He had not yet become good in his own eyes. He now learns that it is God's plan to save sinners who simply believe. To him the Gospel is a revelation of mercy. He is charmed with the method of grace. He gives all honour to the Redeemer, and is willing to be counted the chief of sinners. He no longer goes about to establish his own righteousness, which is of the law. His own merits he counts as nothing. He simply wishes to be found in Christ. His song is of free unmerited grace. He is no longer wedded to the law, as a means of justification, but he is married to Christ, who is now all his salvation. He works, indeed, but it is from love to the Saviour. He says, "What I am, I am by the grace of God." He casts his crown at the Saviour's feet. He expects all from the grace of Christ. A clergyman once represented the conduct of awakened sinners towards God's offers of gratuitous salvation thus: A benevolent and rich man had a very poor neighbour, to whom he sent this message; "I wish to make you the gift of a farm." The poor man was pleased with the idea of having a farm, but was too proud at once to receive it as a gift. So he thought of the matter much and anxiously. His desire to have a home of his own was daily growing stronger, but his pride was great. At length he determined to visit him who had made the offer. But a strange delusion about this time seized him, for he imagined that he had a bag of gold. So he came with his bag, and said to the rich man, "I have received your message, and have come to see you. I wish to own the farm, but I wish to pay for it. I will give you a bag of gold for it." "Let us see your gold," said the owner of the farm. The poor man opened his bag and looked, and his countenance was changed, and he said, "Sir, I thought it was gold, but I am sorry to say it is but silver; I will give you my bag of silver for your farm." "Look again; I do not think it is even silver," was the solemn but kind reply. The poor man looked, and as he beheld, his eyes were further opened, and he said, "How I have been deceived. It is not silver but only copper. Will you sell me your farm for my bag of copper? You may have it all." "Look again," was the only reply. The poor man looked, tears stood in his eyes, his delusion seemed to be gone, and he said, "Alas, I am undone. It is not even copper. It is but ashes. How poor I am! I wish to own that farm, but I have nothing to pay. Will you *give* me the farm?" The rich man replied, "Yes, that was my first and only offer. Will you accept it on such terms?" With humility but with eagerness the poor man said, "Yes, and a thousand blessings on you for your kindness." The fable is easily applied. Mather has well expressed the difference between grace and merit in few words; "God was a God to Adam before he fell, but to be a God to sinners, this is grace. He was a God to Adam in innocency by virtue of the covenant of works; but he is not a God to any sinner but in the way of free grace. Now that was the covenant, 'I will be a God to thee and thy seed.' Gen. xvii. 7. Abraham was a sinner and a child of wrath by nature as well as others; yet God was his God truly. For God to be a God to them that never sinned there may be merit; but for God to be a God to those that have sinned this is grace indeed. They, that do not think this is grace, need not argument, but pity and prayer."

The pious John Newton in few words states with great clearness what grace is: "To bestow gifts upon the miserable is bounty; but to bestow them upon rebels is grace. The greatness of the gifts contrasted with the characters of those who receive them, displays the exceeding riches of the Redeemer's grace. He came to save not the unhappy only, but the ungodly. He gives pardon, peace, and eternal life to his enemies; whose minds are so entirely alienated from him that, until he makes them willing, in the day of his power, their minds are determined against accepting any favour from him.'

CHAPTER XIII.

THE PROPERTIES OF GRACE.—IT IS FREE, SUFFICIENT, UNSELFISH, RICH IN BLESSINGS.

IN many things the grace of God differs from all other manifestations of favour. We should not be surprised at this when we reflect that as the heavens are higher than the earth, so are his ways higher than our ways, and his thoughts than our thoughts. There is none like Jehovah in love, or in majesty, in glory or in condescension. Beyond everything else called grace it is free. It is beyond the power of man to earn it, to deserve it, to purchase it. No price is to be paid for it. To offer anything as an equivalent for it is to insult God. "Without money and without price" is the sole method of its bestowment. This grace is absolutely, everlastingly, immutably free. If you ever secure it, it will not be by paying for it thousands of rivers of oil, the cattle on a thousand hills, the wealth of the world.

This grace is, moreover, all-sufficient. It alone does all. He, who has it is rich beyond the power of want, is strong beyond the possibility of being finally vanquished, is justified so that he can never come into condemnation. It meets every demand of justice, every temptation, every emergency. "My grace is sufficient for thee," are words as sweet as ever reached the ears of mortals.

Another property of divine grace is that it is disinterested and unselfish. It is pure grace. The happiness of the King of kings is not augmented by having kings and priests to bow before him. God is, and was, and shall be blessed for evermore. God's almightiness excludes all want by excluding all weakness. If God could fail in anything, he might cease to be blessed and so cease to be God. When there was as yet no created spirit, and the Spirit increate and eternal existed in solitary grandeur in the universe, that Infinite and Eternal Mind was as happy as it is now, or ever shall be. To the divine blessedness there is no limit, there comes no change. Like his wisdom, power, holiness and truth, his happiness cannot vary. Neither creation nor redemption was undertaken to heighten the bliss of the Godhead. The Bible teaches that if men were even spotlessly holy, they would still be unprofitable servants. "If thou sinnest, what doest thou against him? or if thy transgressions be multiplied, what doest thou against him? If thou be righteous, what givest thou him? or what receiveth he of thine hand? Thy wickedness may hurt a man as thou art; and thy righteousness may profit the son of man. * * Can a man be profitable unto God as he that is wise may be profitable unto himself?" Job xxxv. 6—8 and xxii. 2. God does indeed order all things for his own honour and glory; but that is not for the increase of his infinite blessedness. Pure grace and unbought love have done all for sinners. There is no mixture of God's grace and man's goodness in salvation. God owed nothing, could owe nothing to apostate man. It is a shameful and wicked derogation from the grace of the Gospel to assert that

God intended thereby to make amends to our race for the defects of the covenant of works. That covenant was wise, holy, just and good. Under it the angels enjoy all their bliss. As long as man kept it, he was unspeakably happy. And when he fell under the curse of that covenant, he did it not by any inevitable necessity of nature, but by his own voluntary choice of that which had been forbidden. Nowhere in the Bible is it hinted that God promulged the covenant of grace as something due to us. On the contrary it traces all to divine bountifulness and mercifulness. It speaks on this wise: "God, who is rich in mercy, for his great love wherewith he hath loved us, even when we were dead in sins, hath quickened us together with Christ (by grace are ye saved), and hath raised us up together, and made us sit together in heavenly places in Christ Jesus: that in the ages to come he might show the exceeding riches of his grace, in his kindness toward us through Christ Jesus. For by grace are ye saved through faith, and that not of yourselves; it is the gift of God; not of works, lest any man should boast." Eph. ii. 4—9. Many other portions of Scripture teach the same truth, but this one is so full and explicit that nothing but perversity and blindness can misconstrue its precious doctrine. The peculiar sweetness and excellence of this view of the subject is, first, that it renders illustrious beyond a parallel the mercy of God in Christ, and thus lays a sure foundation for the temple of praise which is now rising to the sovereign love of God. Secondly, this view brings strong consolation to the righteous, because if God had gracious regards towards them when they had no holiness nor good desires, they may assuredly hope that having freely given them new hearts, and having also freely justified them, he will not abandon them to ruin, nor hand them over to condemnation. Nor is this grace in its bestowments limited to a few small items. It would have been unmerited kindness for eternal mercy to have expressed any pity for man. It would have been more than man deserved for God to have given him a respite of a thousand years from the fiery doom, which was before him. It is mere mercy that keeps a sinner out of hell even for an hour. But when God undertook to be gracious, he confined himself to no little work, but devised a plan incomprehensibly great and glorious, running through all coming time, and the eternity beyond that, and embracing in its effects in some way myriads on myriads of happy creatures, who study it, admire it, or taste its abundant provisions. So that on this side of heaven there is no higher exercise of virtue than simply to believe and cordially to rely upon the statements of God's word respecting this greatest of all devices. The first result attained by the works of grace in our world is the securing of an unparalleled revenue of renown to the divine government. *Glory to God in the highest* is an effect peculiar to the work of redemption. To men the results are as happy as to God they are honourable. The fruits of God's grace are so many, and so rich, and so necessary, that we may safely say, without them existence is not desirable; but with them life is a great boon and blessing, though it should be begun by ten thousand years of such affliction as the saints on earth are subject to. God's plan of mercy in Christ secures us against all conceivable ills, except such as shall themselves be made the means of ultimate and eternal gain to us. It also secures the possession of all conceivable good things for this world and the next, and at the best possible time. The tenor of Scripture on these points is unmistakable: "All things are yours; whether Paul, or Apollos, or Cephas, or the world, or life, or death, or things present, or things to come; all are yours; and ye are Christ's; and Christ is God's." 1 Cor. iii. 21—23. Even inspired men seem at a loss for words to convey an adequate conception of any of God's saving mercies. In his gospel John says, "God so loved the world;" and in his first epistle he says, "Behold! what manner of love." Paul breaks out, "Thanks be unto God for his unspeakable gift." With our Lord and his apostles crowns and kingdoms are favourite emblems of the riches of our inheritance in Christ. Nor does God ever revoke any promise made to man in Christ Jesus. "The Lord is not man that he should repent." He never begins to build and finds himself unable to finish. Nor has he affixed to the gospel offer any meritorious condition to be performed by us. Jesus Christ fulfilled the entire conditions of the covenant of grace, so far as satisfying the law and bringing in righteousness are concerned. The fourth property of this grace, then, is that it is exceedingly fruitful in the most precious and most permanent blessings.

CHAPTER XIV.

GOD'S GRACE IS ALSO OF GREAT ANTIQUITY, SOVEREIGN AND DISTINGUISHING.

ANOTHER property of God's grace is that it bears date from the most remote antiquity, even the past eternity of Jehovah. It is not therefore of recent origin, as all human and even angelic friendships are. The plan of showing grace to lost sinners existed before men were lost. It is as old as the plan of the universe. On this subject the language of inspiration is decisive. Paul says to the Ephesians, "Blessed be the God and Father of our Lord Jesus Christ, who hath blessed us with all spiritual blessings in heavenly places in Christ: according as he hath chosen us in him before the foundation of the world, that we should be holy and without blame before him in love; having predestinated us unto the adoption of children by Jesus Christ to himself, according to the good pleasure of his will, to the praise of the glory of his grace, who hath made us accepted in the Beloved." David says: "The mercy of the Lord is from everlasting to everlasting upon them that fear him." Psa. ciii. 17. In Ephesians iii. 11, it is said, we are saved according to an "eternal purpose." The mercies of time are the fruits of the love of eternity. In Jeremiah (xxxi. 3,) the whole work of salvation is ascribed to a divine regard as eternal as the Godhead. "I have loved thee with an everlasting love; therefore with loving kindness have I drawn thee." How precious is the truth that in the counsels of inconceivably distant ages man was not forgotten; but even then Jehovah by his prescience looked upon him in his guilt and vileness and misery, and purposed to raise from the deep and dark abyss of the apostacy a people who should be his church, a people who should ever stand "to the praise of the glory of his grace." Some indeed say that this doctrine encourages sin. But the Bible teaches a very different doctrine. "We love him because he FIRST loved us." "Ye have not chosen me, but I have chosen you, and ordained you, that ye should go and bring forth fruit, and that your fruit should remain." Some say that this view represents God as loving the vile and base and guilty. The answer is that the Scriptures clearly teach as much. "God so loved the world" (guilty, lost and ruined as it was,) "that he gave his only begotten Son that whosoever believeth on him should not perish, but have everlasting life." Indeed they say that this view is not only just and true, but honourable to God. In Romans (v. 8,) Paul says that "God commendeth his love towards us in that while we were yet sinners Christ died for us." Here is one of the brightest glories of the covenant of grace. The stability of the whole plan of redemption is in Scripture said to depend on this great fact: "If while we were enemies we were reconciled by the death of his Son; much more, being reconciled, we shall be saved by his life." Rom. v. 10. God's good will to man, his pity for the lost, his grace to sinners are not novelties to the divine mind. They have run parallel with the divine existence in all past duration.

In contemplating this grace the devout mind finds itself filled with awe and delight at discovering that God's grace is sovereign and distinguishing. Thus our Saviour thought and felt when he said, "I thank thee, O Father, Lord of heaven and earth, because thou hast hid these things from the wise and prudent and hast revealed them unto babes. Even so, Father, for so it seemed good in thy sight." Matt. xi. 25, 26. In this solemn, holy and thankful manner did our blessed Master view this doctrine. Let us imitate him. Let us not rush into doubtful disputations. Let us adore and not cavil. Reason is presumptuous when it revises the decisions of God. Our blessed Lord often insisted on this doctrine, although then as now it was very offensive to the carnal mind. In Luke iv. 25—29 we have this record: "I tell you of a truth, many widows were in Israel in the days of Elias, when the heaven was shut up three years and six months, when great famine was throughout all the land; but unto none of them was Elias sent, save unto Sarepta, a city of Sidon, unto a woman that was a widow. And many lepers were in Israel in the time of Eliseus the prophet; and none of them was cleansed, saving Naaman the Syrian. And all they in the synagogue, when they heard these things, were filled with wrath, and rose up, and thrust him out of the city, and led him unto the brow of the hill (whereon their city was built) that they might cast him down headlong." What shall we then do? If the doctrine so offends men, shall we give it up? Are we to make peace with human wickedness by observing a profound silence on this topic?

Nay, let us rather imitate Christ, who often preached it. The parable of the hired labourers found in Matt. xx. 1—16 is spoken for the express purpose of showing that God will do as he pleases with his own, and that for so doing, he may not be complained of. Indeed by Moses God said, "I will have mercy on whom I will have mercy, and I will have compassion, on whom I will have compassion; so then, it is not of him that willeth, nor of him that runneth, but of God that showeth mercy." As God is abundant in goodness and truth, we see ground of hope and confidence. As he is sovereign in the bestowment of his favours, let us fear before him and adore. He, who will not be pleased with the divine character and government until he can see God waiting on the nod and promptly obeying the mandates of the human will, can never be reconciled to God. "The Lord is a great king and a great God above all gods." "The Lord is king for ever and ever." "The Lord reigneth, let the earth rejoice." "The Lord reigneth, let the people tremble." Jesus Christ not only taught this doctrine, but as the Son of God with power he displayed its truth in calling to himself whom he would for his disciples and apostles, in saving one thief and not the other, in bringing Peter to repentance, and in sending Judas to his own place, in calling and saving Saul of Tarsus and letting Nero persist in sin.

The sovereignty of grace is shown principally in three ways; in the *race* to which mercy is extended, viz: the *human* and not the *angelic*. The heavenly host, who fell, were passed by and left in utter and irretrievable ruin and hopeless sorrow. Compare Jude vi. and John iii. 16. Why this was so we cannot tell.

The loadstone passes by gold and silver and attracts iron. The grace of God passed by angels and came "a little lower," even to man. God also makes known his Gospel and sends his ambassadors to some *nations* and not to others. Thus at first Judea was distinguished from India. Thus now America and Britain are distinguished from Tartary and Japan. And in the same nation, city and family one *person* is taken and another left, one is pardoned, converted, sanctified and received up to glory, while another no worse by nature, dies in his sins. This sovereignty is exercised solely "according to the good pleasure of his will," and not at all on account of any goodness belonging to us, or foreseen in us. Very explicitly and conclusively does Paul prove this: "For *the children* being not yet born, neither having done any good or evil, that the purpose of God according to election might stand, not of works, but of him that calleth; it was said unto her, The elder shall serve the younger. As it is written, Jacob have I loved, but Esau have I hated. What shall we say then? Is there unrighteousness with God? God forbid. For he saith to Moses, I will have mercy on whom I will have mercy, and I will have compassion on whom I will have compassion. So then it is not of him that willeth, nor of him that runneth, but of God that showeth mercy. For the Scripture saith unto Pharaoh, Even for this same purpose have I raised thee up, that I might show my power in thee, and that my name might be declared throughout all the earth. Therefore hath he mercy on whom he will have mercy, and whom he will he hardeneth. Thou wilt say then unto me, Why doth he yet find fault? For who hath resisted his will? Nay but, O man, who art thou that repliest against God? Shall the thing formed say to him that formed it, Why hast thou made me thus? Hath not the potter power over the clay, of the same lump to make one vessel unto honour, and another unto dishonour? What if God, willing to show his wrath, and to make his power known, endured with much long-suffering the vessels of wrath fitted to destruction: and that he might make known the riches of his glory on the vessels of mercy, which he had afore prepared unto glory"—Is not such teaching conclusive? Who can resist it, without refusing to believe God? In rebuking some, who persisted in asserting that God dispenses his grace among men, according to his foreknowledge of the good use which they will severally make of it, Augustine says: "Who but must wonder that this most ingenious sense should escape the Apostle? For after proposing what was suited to excite astonishment respecting those children yet unborn, he started to himself by way of objection, the following question. What then, is there unrighteousness with God? It was the place for him to answer, that God foresaw the deserts of each of them, yet he says nothing of this, but resorts to the decrees and mercy of God."

Indeed on the day of Pentecost the whole weight of Peter's argument in convincing his hearers of their sin was in connection with this doctrine. Speaking of Christ, Peter said: "Him being delivered by the determinate counsel and foreknowledge of God, ye have taken, and by wicked hands have crucified and slain." Acts ii. 23. Now, if he had failed to convince them that in putting Christ to death they had fulfilled the eternal purpose, the determinate counsel of God, he would have failed to convince them of Christ's Messiahship. Or if he had failed to convince them that in doing this of envy and unbelief and enmity they were wicked, then his preaching would have been in vain. There is no escaping from these conclusions. To fulfil God's decrees with a wicked heart is wicked, is the height of wickedness.

That the doctrine of election is a ground of encouragement to pious preachers of the Gospel is certain. Thousands have told us so. It was so to Paul. "Then spake the Lord to Paul in the night by a vision, Be not afraid, but speak, and hold not thy peace: for I am with thee, and no man shall set on thee to hurt thee: FOR I HAVE MUCH PEOPLE IN THIS CITY." Acts xviii. 9, 10. The previous context shows that the Jews at Corinth "opposed themselves and blasphemed." In fact the work of founding a church there was but just begun. Yet God says, "I have much people in this city." No man will say that God merely designed to inform Paul that Corinth was populous. He knew this already. The only fair logical meaning is that among the crowds of the ungodly in that city, were many of God's elect, whom he purposed by Paul's ministry soon to bring to a saving knowledge of Christ. The doctrine of election, *rightly understood*, holds out the only ground of encouragement, which we have, for preaching the blessed Gospel. If God has no elect, we preach in vain.

CHAPTER XV.

GOD'S PURPOSE OF GRACE.

"ALL Scripture is given by inspiration of God, and is profitable for doctrine, for reproof, for correction, for instruction in righteousness." If this be so we should very carefully guard our hearts that we indulge in no prejudices against any portion of divine truth. If God has revealed anything to us, it will do us good to receive it with meekness and fear.

It is not possible for any candid person to deny that the Bible uses words, which seem to teach that God governs the world by a fixed plan, and that events occurring in a manner to us accidental, or brought about by human agency were foreseen and pre-ordained by God. Without dealing in general assertions, let us come at once to God's word. There we find *first* the word *decree* applied to God's plan. The reason why the sea is contained within certain limits is that God has determined it shall be so. "He gave the sea his decree, that the waters should not pass his commandment." Prov. viii. 29. He has "placed the sand for the bound of the sea by a perpetual decree." Jer. v. 22. Elsewhere the same thing is taught in almost the same words. It cannot therefore be denied that God holds the sea in bounds by his unchangeable decree. The Scriptures also declare that it is the fixed decree of God, which nothing can alter, that his Son should be the Mediator. "Yet have I set my King upon my holy hill of Zion. I will declare the decree: The LORD hath said unto me, Thou art my Son, this day have I begotten thee." None will deny that the mediatorial throne has its stability in the everlasting unchangeable purpose of God. So likewise Daniel declares that Nebuchadnezzar was expelled from among men "by the decree of the Most High." Dan. iv. 24.

The Scriptures also use the word *appoint* as expressive of the same idea. Thus Christ says: "I appoint unto you a kingdom, as my Father hath appointed unto me." Luke xxii. 29. Men must have made great advances in boldness before they can deny that all Christ's exaltation and glory are fixed and given him by the unchangeable appointment of God, and yet by an appointment of the same kind all his people shall have a kingdom. So also the day of judgment is fixed. Nothing can hasten it; nothing can defer it: "He hath appointed a day, in the which he will judge the world." Acts xvii. 31. So also no man can die a moment sooner, or live a moment longer than God pleases, and his pleasure and his counsel always agree. "Is there not an appointed time to man upon earth?" "Seeing his days are determined, the number of his months is with thee, thou hast appointed his bounds that he cannot pass." Job vii. 1 and xiv. 5. Nor is this doctrine offensive to the pious. Job says: "All the days of my appointed time will I wait, till my change come." Job xiv. 14. The subversion of the plots of the wicked is in Scripture ascribed to their running counter to God's fixed plan. "For the LORD had appointed to defeat the good counsel of Ahithophel, to the intent that the Lord might bring evil upon Absalom." 2 Sam. xvii. 14. God's word no less clearly declares that the wicked rejection of Jesus Christ by sinners, instead of defeating, is executing God's plan. For he is "a stone of stumbling, and a rock of offence, even to them, which stumble at the word, being disobedient: whereunto also they were appointed." 1 Pet. ii. 8.

Again: the Scriptures call God's fixed plan his counsel and declare its unchangeableness. If it could be changed, it would be either for the better, or for the worse. If it could be changed for the better, it is now imperfect. If it should be changed for the worse it would become imperfect. In either case, it would be unworthy of God. But it cannot be changed: "I am God and there is none like me, declaring the end from the beginning, and from ancient times the things that are not yet done, saying, My counsel shall stand, and I will do all my pleasure." Isa. xlvi. 9, 10. "The counsel of the Lord standeth for ever, the thoughts of his heart to all generations." Psa. xxxiii. 11. No plotting and ingenuity and malice of man can hinder what God will do. "There are many devices in a man's heart; nevertheless the counsel of the LORD, that shall stand." Prov. xix. 21. The Apostles held that God's plan was carried out, even in the wickedness shown towards Christ, and they adoringly said that his enemies "were gathered together for to do whatsoever thy hand and thy counsel determined before to be done." Acts iv. 28. Indeed Paul says that God does "all things after the counsel of his own will." Eph. i. 11. He also says that God has taken great care "to show unto the heirs of promise the immutability of his counsel." Heb. vi. 17.

In like manner the Bible speaks of God's purpose; and says that our conversion is in fulfilment of it—"called according to his purpose." It declares that this purpose embraces the destinies of men. Before Rebecca had given birth to any child it was said, "The elder shall serve the younger," and all this Paul says was, "that the purpose of God according to election might stand." Rom. viii. 28 and ix. 11. Nor is God's purpose temporal, or mutable, but he conducts all things "according to the eternal purpose which he purposed in Christ Jesus our Lord." Eph. iii. 11. Here is the foundation of all our hopes of life; for he "hath saved us, and called us with a holy calling, not according to our works, but according to his own purpose and grace, which was given us in Christ Jesus before the world began." 2 Tim. i. 9.

Nor are inspired writers afraid of the word, predestination, or of the doctrine taught thereby: "Whom he did foreknow, he also did predestinate to be conformed to the image of his Son, that he might be the first-born among many brethren. Moreover, whom he did predestinate, them he also called; and whom he called, them he also justified; and whom he justified, them he also glorified." Rom. viii. 29, 30. "Having predestinated us unto the adoption of children by Jesus Christ to himself, according to the good pleasure of his will." Eph. i. 5. See also verses 11 and 12.

We also find election taught throughout God's word and in many ways. 1. God's well-beloved and eternal Son was chosen out of all in the universe to be the Redeemer of lost men. Accordingly in Isaiah xlii. 1, and in 1 Pet. ii. 6, Christ is called God's elect. I have never seen the professing Christian, who was bold enough to deny that our Saviour was "chosen of God." Augustine well says: "The highest illustration of predestination and grace, is in the Saviour himself, the man Christ Jesus, who has acquired this character in his human nature, without any previous merit either of works or of faith." 2. Election extends to the angels, some of whom are holy and happy, others sinful and miserable. The holy ones are expressly called "elect angels." 1 Tim. v. 21. 3. When some angels and all men had fallen under condemnation, God's electing love turned towards sinners of the human race and not at all towards fallen angels. John iii. 16; 2 Pet. ii. 4. 4. When all nations were rapidly hastening to idolatry and gross corruption, God selected one man and granted to him and his descendants peculiar privileges and mercies. "He did choose Abram and did bring him forth out of Ur of the Chaldees." From that time for generations this family was often spoken of as the chosen, the elect of God. Deut. iv. 37 and vii. 6—8; 1 Chron. xvi. 13, 14; Psa. xxxii. 12, and in many other places. 5. God also exercises his choice as to the heirs of salvation. They are called "God's elect." Rom. viii. 33. Christ calls them "the elect." Matt. xxiv. 22, 24, 31; Luke xviii. 7. Paul says, "God hath chosen us in Christ before the foundation of the world that we should be holy and without blame before him in love." Eph. i. 4. How any man can dispose of all these texts without rejecting God's word, and yet refuse to admit decrees, predestination and election, it is not easy to tell. Is anything more fixed than the events of death, judgment and eternity with all that shall be done therein? Every man plans, purposes, predestinates, before he acts or builds. Has the Builder of the universe no plan, no purpose? As to whether we first chose Christ, or Christ us, what Christian can have a doubt, when he remembers his own vile wanderings, and Christ's explicit teachings? "Ye have not chosen me, but I have chosen you." John xv. 16. Indeed what is a prophecy but a revealed decree? What is a decree but a purpose not revealed, not made known in prophecy?

The consent of the people of God in all periods of the Christian Church has been as remarkably in favour of the doctrine here maintained as in regard to any other. Formal opposition to it by those, who otherwise stood fair in God's Church, was unknown to the ancients. How clearly this doctrine was taught by Augustine all well-informed people know: "Intra mundum facti sumus, et ante mundum electi sumus." "We are made in time, but we were chosen before the world began." "Before he made us, he foreknew us, and he chose us in his foreknowledge when he had not as yet made us." "Out of those to whom the righteous Lord had adjudged punishment, according to the unspeakable mercy of his hidden dispensation, he chose out vessels, which he might fit for honour." Augustine also quotes the following from Ambrose's book on predestination: "Whom Christ has mercy on, him he calls. Those who were indevout, he could, if he would, have made devout. But God calls whom he pleases, and makes whom he will religious." Augustine took the right view of this doctrine when he said: "Do you wish to dispute with me? Rather unite with me in admiration, and exclaim, O the depth! Let us both agree in fear, lest we perish in error." More explicit statements he could not make.

Fulgentius says: "God, who has made man, did himself prepare, in his predestination, both the gift of illumination to believe, and the gift of perseverance to profit and persevere, and the gift of glorification to reign, for those to whom he pleased to give it; who also does not any otherwise perform indeed, than was ordained by his eternal and unchangeable will. The truth of which predestination, whereby the Apostle witnesseth, we were predestinated in Christ before the foundation of the world," &c. &c.

Prosper says: "Predestinationem Dei nullus catholicus negat." "No catholic denies the predestination of God." "The belief of predestination is confirmed by abundant authority of the holy Scriptures," &c. "From the punishment of the sin of our first parent none is freed but by the grace of our Lord Jesus Christ, prepared and predestinated in the eternal counsel of God before the foundation of the world."

The Latter Confession of Helvetia says: "God hath from the beginning, and of his mere grace, without any respect of men, predestinated or elected the saints, whom he will save in Christ," and quotes Eph. i. 4, and 2 Tim. i. 9, 10. "Therefore, though not for any merit of ours, yet not without a means, but in Christ, and for Christ, did God choose us; and they who are now engrafted into Christ, the same also were elected."

The Confession of Basle says: "We confess, that God, before he had created the world, had chosen all those to whom he would freely give the inheritance of eternal blessedness," and quotes Rom. viii. 29, 30, and Eph. i. 4—6.

The Confession of France says: "We believe that

out of this universal corruption and condemnation, wherein by nature all men are drowned, God did deliver and preserve some, whom, by his eternal and immutable counsel, of his own goodness and mercy, without any respect of their works, he did choose in Christ Jesus; and others he left in that corruption and condemnation, in whom he might make manifest his justice, by condemning them justly in their time, as well as declare the riches of his mercy in the others. For some are not better than others, till such time as the Lord doth make a difference, according to that immutable counsel, which he had decreed in Christ Jesus before the creation of the world."

The Confession of Scotland says: "That same eternal God, who of mere grace elected us in Christ Jesus his Son, before the foundation of the world was laid, (Eph. i. 11, 12,) appointed him to be our head," &c.

The Confession of Belgia says: "We believe that God * * hath showed himself to be both merciful and just: merciful, by delivering and saving those from condemnation and from death, whom, in his eternal counsel, of his own free goodness, he hath chosen in Jesus Christ our Lord, without any regard at all of their works; but just, in leaving others in that their fall and perdition, whereinto they had thrown themselves headlong."

The Synod of Dort says: "Election is the unchangeable purpose of God, by which, before the foundation of the world, according to the most free pleasure of his will, and of his mere grace, out of all mankind (fallen through their own fault from their first integrity into sin and destruction) he hath chosen in Christ unto salvation a set number of certain men, neither better nor more worthy than others, but lying in the common misery with others." In subsequent sections many explanations are given, as that this election is not manifold, but one; that it was not made upon the foresight of faith or good works, but was unto faith and holiness; that the true cause of this free election is the good pleasure of God; that it cannot be interrupted, changed, revoked, or disannulled; that this doctrine is to be reverently received, &c. &c.

The Church of England in her 17th Article says: "Predestination to life is the everlasting purpose of God, whereby (before the foundations of the earth were laid) he hath constantly decreed by his counsel, secret to us, to deliver from curse and damnation those, whom he hath chosen in Christ out of mankind, and to bring them by Christ to everlasting salvation, as vessels made to honour. Wherefore, they which be endued with so excellent a benefit of God, be called according to God's purpose by his Spirit working in due season: they through grace obey the calling: they be justified freely: they be made sons of God by adoption: they be made like the image of his only begotten Son, Jesus Christ: they walk religiously in good works: and at length, by God's mercy, they attain to everlasting felicity.

"As the godly consideration of predestination, and our election in Christ, is full of sweet, pleasant, and unspeakable comfort to godly persons, and such as feel in themselves the working of the Spirit of Christ, mortifying the works of the flesh, and their earthly members, and drawing up their mind to high and heavenly things, (as well because it doth greatly establish and confirm their faith of eternal salvation to be enjoyed through Christ, as because it doth fervently kindle their love towards God;) so, for curious and carnal persons, lacking the Spirit of Christ, to have continually before their eyes the sentence of God's predestination, is a most dangerous downfall, whereby the devil doth thrust them either into desperation, or into wretchedness of most unclean living, no less perilous than desperation.

"Furthermore, we must receive God's promises in such wise as they be generally set forth to us in holy Scripture. And in our doings that will of God is to be followed, which we have expressly declared unto us in the word of God."

The Church of Ireland has made up her Article on "God's eternal decree and predestination," from three sources; 1. The Confession of the Westminster Assembly; 2. The 17th Article of the Church of England; and 3. The celebrated Lambeth Articles. That the reader may have a conception of the strength and clearness of these last, a few of them are inserted. They were agreed upon at Lambeth, the 20th of November, A. D. 1595. Archbishop Whitgift and Bishops Bancroft and Vaughan were among the able and staunch friends of these Articles; "By the same eternal counsel, God hath predestinated some unto life, and reprobated some unto death; of both which there is a certain number, which can neither be increased nor diminished. The cause moving God to predestinate unto life, is not the foreseeing of faith, or good works, or of anything, which is in the person predestinated, but only the good pleasure of God himself. But such as are not predestinated to salvation, shall finally be condemned for their sins." The Westminster Confession says that "God from all eternity did, by the most wise and holy counsel of his own will, freely and unchangeably ordain whatsoever comes to pass: yet so as thereby neither is God the author of sin, nor is violence offered to the will of the creatures, nor is the liberty or contingency of second causes taken away, but rather established." Much more is said to the same purpose, but quite coincident with what has been already quoted from the same and other symbols.

The great lights of the Church in modern times have also spoken with much force on this subject. Luther, in commenting on the words "who separated me from my mother's womb," (Gal. i. 15,) says: "This is a Hebrew phrase; as if he said, Who had sanctified, ordained and prepared me. That is, God had appointed, when I was yet in my mother's womb, that I should so rage against his Church, and that afterward he would mercifully call me back again from the midst of my cruelty and blasphemy, by his mere grace, into the way of truth and salvation. To be short, when I was not yet born, I was an apostle in the sight of God, and when the time was come, I was declared an apostle before the whole world.

"Thus Paul cutteth off all deserts, and giveth glory to God alone, but to himself shame and confusion. As though he would say, All the gifts, both small and great, as well spiritual as temporal, which God purposed to give unto me, and all the good things, which at any time in all my life I should do, God himself had before appointed when I was yet in my mother's womb, where I could neither wish, nor think, nor do any good thing. Therefore this gift also came unto me by the mere predestination and free mercy of God, before I was born."

Calvin says: "We shall never be convinced as we ought to be, that our salvation flows from the fountain of God's free mercy, till we are acquainted with his eternal election, which illustrates the grace of God by this comparison, that he adopts not all promiscuously to the hope of salvation, but gives to some what he refuses to others. Ignorance of this principle evidently detracts from the divine glory, and diminishes real humility."

Beveridge says: "If God hath elected us, it is in vain for men or devils to accuse us; if he be our friend, it is in vain for any one to be our foe."

Charnock says: "Conformity to God in purity is the fruit of electing love. *He hath chosen us that we should be holy.* Eph. i. 4. The goodness of the fruit evidences the nature of the root; this is the seal that assures us the patent is the authentic grant of the prince."

John Newton says: "Admitting the total depravity of human nature, how can we account for the conversion of a soul to God, unless we likewise admit an election of grace? The work must begin somewhere. Either the sinner first seeks the Lord, or the Lord first seeks the sinner. The former is impossible, if by nature we are dead in trespasses and sins. * * Let me appeal to yourself. I think you know yourself too well to say that you either sought or loved the Lord first."

Flavel says: "God hath chosen some to salvation and passed by others." "God's choice was not on foreseen works, but merely of his grace, and good pleasure of his will."

Leighton says: "The foreknowledge of God is no other than that eternal love of God, or decree of election, by which some are appointed unto life, and being foreknown or elected to that end, are predestinate tc the way of it." "That thus he chooseth some, and rejecteth others, is for that great end, to manifest and magnify his mercy and justice: but why he appointed this man for the one, and that man for the other, made Peter a vessel of this mercy, and Judas of wrath, this is even so, because it seemed good to him. This if it be harsh, yet is apostolic doctrine. *Hath not the potter* (saith St. Paul) *power over the clay, of the same lump to make one vessel unto honour and another unto dishonour?* This deep we must admire, and always, in considering it, close with this: *O the depth of the riches, both of the wisdom and knowledge of God!*"

A class of honest but timid people, who embrace these views, yet ask, Should this doctrine be preached? The answer is in the affirmative; 1. Because Christ and his Apostles preached it. Their example is safe. 2. It is conducive to holiness when rightly understood and sincerely loved. 3. It is full of comfort to the humble. But then it should be preached as Christ and his Apostles preached it. Augustine says: "Both the grace of free election and predestination, and also wholesome admonitions and doctrines are to be preached."

CHAPTER XVI.

GOD'S WORD TEACHES THE DOCTRINES OF GRACE.—THE FATHERS ALSO.

THE doctrine of gratuitous salvation is prominent in the teachings of inspired men. It is implied in the whole structure of revelation. It is expressly taught in many places. Even on Mount Sinai, amidst all the grandeur and terror of that scene, the LORD passed by and proclaimed himself, "The Lord, the Lord God, merciful and gracious, long-suffering, and abundant in goodness and truth, keeping mercy for thousands, forgiving iniquity, transgression and sin, and that will by no means clear the guilty." Exod. xxxiv. 6, 7. Although in this passage we have a clear revelation of God's inflexible justice, yet we have also a rich variety of expression revealing his grace. That great patriot, soldier, and statesman, renowned for his piety in days of general wickedness, Nehemiah, having given an account of all his labours, perils and sufferings says: "Remember me, O my God, concerning this also, and spare me according to the greatness of thy mercy." Neh. xiii. 22. To this day convinced and penitent sinners find no language more appropriate to their wants, when pleading for mercy and asking for grace, than that used by David, by Daniel, and other Old Testament saints. The wants of sinners as such are in all ages the same. The parable of the pharisee and the publican, the parable of the prodigal son, the parable of the two debtors, and many other teachings of Jesus Christ, clearly show that he led men to hope for salvation as a gift, and in no other way. One of our Lord's sayings has been very dear to afflicted consciences ever since it was uttered, and shall be so while the world stands: "God so loved the world, that he gave his only begotten Son, that whosoever believeth in him should not perish, but have everlasting life."

But in the Epistles, especially those of Paul, the doctrines of grace are stated with great clearness and fulness. In particular the fact of our salvation being a gratuity is unmistakably announced. The following texts are considered sufficient: "But now the righteousness of God without the law is manifested, being witnessed by the law and the prophets; even the righteousness of God, which is by faith of Jesus Christ unto all, and upon all them that believe; for there is no difference: for all have sinned and come short of the glory of God; being justified freely by his grace, through the redemption that is in Christ Jesus; whom God hath set forth to be a propitiation, through faith in his blood, to declare his righteousness for the remission of sins that are past, through the forbearance of God; to declare, I say, at this time his righteousness: that he might be just, and the justifier of him, which believeth in Jesus. Where is boasting then? It is excluded. By what law? of works? Nay: but by the law of faith." Rom. iii. 21—27. Here we are taught 1. that the righteousness of God is without the law; 2. that it yet meets the demands of law, for God is just, when he justifies; 3. that boasting is, by God's method of saving, cut off in every case; and 4. that this is done not by works but by faith. Soon afterwards Paul speaks thus: "Now to him that worketh, is the reward not reckoned of grace, but of debt. But to him that worketh not, but believeth on Him that justifieth the ungodly, his faith is counted for righteousness." Rom. iv. 4, 5. Here whatever works mean, faith is just the opposite; whatever debt is, grace is its opposite. If you owe a man a shilling and pay it, you do not bestow on him a gift. If you owe him nothing and hand him a shilling, it is not paying a debt. The same thing cannot be both a gratuity and the payment of a debt.

Again: "Where sin abounded, grace did much more abound, that as sin hath reigned unto death, even so might grace reign through righteousness unto eternal life, by Jesus Christ our Lord." Rom. v. 20, 21. Here we have, 1. the utter ruin of man—"sin abounded;" 2. the glory and fulness of God's scheme for saving men—"grace did much more abound;" 3. God saves not by trampling on justice, but "grace reigns through righteousness;" 4. the salvation of the gospel is not limited by the temporal blessings it brings—grace reigns "unto eternal life;" and 5. no man is the author of his own salvation, but it is all "by Jesus Christ our Lord." Again: "The gift of God is eternal life through Jesus Christ our Lord." Rom. vi. 23. Nor did Paul teach one doctrine to the Romans, and a different doctrine to other churches. To the Galatians he says: "We who are Jews by nature, and not sinners of the Gentiles, knowing that a man is not justified by the works of the law, but by the faith of Jesus Christ, even we have believed in Jesus Christ, that we might be justified by the faith of Christ, and not by the works of the law; for by the works of the law shall no flesh be justified. * * The life which I now live, I live by the faith of the Son of God, who loved me and gave himself for me. I do not frustrate the grace of God: for if righteousness were by the law, then Christ is dead in vain." Gal. ii. 15, 16, 20, 21. He could not more clearly teach that a denial of gratuitous salvation subverts the whole gospel scheme. Indeed he teaches at large that "as many as are of the works of the law, are under the curse: for it is written, "Cursed is every one that continueth not in all things, which are written in the book of the law, to do them. But that no man is justified by the law in the sight of God, it is evident for, The just shall live by faith." Gal. iii. 10, 11. Again: "Christ is become of no effect unto you, whosoever of you are justified by the law; ye are fallen from grace. For we through the Spirit wait for the hope of righteousness by faith." Gal. v. 4, 5. To the Corinthians he says: "By the grace of God I am what I am." 1 Cor. xv. 10. To a fourth church he twice says: "By grace are ye saved." Eph. ii. 5, 8. To another he says that God even our Father "hath loved us, and given us everlasting consolation and good hope through grace." 2 Thess. ii. 16. To Titus he says that "not by works of righteousness which we have done, but according to his mercy hath he saved us." If any want yet other proofs they can consult Rom. iii. 24; v. 4, 8, 15, 17, 20, and 21. Paul takes pains to remind us that grace excludes works, and works grace. He argues that if salvation be "by grace, then it is no more by works: otherwise grace is no more grace. But if it be of works, then it is no more grace: otherwise work is no more work. Rom.

xi. 6. Wages is one thing, a debt is another thing. The merits of men, if pleaded for righteousness, exclude the merits of Christ. The merits of Christ, if accepted for salvation, exclude our own merits.

It is truly refreshing to find the early writers of the Christian church, after the apostles' days, speaking so clearly as they often do on this subject. Clement of Rome, a cotemporary and fellow labourer of Paul, referring to the Old Testament Fathers says: "All were glorified and exalted, not by themselves, nor by their works, nor by the righteousness they have wrought out, but by his will. We, therefore, being called by his will in Christ, are not justified by ourselves, nor by our own wisdom, understanding or piety, nor by any works, which we have wrought in the holiness of our hearts; but we are justified by faith, by which God Almighty has justified all from the beginning of the world." Polycarp, the disciple of John and the venerable witness of Christ, says: "Let us incessantly and steadfastly adhere to Him, who is our hope, and the earnest of our righteousness, Jesus Christ, who bore our sins in his own body on the tree: who did no sin, neither was guile found in his mouth, but he suffered all on our account, that we might live in him." Justin Martyr says that God "gave his own Son a propitiation for us, the Holy One for transgressors, the innocent for the guilty, the just for the unjust, the incorruptible for the corrupt, for what else could cover our sins but his righteousness? In whom was it possible that we, who are guilty and ungodly, could be justified, except in the Son of God alone? O unsearchable wonder! O unexpected benefit! that the sins of many should be hid in one, and that the righteousness of one should justify many transgressors." Macarius says that, "whatever good a man does by natural strength can never save him without the grace of Jesus Christ." Ambrose says, "If so be that justification, which is by grace, were due unto merits going before, so that it should not be a gift of the giver, but a reward of the worker, the redemption by the blood of Christ would grow to be of small account, and the prerogative of man's works would not yield unto the mercies of God." Again: "They are evidently blessed, whose iniquities are forgiven, without any labour or work, and whose sins are covered, no help of repentance being required of them, but only this that they believe." Again: "They are justified freely, because that working nothing, nor requiting anything, by faith alone they are justified, by the gift of God." Hilary says: "It offended the Scribes, that man should forgive sin, (for they beheld nothing but man in Jesus Christ) and that he should forgive that which the law could not release. For faith alone doth justify." Chrysostom says: "Our works, if there be any consequent on God's gratuitous vocation, are a retribution and a debt; but the gifts of God are grace, beneficence, and immense liberality." In remarking on these words, "that we might be made the righteousness of God in him," he exclaims, "What a saying! what mind can comprehend it? For he made a just person a sinner, that he might make sinners just! rather I should say, he says more: he doth not say, he made him a sinner, but sin, that we might be made not righteous, but righteousness, even the righteousness of God. For it is of God, since not of works (which would require spotless perfection) but by grace we are justified, where all sin is blotted out." And as Paul among inspired men, so Augustine among the Fathers stands out the great champion of the doctrines of grace. He says: "Let human merit, which was lost by Adam, here be silent, and let the grace of God reign through Jesus Christ." "The saints ascribe nothing to their own merits; they will ascribe all, O God, only to thy mercy." "And when a man sees that whatever good he has, he has it not from himself, but from his God, he sees that all that is commended in him, proceeds not from his own merits, but from the divine mercy." "Thou canst not deliver thyself. Thou hast need of a Saviour. Why dost thou vaunt thyself? What maketh thee to presume of the law and of righteousness? Seest thou not that which doth fight within thee? Dost thou not hear one that striveth, and confesseth his weakness, and desireth aid in the battle, saying 'O wretched man that I am, who shall deliver me?'" &c.

CHAPTER XVII.

WHAT THE MARTYRS THOUGHT.—THE REFORMERS.—OTHER GOOD MEN.

Did you ever hear of a martyr dying in the triumphs of self-righteousness, giving glory to nature, lauding his own ability, extolling his own works? All those faithful witnesses held one doctrine, viz. that works are in our case nothing, and grace is everything. Hear blessed old Tyndall: "If thou wouldst obtain heaven by the merits and deservings of thy own works, thou wrongest and shamest the blood of Christ. Faith only justifieth. In believing we receive the Spirit of God, which is the earnest of eternal life; and we are in eternal life already, and already feel in our heart the sweetness thereof, and are overcome with the kindness of God, and of Christ, and therefore we love the will of God, and of love are ready to work freely." And that ever-honoured man, great Patrick Hamilton, burned at St. Andrews in the year 1527, spake no less decisively. He said: "No man is justified by the deeds of the law, but by the faith of Christ. He was punished for thee, and therefore thou shalt not be punished. I do not say we ought to do no good deeds; but I say we should do no good works to the intent to obtain remission of sins, and the inheritance of heaven, for God saith, Thy sins are forgiven thee for my Son's sake, and thou shalt have the inheritance of heaven for my Son's sake. I condemn not good deeds, but I condemn trust in any works; for all the works, wherein a man putteth any confidence, are by his confidence poisoned, and become evil; wherefore thou must do good works, and beware of doing them with the view to deserve any good for them. In a Christian man's life, and in order of doctrine, there is the law, repentance, hope, charity, and the deeds of charity; yet in the act of justification there is nothing else in man that hath part or place but faith alone, apprehending the object, which is Christ crucified, in whom is all the worthiness and fulness of our salvation." Robert Barnes, an English martyr of great eminence, says: "All the merits and goodness, grace and favour, and all that is in Christ to our salvation, is imputed and reckoned unto us because we hang and believe on him." Cranmer says that when we believe, "God doth no more impute unto us our former sins, but he doth impute and give unto us the justice and righteousness of his Son Jesus Christ, which suffered for us."

The Marquis of Argyle on the scaffold said, "Many look on my condition as a suffering condition; but I bless the Lord, that he that hath gone before me, hath trod the wine-press of the Father's wrath; by whose sufferings, I hope that my sufferings shall not be eternal. I bless him that hath taken away the sting of my sufferings: I may say that my charter was sealed to-day; for the Lord hath said to me, 'Son, be of good cheer, thy sins are freely forgiven thee;' and so I hope my sufferings shall be very easy." James Guthrie on the scaffold said, "I bless God and die not as a fool; not that I have anything wherein to glory in myself; I acknowledge that I am a sinner, yea, one of the greatest and vilest that has owned a profession of religion, and one of the most unworthy that has preached the gospel; my corruptions have been strong and many, and have made me a sinner in all things, yea, even in following my duty; and therefore, righteousness have I none of mine own; all is vile; but I do believe that 'Jesus Christ came into the world to save sinners, of whom I am chief.' Through faith in his righteousness and blood have I obtained mercy; and through him and him alone have I the hope of a blessed conquest and victory over sin, and Satan, and hell, and death."

In Rev. vii. 9—17, John gives us the following account of the martyrs in glory, corresponding exactly with the foregoing views of the martyrs on earth. "After this I beheld, and, lo, a great multitude, which no man could number, of all nations, and kindreds, and people, and tongues, stood before the throne, and before the Lamb, clothed with white robes, and palms in their hands; and cried with a loud voice, saying, Salvation to our God which sitteth upon the throne, and unto the Lamb. And all the angels stood round about the throne, and about the elders and the four beasts, and fell before the throne on their faces, and worshipped God, saying, Amen: Blessing, and glory, and wisdom, and thanksgiving, and honour, and power, and might, be unto our God for ever and ever. Amen. And one of the elders answered, saying unto me, What are these which are arrayed in white robes? and whence came they? And I said unto him, Sir, thou knowest. And he said to me, These are they which came out of great tribulation, and have washed their robes, and made them white in the blood of the

Lamb. Therefore are they before the throne of God, and serve him day and night in his temple: and he that sitteth on the throne shall dwell among them. They shall hunger no more, neither thirst any more; neither shall the sun light on them, nor any heat: for the Lamb which is in the midst of the throne shall feed them, and shall lead them unto living fountains of waters: and God shall wipe away all tears from their eyes."

Many other great men, whose praise has long been in the churches speak the same things. In his protestation upon the article of Justification, Luther says: "This is the true gospel, Jesus Christ redeemed us from our sins, and he only. This most firm and certain truth is the voice of Scripture, though the world and all the devils rage and roar. If Christ alone take away our sins, we cannot do this with our works; and as it is impossible to embrace Christ but by faith, it is therefore impossible to apprehend him by works. If, then, faith alone must apprehend Christ before works can follow, the conclusion is irrefragable, that faith alone apprehends him, before and without the consideration of works; and this is our justification and deliverance from sin. Then, and not till then, good works follow faith, as its necessary and inseparable fruit."

Calvin in his last will says: "I witness and declare that I intend not to seek any other aid or refuge for salvation, than his free adoption, in which alone salvation resteth; and with my whole heart I embrace the mercy which he hath used with me for Jesus Christ's sake, recompensing my faults with the merit of his death and passion, that satisfaction might be made by this means for all my sins and crimes, and the remembrance of them be blotted out. I witness also and declare, that I humbly beg of him, that being washed and cleansed in the blood of that highest Redeemer shed for the sins of mankind, I may stand at the judgment-seat under the image of my Redeemer."

Zuingle in his famous LXVII Articles issued in 1523, says: (Art. III.) "Christ is the only way of salvation to all who ever have lived, are living now, or ever shall live." Again, (Art. XXII.) "Christ is our righteousness. Hence it follows that our works are so far good, as they are of Christ; but as far as they are ours, they are not truly good."

Peter Martyr says: "If faith itself be considered as our act, it is impossible we should be justified by it, because faith, in this view of it, is lame and imperfect, and falls short of that completeness which the law requires; but we are said to be justified by faith because it is by faith that we lay hold upon, and apply to ourselves the promises of God, and the righteousness and merits of Christ."

Leighton says: "Free grace, being rightly apprehended, is that which stays the heart in all estates. What though there be nothing in myself but matter of sorrow and discomfort; it cannot be otherwise. It is not from myself I look for comfort at any time, but from my God and his free grace. Here is comfort enough for all times! When I am at the best, I ought not, I dare not, rely on myself. When at the worst, I may and should rely upon Christ, and his sufficient grace."

Whitefield says that some "are for doing what they can themselves and then Jesus Christ is to make up the deficiencies of their righteousness. This is the sum and substance of our modern divinity. And was it possible for me to know the thoughts of most that hear me this day, I believe they would tell me this was the scheme they had laid, and perhaps depended on, for some years, for their eternal salvation. Is it not then high time, my brethren, for you to entertain quite different thoughts concerning justification by Jesus Christ? * * * Salvation is the free gift of God. I know no fitness in man but a fitness to be cast into the lake of fire and brimstone for ever. Our righteousnesses in God's sight are but as filthy rags. He cannot away with them. Our holiness, if we have any, is not the cause, but the effect of our justification in God's sight. 'We love him because he first loved us.' * * Our salvation is all of God from the beginning to the end; it is not of works lest any man should boast. Man has no hand in it."

Pemble says that our assent to the promise of God must be "of the whole heart, in trust, reliance, dependence, adherence, affiance, or, if there be any other word, expressing that action of the soul, whereby it casteth and reposeth itself only upon God's promise in Christ for obtaining eternal happiness. The heart, touched with the spirit of grace, throws itself into Christ's arms, grasping him with all its might. Hiding itself in the clefts of this rock from the storms of God's furious indignation, it bespeaks Christ in all the terms of confidence and affiance, *my* Lord, *my* God, *my* hope, *my* fortress, *my* rock, *my* strength."

Beart in his treatise entitled the Eternal Law and Everlasting Gospel says: "The essence of the Gospel is a free promise, free gift, free grace: A Saviour! A

Saviour! is the loud proclamation of the Gospel. Justification, as it is the application of the righteousness of Christ, in the Spirit's working faith, hath an unbelieving ungodly man for its object; as it is an acquittance or declaring righteous, so it has a believer for its object, God, who justifies the ungodly, the justifier of him who believes in Jesus. That faith in Christ as a priest is the foundation of all obedience to him as a king, must be inculcated. O here lies God's order, to bring a soul to Christ, and then he is brought to holiness! Man's order is, to bring him to holiness, that he may come to Christ. But this is to try to wash the Ethiopian white."

Toplady says: "Fallen man can never know what it is to speed his way to the kingdom of heaven, and make large advances in sanctification, till his progress is disembarrassed by a full submission to the righteousness of God the Son, as the sole procuring cause of eternal blessedness."

Among the dying words of John Brown of Haddington were these: "The command is 'Owe no man anything.' What a mercy that there is no such precept as this: Owe a Saviour nothing; or even this: Study to owe him as little as possible." "O what a mercy that my admission into eternal life does not in the least depend on my ability for anything; but I, as a poor sinner, will win in leaning on Christ, as the Lord my righteousness; on Christ 'made of God unto me righteousness, sanctification and redemption.' I have nothing to sink my spirits but my sins; and these need not sink me either, since the great God is my Saviour." "I have altered my mind about many things; but I am now of the same mind that ever I was, as to grace and salvation through Christ." One of Nevins's dying sayings was: "I recommend Christ to you; I have nothing else to recommend." And blessed McCheyne said: "Live within sight of Calvary and you will live within sight of glory." Vinet says, "Grace, as it is manifested in the Gospel, is the most splendid homage which the law can receive. * * The same act proclaims the compassion of God, and the inflexibility of his justice." As Dr. Nettleton drew very near his end, he said "the great truths of the Gospel appear more precious than ever; and they are the truths which now sustain my soul." Again: "I do not need anybody to tell me that the doctrines of grace are true. I am fully convinced of their truth by my own experience."

CHAPTER XVIII.

THE GRACE OF CHRIST NOT DIFFERENT FROM THAT OF THE FATHER OR SPIRIT.

IT would be a great mistake if any should suppose that the grace of Christ is greater than that of the Father or of the Spirit, or that the love of Christ differs from the love of the first and third persons of the Trinity. The truth is, the grace of each person of the Godhead in man's salvation is absolutely infinite and amazing. The "help of the Spirit," and "the love of the Spirit," are forms of expression as dear to the church of God as any found in Scripture. So also when "grace, mercy and peace from God the Father and the Lord Jesus Christ," are brought to our notice, we see at once how inspiration refuses to separate between the love and grace of one person, and the love and grace of another person of the Godhead. Sometimes all three persons are spoken of in one verse, as in 2 Cor. xiii. 14. "The grace of our Lord Jesus Christ, the love of God, and the communion of the Holy Ghost be with you all." The concord of the divine persons is no less than the harmony of the divine attributes in the work of man's salvation. The Father pitied our case, and gave his Son, and sends his Spirit. The Son loved us, came and died for us, is ascended up on high to plead for us, and unites with the Father in sending the Spirit. The Holy Ghost loved us, inspired the prophets to speak and write as they did, dwelt abundantly in the man Christ Jesus, and illuminates, regenerates, sanctifies and comforts all the people of God. So that while the phrase "grace of God" has at times, no doubt, special reference to the kindness of the Father it yet appropriately expresses the mercy and favour of the entire Godhead. The Bible no where represents to us a Trinity divided in counsels, in purposes, in works, in being or in glory. Creation, providence and redemption are the works of all united. In all of these each person has equal and undivided honours. The death of the man Christ Jesus, was the fruit and not the cause of the love of the Father, and of the Son, and of the Spirit towards our race. The first and third persons of the Trinity are as compassionate and loving as is the second. The love of Father, Son and Holy Ghost is shown in Christ Jesus, being the way, the truth and the life. Yet nothing here said is designed to diminish our love for Christ, but on the contrary to heighten it. His grace is indeed an expression of the unfailing good will of the Creator of the ends of the earth. To them who believe Christ is precious. Calvin well says "Since we see that the whole of our salvation, and all the branches of it, are comprehended in Christ, we must be cautious not to alienate from him the least possible portion of it. If we seek salvation, we are taught by the name of JESUS that it is in him; if we seek any other gifts of the Spirit, they are found in his unction; strength, in his dominion; purity, in his conception; indulgence discovers itself in his nativity; by which he was made to resem ble us in all things, that he might learn to condole with us. If we seek redemption, it will be found in his passion; absolution, in his condemnation; remission of the curse, in his cross; sanctification, in his sacrifice; purification, in his blood; reconciliation, in his descent into hell; mortification of the flesh, in his sepulchre; newness of life and immortality, in his resurrection; the inheritance of the celestial kingdom, in his entrance into heaven; protection, security, abundance and enjoyment of all blessings, in his kingdom; a fearless expectation of the judgment, in the judicial authority committed to him. Finally, blessings of every kind are deposited in him; let us draw from his treasury and from no other source, till our desires are satisfied; for they who, not content with him alone, are driven hither and thither into a variety of hopes, although they fix their eyes principally on him, nevertheless deviate from the right way in the diversion of any part of their attention to another quarter. This distrust however cannot intrude where the plenitude of his blessings hath once been truly known." Nor is it necessary to be continually on our guard lest by giving divine honours to one we should offend the other persons of the Trinity. He who honours the Son, honours the Father. God is one, though subsisting in three persons. Worship offered to one person of the Godhead with the intention of slighting the others would indeed be an abomination. But a heart full of love to the Father for giving his Son, will be sure to love the Son, who came, and the Spirit who anointed him.

CHAPTER XIX.

NO SALVATION BUT BY A REDEEMER, AND NO REDEEMER BUT CHRIST.

THE Lord is a holy God. He hates all sin, yea, he abhors it. His aversion to it is infinite. Moreover, he is a Lawgiver and Governor. In this respect his character must be maintained. God cannot deny himself. He cannot deny his right to rule. He cannot permit transgression in his dominions to go unpunished. He cannot but justify the righteous, and condemn the wicked. When man sinned he fell under the wrath of God, the indignation of the King Eternal. His ruin was entire. What was to be done in his case? The following are the only courses, which can be conceived of.

1. God had power and authority, if he had seen fit, to annihilate the human race. But to this course the objections are numerous and insurmountable. Dreadful as is annihilation, it has never been shown to be an adequate punishment for sin. So far as we know, God never has annihilated, and never will annihilate anything, which he has made. Even the fires of the last day will but change and not destroy the elements on which they will kindle. Had God extinguished our race, he would have left this lower world without an intelligent head. In that case no reasonable service, no song of thanksgiving could ever have been rendered

to the Maker of heaven and earth by any inhabitant of our globe. Besides, who is the Lord, that he should repent? Having begun to build he was able to finish, and he determined to prove that he was neither disappointed nor baffled.

2. A second course, conceivable in our case was that Jehovah should without delay and without mercy consign the entire human family to hopeless, endless misery. This would have been just, gloriously just and right. Our elder brethren, the sinning angels, had received this doom, and all heaven had pronounced their sentence righteous. But had this been done in the case of man, not an individual of our entire race of intelligent beings would have remained a worshipper of the God who made us; nor would earth have ever resounded with a single hosanna. Like hell our globe would have sent up only wailings, howlings, blasphemies, and the smoke of its torment for ever and ever. Men would have been awful monuments of inexorable justice; but none of them would have ever illustrated God's long-suffering, or his loving-kindness. Yet the justice of such a doom being absolute, sentence of eternal banishment pronounced against the entire race would have wronged no one, and, being what had before fallen on rebel angels, could hardly have surprised any one.

3. The third conceivable course for God to pursue was entirely to overlook man's sin, connive at his rebellion, and take him into the divine embrace, though steeped in guilt and reeking in pollution. This is conceivable, but not admissible. For then the universe would have seen the divine government trampled on, and that with impunity, the eternal law broken, and

the Lawgiver consenting to such rebellion. This course must have not only shaken but destroyed all confidence in the rectitude of the divine character. In that case the government of the universe must have been dissolved, and war and anarchy and rebellion have reigned and rioted for ever. Seriously to suppose that God should ever consent to let sin pass unnoticed is to conceive blasphemy.

4. The last conceivable course to be pursued in man's case was to adopt some method, by which to satisfy the demands of law, and yet save the sinner; maintain the glory of divine justice, and yet rescue the criminal offender. What that method of deliverance should be no creature could tell. Sin had wrought such mischief, and was in its nature so deadly and malignant, that God himself is in Scripture represented as wondering that none could provide a remedy. Our case is well described by Jehovah: "When I passed by thee, and looked upon thee, behold thy time was the time of love; and I spread my skirt over thee, and covered thy nakedness; yea, I sware unto thee, and entered into a covenant with thee, saith the Lord God." A ransom, a Mediator were spoken of, but where a sufficient Saviour could be found, no man, no angel could tell. Who could pay a full, an adequate redemption price? The law violated and dishonoured by transgression, the law to be satisfied and magnified in man's recovery was glorious in holiness, absolutely incapable of amendment, and infinitely perfect. It was suited and intended to be universal, binding every rational creature to all eternity. The only perfectly happy society that ever existed was a community wholly conformed to its precepts. The only absolutely

miserable and intolerable state of personal or social existence ever known was where all the precepts of this law were constantly broken. How could reparation be made to such a government violated? How could a ransom be provided for such transgressors?

Suppose man should offer to God all the products of the earth, all its grain and all its mines, all its fruits and all its cattle. At the very best, man could offer but *some* of these, for he must use a part in order to subsist. The residue he might indeed offer. But if men come with any decent regard to truth in making such offerings they would say as David of old: "Who am I, and what is my people, that we should be able to offer so willingly after this sort? for all things come of thee, and of thine own have we given thee." 1 Chron. xxix. 14. A company of beggars in going to ask alms of a rich man might drive up his flocks and his herds to stand before him, or might bring the fruits of his fields and lay them at his feet, but these were all his before they brought them before him, and so could not purchase anything from him. So God says, "the earth is mine and the cattle upon a thousand hills." The gifts we can bring from the store-house of nature all belong to God already, and so can make no atonement, can be no price which he will accept as from us.

A citizen of a free and sovereign State lawfully gets into his possession five millions of her funds, and then not only embezzles the whole amount, but also commits treason and is arrested and brought to trial. He proposes to arrest all legal proceedings by delivering up all the money except one thousand dollars, which sum he has spent, and has nothing besides. Can the government accede to his proposal? It may be in great straits for funds, it may see no way of escaping bankruptcy unless it can recover the sum lost or near that amount; it may see that without the consent of the guilty man it can recover nothing. Under these circumstances it may accept his offer, but when it does, it clearly admits its own weakness and imperfection. It declares that there are cases of atrocious crime and novel difficulty, where it cannot bring the law to bear, except by sustaining a loss too great for its own resources. The divine government could never accede to such a compounding of crime. It would tarnish all its glory. It can bring every offender to justice. It holds all the wicked in the grasp of its omnipotence. It knows all their secrets, all their accomplices, all their hiding-places. It is never in straits. To allow men to redeem themselves by silver and gold or the fruits of the earth would have been a mockery of all justice.

Nor could bloody sacrifices of animals have been a ransom. As property the animals slain belonged to God already: and as sacrifices they never did nor could have any efficacy in setting aside the penalty of the moral law. They never were at all acceptable to God except as appointed by himself to be the types of the sacrifice of his Son. Viewed in any other light, "he, that killeth an ox, is as if he slew a man; he, that sacrificeth a lamb, as if he cut off a dog's neck; he, that offereth an oblation, as if he offered swine's blood; he, that burneth incense, as if he blessed an idol." Isa. lxvi. 3. So that it was impossible to make satisfaction in this way.

Nor could man by voluntary suffering, self-inflicted, work out his own redemption. He cannot do this when he has offended a merely human government. The murderer found guilty and sentenced to death is never permitted by total or partial fasting, by sighing and groaning, by beating himself with rods, or tearing himself with pincers to set aside the penalty of the law. The reason is that all these sufferings do not satisfy the law. They are not the penalty provided. So under the government of God voluntary humility and dishonouring of the body, though in the eyes of the simple they have a show of wisdom, can never redeem a soul, can never satisfy God's law.

Nor can *present* or *future* reformation atone for *past* sins. The very best obedience, which can possibly be rendered, is due, always was due, always will be due to God. He, who owes a thousand pounds, cannot discharge that debt by being careful to contract no new obligations with the same house. A man may have lived a blameless life for half a century. He may then commit murder, and if it is proven on him, he cannot plead his former good conduct, nor give the amplest security for future good behaviour, *in order to set aside the penalty incurred by murder.* Under God's government all our obedience is God's right, and to give him his right at one time cannot redeem us from the guilt of transgression at another.

Nor can one man redeem another. All men are guilty and have forfeited their lives by their own sins. When two pirates are condemned to death, one of them cannot die for the other, for the reason that he has to die for himself. Two manslayers are sentenced for life to close prison. One cannot take the place of the other, and so let him go free. Redemption, therefore, by any human means or merits was absolutely out of the question.

Nor could *angels* atone for men. Of course the sufferings of *fallen* angels, though they are the pains of hell, being due for their own transgressions, could be no ransom for us. Nor could *holy* angels make atonement or bring in righteousness for others. All the obedience they can render is due for themselves. They could therefore never supererogate. They can have no surplus of merit beyond their own wants. Nor could they by suffering ever exhaust the penalty due for man's sins. An angel is finite. The law violated and the justice offended are infinite. Sin is therefore an infinite evil. In an angel an eternity of suffering would be necessary to redeem one man from hell. The sin of even one man would, if imputed to an angel, send him to prison for ever. Had his mediation been admitted, where would have been the gain in the happiness of the universe? Then too a sinner pardoned would have been bound for ever to ascribe his redemption not only to a mere creature, but to that creature ever suffering in hell the penalty due to the ransomed spirit, whose substitute he had become. In this way no end would ever be made of transgression. The suffering substitute could never rise triumphant and say, "It is finished." And the redeemed would have praised in the highest notes and with the deepest sense of obligation their deliverer, and that deliverer would have still been enduring the penalty. Such would have been the confusion, disorder, and idolatry of admitting an angel or angels to undertake the work of redemption.

Besides, any holy angel must have been for ever

unfit for the work of mediation, as he is not able as a days-man to lay his hand upon both God and man. The highest created angel is infinitely inferior to God. For him to claim equality with God would have been robbery indeed. He never could have appeared before God with authority, asserting a right to dominion over any part of his works. He never could have been admitted into the counsels of eternity. He would have been looked upon with a righteous jealousy by God himself as a rival in his kingdom and for his throne. His intercessions must therefore have failed. He never could have said, "Father, I WILL," without great presumption.

Nor could any holy angel ever have sympathized with man, either as a sufferer or as a sinner, to such an extent as would have fitted him to be a Redeemer. Angels know not what suffering is. In their natures they are quite ignorant of what are the real feelings of men. They know nothing by experience of the natural affections of men. They understand not the hard pressure of poverty, or shame. Being holy and yet finite in their compassions, no one of them could endure the recital of our offences without utter dislike to our persons. Before he had learned half of the details and aggravating circumstances of any one's crimes, he would have turned away with unspeakable loathing from the shocking tale of human guilt. He would have said, "Such a sinner ought to perish—must perish—I can have no sympathy with him." It is indeed well for us that our salvation does not depend on the mercies of an angel. If it did, our doom would soon be sealed. The reason is that our case requires a height, a depth, a length and a breadth of compassion and grace to be found in but one being in the universe. "It is of the LORD's mercies," yes, "it is of the LORD's mercies that we are not consumed."

Nor upon any admissible supposition could one angel have redeemed many souls. Had one of them become a mediator, he could not have saved any considerable number of the human family. So that still nearly all the inhabitants of earth must have perished, or there must have been millions of redeemers, and consequently as many different objects, to whom loud praises and eternal thanks should have been rendered. And as redemption is a greater blessing than creation, each person thus saved would for ever have felt himself more indebted to a creature than to the Creator, inasmuch as the deliverer of each one would in the case supposed have been a creature. Such are some of the monstrous results, to which the admission of a finite mediator would have led. So that we are shut up to the admission that no finite being could ever fitly or successfully have undertaken our cause. None of these difficulties lie in the way of Christ's mediation. Nor could there be any objection to his undertaking our cause, unless it were one of the following, viz:

1. That God was unwilling to admit any interposition in our behalf. Such unwillingness would have operated no injustice to us. Our mouths must have been for ever stopped, if he had treated us as he treated rebel angels. But God, ever blessed be his name, pitied us, and was willing to save us. He rejoiced to send his Son. He delivered him up freely. He so loved the world that he gave him not grudgingly, nor reluctantly, but freely and benignantly.

God, therefore, as the offended Lawgiver, made no objection to Christ's mediation.

2. Or it would have been a valid objection to Christ's mediation, if he himself had been unwilling to become our surety. For eternal justice to have seized upon any innocent victim and led him forth a reluctant sufferer in the room and stead of others would have been a procedure, which we could never justify. The Spirit of God, knowing how this point would come up before our minds, has mercifully and completely relieved all our apprehensions on the subject. By the Psalmist he declares in the name of Christ, "Lo, I come, I delight to do thy will, O my God." And in the Gospel we are informed by Christ himself that his sufferings were voluntary. His words are: "I lay down my life that I might take it again. No man taketh it from me, but I lay it down of myself. I have power to lay it down, and I have power to take it again." John x. 17, 18. If in any sense Christ was constrained to suffer for us, it was only by his amazing love and mercy to the lost.

3. Or if the satisfaction rendered, or to be rendered, had fallen short of what might justly have been required by the law of God, or by the good of his dominions, this would have been an objection to Christ's mediation. If Christ's interposition was in any way to diminish the due force of law, or the just power of government in any province of God's empire; if, in short, it could be fairly construed as a relaxation of moral obligation, a concession to iniquity, then indeed there would have been a valid objection to Christ's undertaking. But the Son of God gave for man's redemption as heavy a ransom as justice, law, the con-

science of man, the judgment of angels, or the infinite holiness of God demanded. He paid the full price. He drank the cup of bitterness even to the dregs thereof. He magnified the law and made it honourable. God's abhorrence of sin is more clearly expressed in the cross of Christ, than in the flames of hell. Even the most tender and enlightened conscience of the most guilty man says of Christ's satisfaction, whenever it is divinely revealed, "This is enough—I ask no more—I end my quest of atonement here."

CHAPTER XX.

THE CONSTITUTION OF CHRIST'S PERSON.—HIS GRACE THEREIN.

Nothing in the Christian religion has been the subject of so much error as the person of our Lord Jesus Christ. Some have denied that he was God. Some have said that he was a created God. Some have denied that he had a true body, and some that he had a reasonable created soul. Some have held that he had two persons, and some that one of his natures absorbed the other. The apostles were not all dead when Ebion and Cerinthus denied our Lord's divinity. To counteract their dangerous opinions John wrote his Gospel. Their error was revived, though in a form somewhat varied, by Arius and his followers in the fourth century, by the Socinians of the seventeenth century, and by still more modern Unitarians. Most of these perhaps have held simply to Christ's humanity.

Some, however, have spoken of our Lord as a created God. Duly considered, this must appear absurd. The greatest gulf in the universe is that which separates the finite from the infinite, the creature from the Creator. A God, not self-existent, eternal, independent and unchangeable, is no God. He, who has these attributes, is the supreme God. The Manichæans denied that Christ had a true body. Consistency compelled them to deny his death. Others have held that the

Father, Son, and Holy Ghost were one person, became incarnate and suffered on the cross. Indeed the forms of error on this whole subject have been almost countless. The enmity of the human heart against God has brought all its strength, violence and ingenuity to destroy the corner-stone, or to remove it out of our sight. What then is the truth on this subject?

I. Jesus Christ had and has a divine nature. He was truly God. He is expressly called "God," "God and our Saviour Jesus Christ," "The great God and our Saviour Jesus Christ," "the Lord their God," "the true God and eternal life," "Emmanuel, God with us," "Jehovah," "Lord of hosts," "Lord of lords," "King of kings," "the mighty God," "the everlasting Father." That he existed before his incarnation it requires great boldness to deny. He often asserts this truth. "Before Abraham was I am." "And now, O Father, glorify thou me with thine own self with the glory which I had with thee before the world was." "I came down from heaven." "What if ye shall see the Son of man ascend up where he was before." John vi. 38, 62; viii. 58; xvii. 5. Paul says: "He is before all things." Col. i. 17. These texts clearly prove two things: 1. that Christ existed before he was born in the days of Herod. But as his human nature then had its beginning, it must have been in some other nature that he was before Abraham, and had glory with the Father before the world was; and 2. that if he was before all things, he had an uncaused existence, and so was God.

Christ was also the Creator of all things. "All things were made by him, and without him was not anything made that was made." John i. 3. "Thou,

Lord, in the beginning hast laid the foundations of the earth, and the heavens are the work of thy hands." Heb. i. 10. The Maker of all things, of the heaven and of the earth, is God. There is none above him, none more worthy of love and fear. Paul says, that he, "being in the form of God, thought it not robbery to be equal with God." Phil. ii. 6. The only thing which could hinder such a claim from being the most daring robbery was that it was well founded, and that he was God. In Rev. i. 8, he gives this account of himself: "I am Alpha and Omega, the beginning and the ending, saith the Lord, which is, and which was, and which is to come, the Almighty." Is not that being God?

In 1 Tim. iii. 16, Paul says, "God was manifest in the flesh." But God was not manifest in the flesh, unless he was there in the person of him who took our flesh. If any should say that the meaning simply is that virtue, which is conformity to God, was manifest in the flesh of Christ, the reply is at hand; 1. There is not a word said about virtue in the text or context. The words are "God was manifest;" 2. Where would be the propriety of calling virtue a great mystery? Paul says, "Great is the mystery of godliness. God was manifest," &c. 3. This interpretation ill suits the residue of the passage: "He was justified in the Spirit, seen of angels, preached unto the gentiles, believed on in the world, received up into glory."

To Christ belongs also the work of universal providence. "By him all things consist," and "he upholdeth all things by the word of his power." Col. i. 17. Heb. i. 3. Can it be possible that a mere creature can do such things? What can Jehovah do in providence to evince his proper divinity more than to uphold all things by his powerful word?

Christ is also omniscient. He knows what is in man. John ii. 24, 25. He searches the heart and tries the reins. Rev. ii. 23. In short, let any man prove by any scriptural course of argument the divinity of the Father, and by the same process can we establish the divinity of the Son. Is the Father almighty and so divine? So is the Son, Rev. i. 8. Is it a prerogative of the supreme God to forgive sins? Jesus Christ forgives sins. Matt. ix. 2—6. Is the supreme God every where present? So is Christ. "Lo, I am with you always, even unto the end of the world." "Where two or three are gathered together in my name there am I in the midst of them." Matt. xviii. 20; xxviii. 20. If the divinity and supremacy of Jehovah were proven by the miracles in Egypt and the wilderness, the divinity and supremacy of Christ were proven by the miracles in Palestine. They were many; (John xxi. 25,) were wrought for his own glory; (John ii. 11,) were of a stupendous nature; (John ix. 30—33,) and were all wrought in his own name, and not in the name of some other person. See every account. Is the Father worshipped by all the holy angels? So is the Son. "When he bringeth the first-begotten into the world, he saith, And let all the angels of God worship him." Heb. i. 5. Did David devoutly say of Jehovah, "Thou art my God?" Thomas addressed Jesus, saying, "My Lord and my God." John xx. 28. Is the Father now worshipped in heaven? So is the Son. Rev. v. 12—14. So that Jesus Christ is in his pre-existent nature God, the true God, equal with the Father. Our Saviour is truly divine.

II. Christ is as to his created nature truly and properly a man. He had entire humanity, as fully as Moses, Paul, or any other man. In proof inspired writers call him a man. "A man shall be as an hiding-place," "A man approved of God," "A man of sorrows," "There is one God and one Mediator, the man Christ Jesus." He is often called the Son of Man. This phrase teaches his humanity. Thus we read: "The Son of Man hath power to forgive sins," "The Son of Man is Lord even of the Sabbath-day," "Now is the Son of Man glorified." The objection of some that he was not truly a man, because he had no father according to the flesh is of no force, for 1. he derived his human nature from his mother, and was made of her substance as much as any child derives its nature from its parents. 2. If it is essential to humanity entire and complete, that it be derived from a pair, then Eve, the mother of all living, was not a human being, for she derived her nature through Adam alone. 3. By parity of reasoning, yea, by still stronger reasoning, Adam was not a human being, for he had neither father nor mother. Such are some of the conclusions to which this objection would lead us.

Christ's humanity is also proved by many plain texts of Scripture. "He was made in the likeness of men," "He was found in fashion as a man," "His visage was so marred more than any man." He had eyes, and saw the beauties of nature, even of the lilies of the field. He had ears, and heard the words of friends and of foes. He had all the senses of a man. He ate, he drank, he slept, he awaked, he walked, he rested, he was weary, he was hungry, was thirsty, he was handled, was bound, was scourged, was smitten, was spit upon, was crowned with thorns, and crucified. He was born, he wept, he bled, he died, he was dead. Prophecy promised him a body; (Heb. x. 5, and Psal. xl. 6—8,) and Providence gave him a body.

Jesus Christ had a soul also, a human soul, a true rational soul. The proof is that he had sentiments of joy and sorrow, of indignation and grief, of compassion and pity, of hope and fear. He had the mental trials and sorrows of men. "He was tempted in all points like as we are." As a son and as a friend none ever more clearly showed that he had true human affections. As he had the body and affections, so also he had the intellect of man. He grew from infancy to manhood, not only in stature but in the strength and scope of his faculties, as other children do, except that he had better religious teaching than many, and far more abundant influences of the Spirit than all other children. He had the Spirit without measure. So that his growth in holy wisdom was extraordinary and unparalleled. That he had a human mind is as clear as that he had a human body; and that he had both is as certain as that any other person ever had them. To suppose the contrary is to charge him with imposture, and this is blasphemy. If Christ were not man, how could he be a descendant of Eve; (Gen. iii. 15,) or of Abraham (Gen. xxii. 18,) or of David, as was often promised? or why did Matthew and Luke in their Gospels give the genealogy of our Lord, if they did not intend to teach that he derived his human nature through a long line of ancestors from Abraham and from Adam?

Some would lead us to suppose that Christ had no human soul, but that he merely had a human body, inhabited by his heavenly or pre-existent nature, and in proof they quote such expressions as these: "God was manifest in the *flesh*," and "The word was made *flesh*." They contend that the word, *flesh*, includes the body only. If this is so, their objection has force. Let us see what the truth is. Admitting that the primary meaning of the word was that of the body, yet this was far from being its usual signification. By *flesh* Paul understands the depraved moral nature of man: "They that are in the flesh cannot please God." The word is often applied to men, as men, so that in the following cases, "all flesh" simply means "all men:" "All flesh had corrupted his way;" "Unto thee shall all flesh come;" "Let all flesh bless his holy name for ever and ever;" "All flesh shall see the salvation of God." Paul therefore intends to teach that "God was manifest in the" *man*, Christ Jesus. John in saying "the Word was made flesh," &c., teaches that the Word, which was God, became man, not by the conversion of the divine into the human nature, but by uniting the two. Has it not therefore been shown that Christ had a true, proper, entire human nature, a true body and a reasonable soul?

III. The divine and human natures of Christ are united in one person; so that it is proper to speak of the Lord Jesus in the singular number, and not in the plural. When we address him we say, "thou," and not ye. When we speak of him we say, "he, his, him," not they, theirs, them. When Christ spoke of himself, both before and after his death and ascension, he said, "I, mine, me," not we, ours, us. There is but *one* Christ. He is *a* Lamb, *a* Priest, *a* King, *a* Shepherd, *a* Saviour, *a* Mediator, *a* Surety. Though he has two natures, the human and the divine, yet he is but one person, one Redeemer, one Mediator. His human and divine natures are distinct, not separate; distinguishable, not separable.

His two natures became one person, not by his human nature seeking to be affianced to his divine nature, but by his divine nature seeking union with the human. For the human nature to have sought union with divinity would have been blameworthy ambition. For the divine nature to seek union with the human was great condescension, unspeakable love. Besides, Christ's human nature never existed separately from the divine. The union was formed at his conception in the womb of the virgin. The divine nature existed separately from the human nature, and prior to it, and sought union with it, and assumed it into indissoluble union. So the Scriptures do not say that flesh was made the Word, but that "the Word was made flesh," nor that the flesh was made manifest in God, but that "God was made manifest in the flesh." Human nature did not assume divinity; but the divine nature assumed humanity. So the Scriptures say that "being in the form of God, he thought it not robbery to be equal with God, but made himself of no reputation, and took upon him the form of a servant, and was made in the likeness of men." He was first rich in all the attributes and glories of Divinity, and by taking a body he became poor, for our good, out of love to us. Here is indeed a wonder, a very marvellous thing, but in it nothing is so marvellous as the love and mercy which it reveals; love and mercy so great that none but the wicked reject them; love and mercy so great that even angels do not comprehend them. Here is the light of men, the life of the world.

In this union the natures of Christ are not confused, compounded, or converted one into the other, or absorbed one by the other. His body was and is a true human body, not mixed with his soul or divinity, nor converted into them, yet it is for ever united with both. His human soul is as truly a human soul as that of Enoch or Abraham, and will for ever so remain. It is not absorbed by his divinity, nor mingled with it, but united with it. So that Christ is the "God-man," possessing at once and henceforth for ever the image of the invisible God and the likeness of men. Thus is constituted the person of our one Lord Jesus Christ, our one Mediator. This is the Bible doctrine on the subject. His conception and birth were miraculous, so that he was born free from the guilt and defilement of original sin. Accordingly Gabriel said unto Mary: "that holy thing which shall be born of thee, shall be called the Son of God." He was and is in his entire nature holy, harmless, undefiled, and separate from sinners.

This view of his person gives us the key, by which to unlock the mystery of any text of Scripture relating to that subject. Thus when it is said, he thirsted, he walked, he slept, he ate, the reference is to his body. After his resurrection he said "handle me and see, for a spirit hath not flesh and bones as ye see me have." Surely he thus intended to convince them of the truth and reality of his body. There was no deception in the case. Both before his death and after his resurrection he gave infallible proof of his having a body. There is no absurdity or contradiction here. Corporeally he did as other men do.

Another class of texts relates to his human soul.

Thus it is said, "He rejoiced in spirit," "he was grieved for the hardness of their hearts," "he began to be sorrowful and very heavy." All these are the acts and exercises of his reasonable human soul, and are in themselves no more inscrutable than the same things said of any other man.

Sometimes the Scriptures speak of his entire human nature, soul and body, in the same verse. Thus: "The child grew and waxed strong in spirit, filled with wisdom." Again: "Jesus increased in wisdom and stature, and in favour with God and man." There is nothing more mysterious in this than if the same had been said of any other healthy, pious, amiable child. Again: "He beheld the city and wept over it." Beholding and weeping were bodily acts. But shedding tears, accompanied by his lament over the city, showed that his whole human nature, soul and body, was united, his soul being moved by prophetic visions and heavenly compassions, and his body agitated by his thoughts and pure affections. This is all plain. Thus we all speak and weep, when we think strongly and feel exquisitely.

Again we read, "in the beginning was the Word, and the Word was with God, and the Word was God. All things were made by him, and without him was not anything made that was made." This plainly and clearly belongs to his divine nature alone. His human nature was not in the beginning with God, and had no part in the work of creation.

But "the Word was made flesh and dwelt among us, (and we beheld his glory, the glory as of the only begotten of the Father) full of grace and truth." "God was manifest in the flesh." Thus the person of the Mediator was constituted. He was found in fashion as a man. He was made a little lower than the angels. He humbled himself and became obedient unto death. It is of himself as the Mediator and in a low condition that he says, "The Father is greater than I." But lest this language should mislead any one, and cause them to think that in his divine nature he was inferior to the Father, he said, "I and the Father are one," "He that hath seen me hath seen the Father." To him as Mediator in his exaltation "all power is given in heaven and earth;" "All judgment is committed." By his divine nature and by divine right he was fit to be judge of the world; but he who was pierced shall be on the throne. The entire person of the Mediator, the man Christ Jesus, shall judge the world. Thus and thus only every text referring to him has a full, fair, plain, consistent sense given to it.

This union of the two natures in Christ is most intimate. No union could be more perfect. If the term, *one person*, can be properly applied to any being in the universe, that being is Christ Jesus, the Lord. So the Scriptures uniformly teach by speaking of him always in the singular. So perfect is this union, that although his divine nature, because divine, could neither suffer nor die, yet we properly speak of him as a divine sufferer. Paul calls his blood the blood of God. "Feed the church of God, which he hath purchased with his own blood." The same person is God and man for ever. If any say this is a great mystery, the Bible said the same long ago: "Great is the mystery of godliness; God was manifest in the flesh." Anything, which we do not comprehend, is mysterious. But because a thing is incomprehensible, it is not therefore absurd or false. No man comprehends how his soul and body are united; yet no sober man doubts their union. No man knows how an animal frame is nourished by food, yet we all know the fact. How the human will can in any case control the muscles of the body is inexplicable, yet the fact is indisputable. Mysteriousness, so far from disproving a fact, is a property of every fact known to us. Our Lord Jesus undertook the greatest work ever devised, viz., to reconcile God and man. In doing this none but shallow thinkers will expect everything to be level to their comprehension, and none but the unbelieving and abominable will reject his grace, because they discover a mystery in the constitution of his person.

The Westminster Assembly thus expresses the whole doctrine of this chapter. "The Son of God, the second person in the Trinity, being very and eternal God, of one substance and equal with the Father, did, when the fulness of time was come, take upon him man's nature, and all the essential properties and common infirmities thereof, yet without sin: being conceived by the power of the Holy Ghost, in the womb of the virgin Mary, of her substance. So that two whole, perfect, distinct natures, the Godhead and the manhood, were inseparably joined together in one person, without conversion, composition or confusion. Which person is very God and very man, yet one Christ, the only Mediator between God and man."

Without giving extended quotations from symbols of faith on this head, it is deemed sufficient to say that the doctrine of this chapter is not controverted in any but Arian, Socinian or Unitarian churches. It is thought, however, that the following extract from the Confession of Belgia may be useful to some: "We believe also, that the person of the Son [he had just been called God's only and eternal Son] was, by his conception, inseparably united and coupled with the human nature; yet so that there be not two Sons of God, nor two persons, but two natures joined together in one person; both which natures do still retain their own properties. So that, as the divine nature hath remained always uncreated, without beginning of days or term of life, filling both heaven and earth; so the human nature hath not lost its properties, but hath remained still a creature, having both beginning of days and a finite nature. For whatsoever doth agree unto a true body, that it still retaineth: and although Christ, by his resurrection, hath bestowed immortality upon it, yet notwithstanding, he hath neither taken away the truth of the human nature, nor altered it. For both our salvation, and also our resurrection depend upon the truth of Christ's body. Yet these two natures are so united and coupled in one person, that they could not, no not in his death, be separated one from the other. Wherefore that, which in his death he commended unto his Father, was indeed a human spirit, departing out of his body; but in the mean time, the divine nature did always remain joined to the human, even then when he lay in the grave; so that his Deity was no less in him at that time, than when as yet he was an infant, although for a small season it did not show forth itself. Wherefore, we confess that he is true God, and true man; true God, that by his power he might overcome death; and true man, that in the infirmity of his flesh he might die for us."

Let us dwell a moment on the grace and mercy of Christ in the constitution of his person. Duly considered his incarnation is the most amazing step in his humiliation. His first becoming a man is more surprising than his sufferings and death after he became man. Having assumed our nature, we should expect that he would submit to all else necessary for our deliverance. But the marvel is that he should have ever married our nature. Here is the mystery of mysteries, the wonder of wonders. The conduct of the heavenly host at his birth seems to justify such views as this. Many things in Scripture look the same way. The following is but a sample of the way in which inspired men treat the whole subject of his humiliation: "Ye know the grace of our Lord Jesus Christ, that though he was rich, yet for your sakes he became poor, that ye through his poverty might be rich." In his incarnation the Son of God stooped to a union with the lowest intelligent nature, and that nature all in ruin and rebellion. In dying it was the human nature alone that suffered.

CHAPTER XXI.

THE WORK AND SUFFERINGS OF CHRIST.—HIS ACTIVE AND PASSIVE OBEDIENCE.

Our Lord Jesus Christ became incarnate, was made under the law, lived, acted, obeyed, suffered, died and rose again for his people. He came down to earth that they might go up to heaven. He suffered that they might reign. He became a servant that they might become kings and priests unto God. He died that they might live. He bore the cross that their enmity might be slain, and their sins expiated. He loved them that they might love God. He was rich and became poor that they, who were poor, might be made rich. He descended into the lower parts of the earth that they might sit in heavenly places. He emptied himself that they might be filled with all the fulness of God. He took upon him human nature that they might be partakers of the divine nature. He made flesh his dwelling place that they might be an habitation of God through the Spirit. He made himself of no reputation, that they might wear his new name, and be counted an eternal excellency. He became a worm, and no man, that they, who were sinful worms, might be made equal to the angels. He bore the curse of a broken covenant that they might partake of all the blessings of the everlasting covenant, ordered in all things and sure. Though heir of all things, he was willingly despised of the people, that they, who were justly condemned, might obtain an inheritance that is incorruptible, undefiled, and that fadeth not away. His death was a satisfaction to divine justice, a ransom for many, a propitiation for sin, a sweet smelling savour to God, that we, who were an offence to God, might become his sons and daughters. He was made sin for his people that they might be made the righteousness of God in him. Though Lord of all he took the form of a servant, that they, who were the servants of sin, might prevail like princes with God. He, who had made swaddling-bands for the sea, was wrapped in swaddling-clothes that they, who were cast out in their blood, might be clothed in linen white and clean, which is the righteousness of saints. He had not where to lay his head that they who otherwise must have lain down in eternal sorrow, might reach the mansions in his Father's house. He was beset with lions and bulls of Bashan, that his chosen might be compassed about with an innumerable company of angels and of the spirits of just men made perfect. He drank the cup of God's indignation that they might for ever drink of the river of his pleasures. He hungered that they might eat the bread of life. He thirsted that they might drink the water of life. He was numbered with the transgressors that they might stand among the justified, and be counted among his jewels. He made his grave with the wicked that they might sleep in Jesus. Though he was set up from everlasting, from the beginning, or ever the earth was, yet he became a helpless infant, that creatures of yesterday, sentenced to death, might live for ever. He wore a crown of thorns that all, who love his appearing, might wear a crown of life. He wept tears of anguish that his elect might weep tears of repentance not to be repented of. He bore the yoke of obedience unto death that they might find his yoke easy and his burden light. He poured out his soul unto death, lay three days in the heart of the earth, then burst the bars of death, and arose to God, that they, who through fear of death were all their life-time subject to bondage, might obtain the victory over the grave and become partakers of his resurrection.

He exhausted the penalty of the law that his redeemed might have access to the inexhaustible treasures of mercy, wisdom, faithfulness, truth and grace promised by the Lord. He passed from humiliation to humiliation, till he reached the sepulchre of Joseph, that his people might be changed from glory to glory as by the Spirit of the Lord. He was matchless in grace that they might be matchless in gratitude. Though a Son, he became a voluntary exile, that they, who had wickedly wandered afar off, might be brought nigh by his blood. He was compassed about with all their innocent infirmities that he might perfect his strength in their weakness. His visage was so marred more than any man, that his ransomed might be presented before God without spot, or blemish, or wrinkle, or any such thing. For a time he was forsaken of his Father that they, whom he bought with his blood, might behold the light of God's countenance for ever. He came and dwelt with them that they might be for ever with the Lord. He was hung up naked before his insulting foes that all, who believe on his name, might wear a glorious wedding garment, a spotless righteousness. Though he was dead, he is the first-born among many brethren. Through his sorrow his people obtain joy and gladness, and sorrow and sighing flee away. Though he endured the worst things, they do and shall for ever enjoy the best things. Wonderful mystery! God was manifest in the flesh! Here is no absurdity, no contradiction, no fiction, and yet a mystery that baffles all attempts to solve it, and dazzles all human and angelic vision. Blessed is he, who is not offended in Jesus. Blessed is he, who loves the incarnate mystery, and rests upon it. It is a mystery of love, of truth, of grace, of wisdom, of condescension, of power, of salvation. It is *the mystery of Godliness.* It is the great study of the inhabitants of heaven, and shall be while immortality endures.

If it be allowed to take these statements in a general and vague sense, most persons, who are willing to be called evangelical, will at least assent to them. But let us consider more particularly the *work* and the *sufferings* of our Lord, what he did, and what he endured, his obedience to law, and his submission to pain. It is true these things were not separated in him; but it is true that they can be distinguished. Some ignorant persons have seemed to suppose that orthodox Christians held that Christ obeyed one day or hour and suffered another. This is not the teaching of any. Christ was from his birth to his death a sufferer. He was also a servant to do the will of God. He obeyed in suffering. He suffered in obeying. His obedience to the precept and his endurance of the penalty of the law ran parallel to each other. Sound divines have therefore commonly spoken of Christ's *active* and *passive* obedience as comprehending the whole of his work on earth. His active obedience was rendered to the moral law as a rule of life. His passive obedience was his voluntary submission to the penal sufferings provided by the law for the transgressors of its holy commandments. Although a few good men have not favoured this formal distinction, yet the great body of sound writers have approved it. Nor is there any objection to it, if correctly understood. And until a better mode of explaining the mediatorial work of Christ on earth shall be suggested, let the friends of truth hold fast to the established language of sound divinity. It is remarkable that modern writers, who oppose the use of these phrases almost without exception are very erroneous on other points. If a man denies that Christ obeyed the precept of the law for us, it is almost certain that he will deny that he bore the curse or penalty of the law in our stead. Nor is it known that any sound writer has ever rejected the doctrine, which sober divines have always understood to be involved in the active and passive obedience of Christ.

Thus Owen says: "I shall not immix myself in the debate of the distinction between the active and passive obedience of Christ." This might startle some. But the fact is that some writers in his day had tediously dwelt upon the distinction, and had probably conveyed the idea that Christ's active and passive obedience were not only distinguishable but separable. But Owen instantly relieves our minds. His next words are: "For he exercised the highest active obedience in his suffering, when he offered himself to God, through the eternal Spirit. And all his obedience, considering his person, was mixed with suffering, as a part of his ex-inanition [emptying himself] and humiliation;

whence it is said, that 'though he were a Son, yet learned he obedience by the things that he suffered.'" Such an explanation instantly given by the author himself relieves all our concern for his statement; especially when in the same and preceding chapter he speaks thus: "There is no other way whereby the original, immutable law of God may be established, and fulfilled with respect unto us, but by the imputation of the perfect obedience and righteousness of Christ, who is the end of the law for righteousness unto all that do believe." Indeed he enters into a formal argument in defence of "the imputation of the active obedience or righteousness of Christ unto us, as an essential part of that righteousness whereon we are justified before God." His words are: "If it were necessary that the Lord Christ, as our surety should undergo the penalty of the law for us, or in our stead, because we all have sinned; then it was necessary also, that as our surety he should yield obedience unto the preceptive part of the law for us also: and if the imputation of the former be needful for us unto our justification before God, then is the imputation of the latter also necessary unto the same end and purpose." "And as we are no more able of ourselves to fulfil the law, in a way of obedience, than to undergo the penalty of it, so as that we may be justified thereby; so no reason can be given, why God is not as much concerned in honour and glory, that the preceptive power and part of the law be complied withal, by perfect obedience, as that the sanction of it be established by undergoing the penalty of it." Very much more he says to the same purport. Indeed he alleges that in this matter "our principal difference is with the Socinians," and he states and refutes their answers at length. In truth Socinus and his followers exhausted all the arguments that could be brought against Christ's complete satisfaction. Owen having made a long quotation from that dangerous heretic on this subject adds: "I have transcribed his words, that it may appear with whose weapons some young disputers, among ourselves, do contend against the truth." This remark is as applicable to errorists in the middle of the nineteenth century as it was to their predecessors two hundred years ago. The same is true of the following remark: "There is nothing in the whole doctrine of justification, which meets with a more fierce and various opposition."

That Charnock held the same doctrine is very clear; for in extolling the work of the Mediator, he thus dwells on "His *obedience* to his Father. It is a signal testimony given him, that he was *obedient even to the death of the cross*. Phil. ii. 8. The sharper then his circumstances were upon the cross, the more illustrious his obedience was. The lustre of obedience is seen in engaging upon command with the most affrighting difficulties." He subsequently dwells at length on the *sufferings* of Christ.

Archbishop Leighton speaking on 1 Cor. i. 30, "he is made of God unto us righteousness," &c., says: "This doubtless is meant of the righteousness by which we are justified before God; and as he is *made this to us*, applied by faith, *his righteousness becomes ours*. That exchange made, our sins are laid over on him, and his obedience put upon us."

The Rev. Thomas Boston says that Christ's obedience to the law for his people included "these three things following: 1. 'That he, as the second ADAM, should obey the whole law, in the name of those he represented.' This was a debt owing by them all, and was required of them, by the law, as a condition of life." "It was provided, that Christ, as their representative, should give obedience to the whole law for them; that both tables of the law, and each command of each table, should have the due obedience from him; that the law being laid before him, in its spirituality and full extent, he should fully answer it, in internal and external obedience, in his mind, will and affections, in thought, word and deed: that he should conform himself to the whole natural law, and to all divine institutions, ceremonial or political, so as to be circumcised, keep the passover, to be baptized, to be a servant or subject to rulers, pay tribute to whom it was due, and the like." [In fact the very reason Christ gave for being baptized was that "thus it becometh us to fulfil all righteousness."]

2. "That every part of that obedience should be carried to the highest pitch and degree. This the law required of them, as a condition of life.

"Lastly, that all this should be continued to the end, without the least failure in one jot of parts, or degrees of obedience. This also was a condition of life." * * It was agreed that the second ADAM should, in the name of those he represented, 'continue in all things, written in the book of the law to do them' even to the end. All which he did accordingly fulfil, being 'obedient unto death.'" Phil. ii. 8.

Ridgley says: "Satisfaction must bear some similitude, or resemblance, as to the matter of it, to that debt which was due from those for whom it was to be given. Here we must consider what was the debt due from us, for which a demand of satisfaction was made; this was twofold.

"1st. A debt of perfect and sinless obedience, whereby the glory of God's sovereignty might be secured, and the honour of his law maintained. This debt it was morally impossible for man to pay, after his fall; for it implies a contradiction to say that a fallen creature can yield a sinless obedience; nevertheless it was demanded of us, though fallen; for the obligation could not be disannulled by our disability to perform it.

"2dly. There was a debt of punishment, which we were liable to, in proportion to the demerit of sin, as the result of the condemning sentence of the law, which threatened death for every transgression and disobedience. Now, to be satisfaction to the justice of God, it must have these ingredients in it."

Dr. A. Alexander says: "By the righteousness of Christ, we mean all that he did and suffered to satisfy the broken law of God, for those whose salvation he undertook to secure. It has been shown that the law has a double demand upon us, both of which must be satisfied before a sentence of justification can righteously be pronounced." The "double demand" here spoken of is explained to be obedience to the precept, and endurance of the penalty of the law.

Indeed so precious is the doctrine of the full and perfect obedience of Christ, both in *doing* and *suffering*, in meeting the demands of both the *precept* and the *penalty* of the law, that in experience no enlightened mind can rest satisfied until it is assured of the truth of the positions here maintained. Some indeed object and say Christ's obedience to the precept of the law was due from him for himself, his human nature being under natural and indissoluble obligations to holiness. It is indeed true that Christ's human nature was bound for itself after being in existence to obey the law. And so was Adam in the garden of Eden. Yet if he had stood faithful to the end of his probation, his obedience would have been counted not only for himself but for us also. So the obedience of Christ not only caused the Father to say "This is my beloved Son in whom I am well pleased," but also for his sake to promise eternal life to as many as are found in him, clothed with his righteousness. Besides the person of the Mediator was constituted of a divine and a human nature. In his divine nature he was the lawgiver, the Lord of the Sabbath day, and the King universal. This gave to his obedience both to the precept and penalty of the law, a value transcending all our conceptions of merit as obtained even by angels who never sinned.

This is the very doctrine of the Scriptures. The reader has already had the interpretation of Charnock and Boston of the phrase "obedient unto death." Phil. ii. 8. Ridgley interprets the phrase the same way, viz: to signify Christ's active obedience, even in dying. That this is the correct mode of interpreting the text has long been held by the Church of God. The same doctrine is clearly taught by Paul in Rom. v. 12—19. There our justification is clearly stated to be "by the obedience of one," by the righteousness of one." To say that "obedience" and "righteousness" mean death, and death only is taking such a liberty with terms as, if carried out, will enable us to subvert every truth of Scripture, every record of history. If Christ's "obedience," in Romans v. has any meaning, it is the opposite of Adam's "disobedience." Christ's "righteousness" is the opposite of Adam's "offence." If Christ's obedience means simply his death, then Adam's disobedience means simply his life. If Christ's righteousness includes nothing but his suffering on the cross, Adam's offence must be that he did not suffer for us. In fine, no more unwarrantable liberties are taken with God's word than by the enemies of the doctrine of Christ's active obedience. In Gal. iv. 4, 5, Paul says: "God sent forth his Son, made of a woman, made under the law, to redeem them that were under the law." A law consists of two parts; 1. a precept, a rule to be followed, a canon; and 2. a sanction, a penalty for the transgressor. Now, was Jesus Christ made under the precept only, or the penalty only? One errorist will perhaps say one thing, and another a different thing. Some very bold heretics will deny that he was placed either under the precept or the penalty for us; but from the days of Paul to the present the Church of God has held that Christ was made under both the precept and the penalty of the law for us. Indeed it is well worthy of notice that as error never stops of its own accord, as its nature is to sink lower and lower, so it is very common, yea, almost universal to find those, who object to Christ's active obedience soon subverting all his righteousness, and even denying that he bore the penalty of the law for us, and contending that even his death was but a show of what God could do when he chose to express his indignation against his well beloved Son. But of Christ's death, and the atonement thereby made the next chapter will treat.

CHAPTER XXII.

THE DEATH OF CHRIST.—THE ATONEMENT.

WHEN we speak of the cross and death of Christ, we intend to set forth all his expiatory work. Christ's sufferings did not begin at the time of his crucifixion. Nor were his last sufferings alone possessed of value. The flight into Egypt no less than the nailing to the cross, the hunger and subsequent temptation in the wilderness no less than the thirst upon the cross, belonged to the sum of those things, which he endured for others. From most men the time and manner of their death are mercifully concealed until they are about to leave the world. But the Lord Jesus knew the end from the beginning. He had all the revolting circumstances distinctly before his mind for long years before his crucifixion. His life was as a death. He died as it were a thousand times. No words nor acts of our blessed Lord convey more just conceptions of the anguish he endured than that saying of his spoken long before his betrayal: "I have a baptism to be baptized with; and how am I straitened till it be accomplished." Luke xii. 50. Here is one secret of the sorrows of his life. I marvel not that his visage was so marred more than any man, and his form more than the sons of men. No sorrows were ever so keen, so consuming, and so long continued as his. Well may we blush to have made an ado over the comparatively little ills, to which our sins, or our sense of duty may at any time have subjected us.

Yet the actual *death* of Christ was necessary. If it had not been, it would not have occurred. The modes of bringing Christ's mediatorial work on earth into disesteem are countless. Some, using great swelling words, have said that his death was unnecessary, and that one drop of his blood was sufficient to all the ends of his death. But the Scriptures teach no such doctrine. They clearly declare that Christ ought to have suffered all that came upon him, and so to enter into his glory. Such a view is also very derogatory to the character of God. Flavel says: "I dare not affirm, as some do, that by reason of the infinite preciousness of Christ's blood, one drop thereof had been sufficient to have redeemed the whole world: for if one drop had been enough, why was all the rest, even to the last drop, shed? Was God cruel, to exact more from him than was needful and sufficient? Besides, we must remember, that the passions [sufferings] of Christ, which were inflicted on him as the curse of the law, these only are the passions, which are sufficient for our redemption from the curse of the law. Now it was not a drop of blood, but death, which was contained in the curse: this therefore was necessary to be inflicted. But surely as none but God can estimate the weight and evil of sin, so none but he can comprehend the worth and preciousness of the blood of Christ, shed to expiate it." The DEATH of Christ was necessary. The victim, because it stood in the place of the transgressor, must die. "A testament is of force after men are dead: otherwise it is of no strength at all while the testator liveth." While Jews, infidels and

Christians all agree in holding that Christ died, the latter only hold, that without his death we could not be saved.

Of the nature and intention of Christ's sufferings, which terminated in his death, the human mind has indulged many wild and dangerous fancies. There are still men on earth, who boldly deny that Jesus Christ endured the penalty of the law in the room and stead of sinners, or that the sins of any were imputed to him, or that he was a substitute for others, or that his sufferings were strictly vicarious. With very various degrees of ignorance or hatred of the truth, men reject all the established forms in which sound doctrine is taught. Yet all error is dangerous, and all truth is precious. The doctrine of the death of Christ holds a very prominent place in the Christian system. In fact it is a central truth and demands our warmest love.

The common doctrine of the Christian world has been that our sins were imputed to Christ, that he bore the curse due to us for our transgressions, that he endured the penalty of the law in our stead, that his sufferings were those of a substitute for guilty men. It has been the judgment of the people of God for ages on ages that this doctrine is well established in both the Old and the New Testaments.

It is natural to inquire whether our Lord himself explained the nature and object of his own death. In the Gospels we gain light on this point. "The Son of man came not to be ministered unto, but to minister, *and to give his life a ransom for many.*" Matt. xx. 28, and Mark x. 45. In full agreement with this declaration Paul says that Christ "gave himself a ransom for all to be testified in due season." 1 Tim. ii. 6. The words translated *ransom* in these passages are not the same. One is *lutron*, the price of redemption. The other is *antilutron*, which also signifies ransom, the price of redemption. Our Lord then did not die reluctantly, nor as the martyrs died, but he died in *commutation* or *compensation*, as Grotius says. His life was the price of our deliverance. It was all the price demanded. It was the ransom, the full ransom. Robinson's definition of *lutron* is "*loosing-money, a ransom*, the price paid for the release of any one." His definition of *antilutron* is "an equivalent for redemption, i. e. a ransom." Christ paid the price for which many, who had been justly detained as prisoners to sin and death, are released.

Our Lord also said: "This is my blood of the New Testament which is shed for many *for the remission* of sins." Matt. xxvi. 28. Whose blood besides was ever shed for the same end? Isaiah, John the Baptist, Stephen and many others died for the truth, but not for the remission of sins. In full accordance with this Paul says that Christ "purged our sins." Heb. i. 3. "Without shedding of blood is no remission." Heb. ix. 22. Here is the reason why "repentance and remission of sins should be preached in his name among all nations." Luke xxiv. 47. Remission is by no other name given under heaven among men. Not the blood of the prophets, nor of the martyrs, nor of beasts, but only the blood of Christ secures the forgiveness of sins. Rev. i. 5; Acts xx. 28; Heb. ix. 12.

Again, Christ says: "I am the good shepherd; the good shepherd giveth his life for the sheep." John x. 11. "Great and good, just and holy, as he is, he saw his sheep about to perish in their wanderings, and in order to expiate their guilt, and to ransom them from destruction, he not only endured hardship, and encountered danger, but he 'laid down his life for them,' and in their stead!" With the truths thus explicitly taught well agree all those general statements of Christ respecting his mission into this world, such as this, "The Son of man is come to seek and to save that which was lost." Luke xix. 10. He is the Saviour. That is his name. The reason why he bears his name JESUS is that he saves his people from their sins.

The apostles and prophets give an account of the death of Christ every way coincident with that given by the Lord himself. Thus Peter says: "Christ also hath once suffered for sins, the just for the unjust, that he might bring us to God." 1 Pet. iii. 18. All suffering under the moral government of God is in some sense "for sins." "Death by sin." Some suffering is purely by way of condign punishment. Thus lost angels suffer for their own sins. Some suffering is disciplinary, and is designed to wean men from error. Thus the pious Christian often suffers for his follies. Some suffering is exemplary. Thus the old prophets often suffered. James v. 10. But the ground of their suffering was always their own sins. God never permitted a holy angel to be a sufferer. The wicked who are suffering the vengeance of eternal fire, are also an ensample to us, but they suffer justly for their own sins. The last kind of suffering for sin is expiatory, where "the just" suffers "for the unjust." Christ in no sense suffered for himself. In fact the apostle in the next chapter says expressly that "Christ hath suffered FOR US in the flesh." 1 Pet. iv. 1.

In like manner the Scriptures generally and explicitly teach that Christ died for our sins. "He was delivered for our offences." Rom. iv. 25. "He gave himself for our sins." Gal. i. 4. "Christ died for our sins according to the Scriptures." 1 Cor. xv. 3. No words could more clearly teach that Christ's death was because of our offences against God, on account of our rebellion against the Most High. The word of God as clearly expresses the same truth in other language. "While we were yet sinners, Christ died for us." Rom. v. 8. "Christ died for the ungodly." Rom. v. 6. "This is my body, which is broken for you." 1 Cor. xi. 24. Here is substitution taught in the clearest terms. Christ died in the room and stead of us, sinners and ungodly.

By two different writers of Scripture Christ is said to be the propitiation for our sins. "Whom God hath set forth to be a propitiation, through faith in his blood, to declare his righteousness for the remission of sins, that are past." Rom. iii. 25. "He is the propitiation for our sins." 1 John ii. 2. "He loved us, and sent his Son to be the propitiation for our sins." 1 John iv. 10. In the above verses it is not the same word in all places that is rendered propitiation. Paul's word is *hilasterion ;* John's is *hilasmos*. They are, however, both correctly rendered propitiation, meaning an expiation for sin. In full harmony with the foregoing, Paul says that "Christ also hath loved us and hath given himself for us an offering and a sacrifice to God for a sweet-smelling savour." Eph. v. 2. All Christ did he did "for us." In particular when he offered himself a sacrifice it was not for himself, but for us. He needed no expiation on his own account, because he was holy and personally innocent. But just as surely as Abel's firstlings were sacrifices in his room and stead, so surely was Christ a sacrifice "for us." Accordingly he is said to have "offered himself without spot to God." Heb. ix. 14. So also Christ is called "the lamb of God" and "a lamb without blemish and without spot." There is no significancy in any bloody sacrifice unless the victim offered is a substitute for some one.

Christ is also called our Surety. Heb. vii. 22. A surety binds himself to perform something for others, and this obligation is either absolute or conditional. If one be hopelessly insolvent, the surety unconditionally assumes the payment of his debts. This was precisely our case. Our ruin was complete. We were utterly bankrupt, and Christ undertook to extricate us, 1. by obeying the precept of the law for us, and 2. by enduring the punishment due to us for our transgressions. In our helplessness Christ pitied us, voluntarily and lovingly undertook our cause for us, was fully able to accomplish all he engaged to do, and did satisfy all the demands of the law against us as rebels. The Scriptures teach that Christ did all this. "He was manifested to take away our sins, and in him was no sin." 1 John iii. 5. He took away our sins by taking them upon himself. Accordingly the Scriptures clearly assert that he "his own self bare our sins in his own body on the tree." 1 Pet. ii. 24. "Christ was once offered to bear the sins of many." Heb. x. 28. No such language is ever used of any other. Men bear their own sins in many cases. But Christ alone is the offering for the sins of many, to bear them quite away as the scape-goat did.

In Rom. viii. 3, Paul says: "What the law could not do, in that it was weak through the flesh, God sending his own Son in the likeness of sinful flesh and for sin, condemned sin in the flesh." That the word here translated condemned means *punished* is satisfactorily shown by Dr. Hodge in his commentary. That the doctrine thus taught is true many Scriptures declare. God then punished sin, not in those who committed it and who deserved his wrath, but in the flesh of his dear Son. In like manner Paul says: "Christ hath redeemed us from the curse of the law, being made a curse for us." Gal. iii. 13. If language has any force or meaning this passage teaches that Christ has rescued his people from the penalty of the law, and that he did this by enduring the penalty in their room and stead. It is not probable that any man, who will deny that these words teach as much as is here supposed, would be profited by any teachings on the subject, whether from men or from heaven. The curse of the law can mean nothing but the penalty of the law. Christ's being made a curse for us can mean nothing less than that he bore the penalty for us. The Scriptures also expressly teach that Jesus Christ is the sole author of reconciliation between God and sinners, that by him "we have received the atonement" (or reconciliation); Rom. v. 11; that we are "reconciled to God by the death of his Son;" Rom. v. 10; and that God hath reconciled us to himself by Jesus Christ." 2 Cor. v. 18. Now there is no way that the death of God's Son could make reconciliation but by his satisfying divine justice in our place and stead. Christ is our peace.

Having seen what Christ and his apostles taught

respecting the intent of his death, let us look at two portions of the Old Testament, which have been supposed to teach that Christ bore the punishment due to his people for their sins. The first is in the 40th Psalm. "Sacrifice and offering thou didst not desire; mine ears hast thou opened [or bored, as Hebrew masters bored the ears of their servants]: burnt-offering and sin-offering hast thou not required. Then said I, Lo I come, in the volume of the book it is written of me: I delight to do thy will, O my God." The apostle Paul, in Heb. x. 5—12, has given us an inspired and therefore infallible interpretation of this passage. It is fully coincident with what has already been argued.

The other portion of the Old Testament to which attention is here called is the precious 53d chapter of Isaiah, where many of the forms of speech already noticed occur and others are introduced, all teaching that Christ was our substitute, that he was punished for us, that he bore the wrath of God in our stead. The whole chapter is very dear to God's people. But a few quotations must suffice: "Surely he hath borne our grief and carried our sorrows," v. 4. William Lowth says of this: "He hath borne the evils and punishments which were due to our sins. The Hebrew verbs [rendered he *hath borne* and *hath carried*] properly signify to bear the punishment due to sin." Matthew Henry says: "The load was heavy, and the way long, yet he did not tire, but persevered to the end, till he said, *It is finished.*" Dr. Scott says: "He endured our griefs and sorrows, becoming a sufferer to redeem us from eternal sufferings."

The fifth verse of the chapter reads thus: "But he

was wounded for our transgressions, he was bruised for our iniquities; the chastisement of our peace was upon him, and with his stripes we are healed." Lowth says, "He suffered those chastisements or punishments, by which our peace with God was wrought, and satisfaction was made to the divine justice." Scott says, "He was 'wounded,' but it was not for his own, but for our transgressions; he was crushed with most intense agonies of body and soul, but it was for our iniquities." Dr. J. A. Alexander says: "The chastisement of peace is not only that which tends to peace, but that by which peace is procured directly."

"The Lord hath laid on him the iniquity of us all," v. 6. Lowth says: "The letter of the Hebrew runs thus, *The Lord* hath made the iniquities of us all to meet on him, or to fall upon him." Scott says, "The justice of God must be satisfied, before the criminals could be again received into his favour and under his care, and therefore JEHOVAH laid, or 'caused to meet' upon Christ, the Surety, not the punishment only, but the iniquity of them all, imputing it to him, and requiring of him satisfaction for it." Dr. Alexander says that our version "is objectionable only because it is too weak, and suggests the idea of a mild and inoffensive gesture, whereas that conveyed by the Hebrew word is necessarily a violent one, viz. that of causing to strike or fall."

"For the transgression of my people was he stricken," v. 8. Dr. Alexander translates it, "for the transgression of my people (as) a curse for them." Dr. Scott says: "For the transgression of his people, the stroke or punishment was on him."

"It pleased the LORD to bruise him; he hath put

him to grief; when thou shalt make his soul an offering for sin," v. 10. Surely none will blaspheme his blessed name by saying that his soul was an offering for his own sin. He was holy, harmless, undefiled and separate from sinners. As his soul was the offering also, and not merely his body, so it was the sword of the Lord that pierced him much more deeply than the nails or the spear. Zech. xiii. 7. Awake, O sword, and smite the man, that is my fellow, saith Jehovah."

"For he shall bear their iniquities," v. 11. Dr. Alexander on this verse remarks that Christ "becomes a Saviour only by becoming a substitute." His people shall receive his righteousness, "and he shall bear their burdens." Such is a very brief view of the express and precious teachings of this portion of God's word, which makes Matthew Henry say that "this chapter is so replenished with the unsearchable riches of Christ, that it may be called rather, *The Gospel of the evangelist Isaiah*, than *the prophecy of the prophet Isaiah.*"

In teaching the imputation of our sins to Christ no one holds that there is or could be any personal identity between Christ and his people. When we say that he and they are one, we mean that for their sakes and on their account, he was regarded and treated as if he deserved evil, and that for his sake and on his account they are regarded and treated as if they were innocent and deserving of good. Nor is it any portion of sound doctrine that the moral turpitude of our sins was transferred to Christ. This, in the nature of things, is impossible. The moral qualities of personal acts are confined to the acts themselves, or to those who perform them. The defilement of our sins is not imputed to Christ any more than the moral excellence of his acts is imputed to us. Of course Christ felt no consciousness of personal ill-desert, and consequently no remorse. This was as impossible as that we should feel self-complacency for Christ's righteousness imputed to us. A surety is not partaker of the misdeed, which has brought a party into trouble, but he simply agrees to pay the penalty or debt. Bitter as may be the sufferings brought on us by the sins of others, we cannot upbraid ourselves for having committed them. Neither did our Saviour feel the fell gnaw of despair. O no. "For the joy that was set before him he endured the cross, despising the shame, and is set down at the right hand of God." Heb. xii. 2. Neither remorse nor despair was the penalty denounced against transgression. The penalty was death. And although despair and remorse come on those, who are personally depraved, yet this is because they are thus sunk in sin.

It may be well also here to say that Christ's sufferings, though protracted, were not eternal, because of the infinite dignity of his person. "The eternity of punishment," says Charnock, "arises from the condition of the subject suffering, not from the nature of punishment itself. A creature, being a limited nature, cannot give an infinite satisfaction commensurate to an infinite justice, without suffering eternally. Therefore though infinite punishment be due, yet eternal punishment is not in itself due, but falls in, for want of the creature's ability to satisfy the demands of legal justice. Since it cannot satisfy the law by one, or many acts of sufferings, it is always suffering, but never fully satisfies: but the infinite dignity of the person of

Christ transcending all creatures, made the satisfaction he offered valuable without an eternal duration of those torments."

As our Saviour was a voluntary surety there was no injustice in requiring of him the satisfaction due from us. So true and so old is the doctrine that our Lord suffered the just for the unjust, the innocent for the guilty, that to this day we have no better means of illustrating the whole method of pardon and acceptance than by a simple explanation of many of the types, and especially the sacrifices of the Old Testament. The doctrine of the imputation of the sin of one to the person of another is as old as the institution of shedding blood in solemn worship, and slaying victims at earthly altars.

One of the most painful things in the life of a lover of sound doctrine is, that where his own views and feelings would lead him to rejoice and adore, he finds cavillers calling him to refute frivolous objections. "The highest wonder ever exhibited to the world, to angels and men, is the Son of God suffering and dying for sinners." But such is the wickedness of men that instead of being charmed and awed by the glories of redemption by Christ Jesus, they often sit down in cold blood, as did his murderers, and without emotion contemplate the most amazing sufferings ever witnessed. Beware of self-conceit, beware of all opinions on the subject of the atonement, unless you can prove them by the tenor of Scripture.

Respecting the satisfaction of Christ four views have been taken: 1. That he fully satisfied all the claims of the law for all men, and that all shall therefore infallibly be saved. This was the doctrine of the old Universalists. As it is fallen into general disfavour, further notice need not here be taken of it. 2. Another theory is that Christ did not satisfy divine justice for any of the sins of any man. In other words there was no atonement required and none made. This theory teaches that Christ's death was a symbol, a testimony, a display of jüstice against one on whom no sins were laid. The old Socinians held that Christ's death was a mere martyrdom. Is it not strange that they should thus hold, when our Lord gave signs of distress and agony never witnessed in any of his people when called to die for the truth? John Newton says, "No words can be more select and emphatical than those which the evangelists use in describing his consternation in the garden of Gethsemane. How can this his dejection and terror be accounted for by those, who deny that his sufferings and death were a proper atonement of sin; and who suppose, that when he had given to men a perfect rule of life, and commended it to them by his own example, he died merely to confirm the truth of his doctrine, and to encourage his followers to faithfulness under sufferings? Many of his followers, who were thus witnesses for the truth, and patterns of faithfulness to us, have met death in its most terrible forms with composure, yea, with pleasure, yea, with transports of joy. But is the disciple above his Lord? If Christians have triumphed in such circumstances, why did Christ tremble? Not surely because their constancy and courage were greater than his. The causes were entirely different. The martyrs were given up to them, who could kill the body only; but Jesus suffered immediately from the hand of God. One stroke of his mighty hand can bruise the spirit of man more sensibly than the united power of all creatures."

3. Another theory is that Christ satisfied for some of the sins of all men, and left them by their own works and sufferings to satisfy for the rest. This theory is seldom stated in so many words, but it is very pleasing to many, and is the actual scheme of thousands. It is virtually the plan of many Roman Catholics, who add their own merits and those of the saints to the merits of Christ. The Archbishop of Paris dying of wounds, received in fightings, which followed the expulsion of the house of Orleans, said: "O God, I offer to thee my present sufferings as an atonement for the errors of my episcopate." This sounds indeed as if his own sufferings were his sole reliance; but his creed mentions the sufferings and death of Christ.

4. The last theory is that Jesus Christ made satisfaction for all the sins of all his people, that he paid the last farthing of the debt they owed to the broken law and injured government of God, and that in him they are complete and have full redemption. The Westminster Assembly says: "Christ by his death did fully pay the debt of all his people, and did make a proper, real, and full satisfaction to his Father's justice in their behalf." The essence of the atonement consists in this satisfaction, which was *proper*, not figurative, not emblematical; *real*, not imaginary, nor pretended; and *full*, not partial, nor incomplete, not needing our merits to eke it out.

We have already seen how well this doctrine agrees both with the very words and with the general scope of Scripture. Were not this chapter already long, it would be easy to add the concurrent testimony of the best reformed churches and of many great divines. Some of these will hereafter be adduced for the purpose of illustrating other points. In the meantime the foregoing is the plain simple doctrine of the atonement as held in the Presbyterian and many other churches.

CHAPTER XXIII.

JUSTIFICATION BEFORE GOD.

No doctrine is more important than that of justification before God. This has long been the judgment of the Christian world. Luther says: "The article of justification being lost, all Christian doctrine perishes with it." He elsewhere calls justification "the article of a standing or falling church." Melancthon says: "We are brought into danger for the only reason that we deny the Romish doctrine of justification." Calvin says: "If this one head were yielded safe and entire, it would not pay the cost to make any great quarrel about other matters in controversy with Rome." Hooker says: "The grand question, that hangeth in controversy between us and Rome is about the matter of justifying righteousness." John Newman in his Salters-Hall Sermon says: "A sinner's justification before God is a doctrine of great importance in the Christian religion." Usher says: "The strong bastion of our Reformed Church is *justification by faith;* 'erected upon the foundation of the apostles and prophets, Jesus Christ himself being the chief corner-stone.' *That* gone, the temple is taken, the ark is in captivity; 'from the daughter of Zion all her beauty is departed.'" Bishop Hall says: "That point of justification of all others is exceeding important." John Newton says: "The great privilege of the elect, comprehensive of every blessing, is, that they are justified, finally and authoritatively justified.' Dr. Thomas Scott says: "'How should man be just with God?' All our eternal interests depend on the answer, which, in our creed and experience, we return to this question: for if God hath, for the glory of his own name, law, and government, appointed a method of justifying sinners, and revealed it in the gospel; and they in the pride of their hearts, refuse to seek the blessing in this way, but will come for it according to their own devices; he may justly, and will certainly, leave them under merited condemnation." The elder Edwards presents the following considerations in proof of the importance of the doctrine of justification by faith alone: 1. "The Scripture treats of this doctrine as a doctrine of very great importance." 2. "The adverse scheme lays another foundation of man's salvation than God hath laid." 3. "It is in this doctrine that the most essential difference lies between the covenant of grace and the first covenant." 4. "This is the main thing for which fallen men stood in need of a divine revelation, to teach us how we who have sinned may come to be again accepted of God." 5. "The contrary scheme of justification derogates much from the honour of God and the Mediator." 6. "The opposite scheme does most directly tend to lead men to trust in their own righteousness for justification, which is a thing fatal to the soul." Father Paul tells us that the Popish fathers and divines of the Council of Trent admitted that all the alleged errors of Luther could be traced to his views on justification, and that the only way to maintain the other dogmas of Rome was "to overthrow the heresy of justification by faith only." Socinus calls this doctrine base and pernicious, and says it is to be execrated and detested. Swedenborg and his followers direct their strongest efforts against this doctrine. The same is true of nearly all modern heretics. So that by the confession of the friends and the enemies of the true doctrine, the views men entertain on this subject are vastly important and control their belief on other points. Indeed Paul's epistles to the Romans and to the Galatians, written chiefly to teach and establish the truth on this subject, stand imperishable monuments of the judgment of that great and inspired man as to the weighty matter of justification before God. It could not be otherwise. We rise or fall, we live or die, we are saved or lost, according as we are justified, or not. On such a subject we should conduct our inquiries with great candour, and adopt conclusions after much prayer and in the fear of God. He, who heartily loves and adopts the truth here, may indeed be left to some other errors, which will mar the symmetry of his Christian character, impair his usefulness, and diminish his final reward, yet he shall not be cast off at last. But he, who at heart rejects the true ground of justification must finally, utterly, inevitably perish. So teaches Paul: "Other foundation can no man lay than that is laid, which is Jesus Christ. Now if any man build upon this foundation, gold, silver, precious stones, wood, hay, stubble; every man's work shall be made manifest; for the day shall declare it, because it shall be revealed by fire; and the fire shall try every man's work, of what sort it is. If any man's work abide which he hath built thereupon, he shall receive a reward. If any man's work shall be burned, he shall suffer loss: but he himself shall be saved; yet so as by fire." 1 Cor. iii. 11—15. This settles the question.

Justification is the opposite of condemnation. Whatever one is, the other is not. In Scripture they are often set over against each other. "By thy words thou shalt be *justified*, and by thy words, thou shalt be *condemned*." Matt. xii. 37. "He that *justifieth* the wicked, and he that *condemneth* the just, even they both are abomination to the Lord." Prov. xvii. 15. "If there be a controversy between men, and they come unto judgment, that the judges may judge them; then they shall *justify* the righteous, and *condemn* the wicked." Deut. xxv. 1. "If I *justify* myself, mine own mouth shall *condemn* me." Job ix. 20. "As by the offence of one, judgment came upon all men to *condemnation*, even so by the righteousness of one the free gift came upon all men to *justification of life*." Rom. v. 18. These texts not only show that condemnation and justification are opposite to each other, but that these two words are borrowed from judicial proceedings, and so are properly said to be forensic. Justifying is declaring or pronouncing one righteous, as condemning is pronouncing or declaring one guilty. Often in Scripture these terms are said to belong to judicature, as in Psa. xxxvii. 33, "The Lord will not condemn him *when he is judged*;" Matt. xii. 42, "The queen of the south shall rise up *in the judgment* with this generation and shall condemn it;" Psa. cix. 7, "*When he shall be judged*, let him be condemned;" Psa. li. 4, "That thou mightest be justified, when thou speakest, and be clear, *when thou judgest*." Yet, while the term is borrowed from the forum, it is not used precisely in the same sense in theology as when we apply it to judicial proceedings among men. At a human tribunal a man is said to be *justified*, when no crime has been proven against him, but his conduct has met with the approval of those by whom he was judged. But when a man is said to be justified before God, the meaning is that a *sinner* has been *pardoned* and *accepted in the Beloved*. Had man never sinned, he would have been justified as one, who had broken no law, and would have needed no pardon. But being a law-breaker, any trial in the sight of God will show him culpable, and in himself undone. If a sinner is justified, it must be by an act of grace.

The Westminster Assembly thus taught: "Justification is an act of God's free grace unto sinners, in which he pardoneth all their sin, accepteth and accounteth their persons righteous, in his sight; not for anything wrought in them or done by them, but only for the perfect obedience and full satisfaction of Christ, by God imputed to them, and received by faith alone." You will hardly find a better definition than this in uninspired writings. It is true, complete, guarded, comprehensive. Let us consider it somewhat in detail. *First*, justification is an ACT. It is not a work, or series of acts. It is not progressive. The weakest believer and the strongest saint are alike and equally justified. Justification admits of no degrees. A man is either wholly justified or wholly condemned in the sight of God. "There is therefore now NO condemnation to them, which are in Christ Jesus." "Who shall lay ANYTHING to the charge of God's elect?" Rom. viii. 1, 33. And when a soul is condemned it is wholly condemned. "Whosoever shall keep the whole law, and yet offend in one point, he is GUILTY OF ALL." James

ii. 10. "The soul that sinneth, IT SHALL DIE." Ezek. xviii. 4. When it is said in Luke xviii. 14, that the publican "went down to his house justified *rather* than the" pharisee, it does not mean that the pharisee was somewhat justified and the publican more justified. The sense is that the former was justified in preference to the other, to the exclusion of the other. The publican was perfectly justified, the pharisee was not at all justified. There is a moment, when a man is under the curse, and a moment when he comes to be under grace.

Secondly, justification is an act of GOD. He alone is its author. He is called "the Justifier." "It is God that justifieth." "It is one God which shall justify the circumcision by faith, and uncircumcision through faith." Rom. iii. 26, 30, and viii. 33. We should not forget this great truth. We may justify ourselves, our neighbours may call us the excellent of the earth, pretended priests of God may blasphemously pronounce us absolved from all sin, but all this will avail us nothing; "for the LORD seeth not as man seeth; for man looketh on the outward appearance, but the Lord looketh on the heart." 1 Sam. xvi. 17. Christ said to some, "Ye are they which justify yourselves before men; but God knoweth your hearts: for that which is highly esteemed among men is abomination in the sight of God." Luke xvi. 15. Moreover it is one of the highest prerogatives of sovereignty to condemn and to justify. As it is God's government we live under, as it is his law that we have broken, as it is his Son that died, as it is his tribunal, before which we must all appear, so it is right that he and not another should pass sentence upon us. The governor of one state, or the king of one country cannot punish or pardon an offence committed in the territorial limits of another. It is beyond his jurisdiction. In the moral government of the universe, God's authority is sole, supreme, exclusive. He alone is the Lawgiver, he alone is the Judge. No one has jurisdiction but himself. None can really or effectually justify or condemn but he.

Thirdly, justification is more than is of right due to any man. He is a sinner, and whatever good thing comes to him must be of God's mere bounty. It is a gratuity, not a debt. So justification is "an act of God's FREE GRACE UNTO SINNERS." Considered in regard to holy angels, justification would have another signification. They have no sins to pardon. Their innocence is their shield. In the eye of the divine law they stand on the ground of perfect, personal, perpetual obedience. But the question is not, How are holy angels justified? but, How shall *man* be just with God? Had man never sinned he would have stood justified in the same way as his elder brethren in glory. Indeed the natural method of justification for all accountable creatures is by personal righteousness, but since man became a sinner, this door is shut up, and cherubim and a flaming sword forbid his entrance into life by that method. The Scripture does not deny that angels stand before God by their works. But it does say: "By the deeds of the law there shall no FLESH be justified in his sight;" "a MAN is not justified by the works of the law:" "by the works of the law shall no FLESH be justified." Rom. iii. 20, and Gal. ii. 16. Paul expressly teaches that God "justifieth the ungodly." Rom. iv. 5. To say that the power of sight in the blind, whose eyes Christ opened, was the cause of the miracle by which they obtained vision is absurd. Their ability to see came only from the love and power of the Son of God. To say that a sound condition of the body was the cause of the expulsion of the fever from the veins of Peter's wife's mother, is to speak foolishness. That disease was removed by Christ alone. Health did not precede, it followed the act of Christ. So God looks on sinners as *ungodly*, and in their *ruin* he pities them, and graciously pardons and accepts them. This doctrine must be insisted on at all times and at all hazards for three reasons. *First*, it is the only doctrine, which can properly be called Gospel, good news to sinners; *secondly*, God's honour is more completely staked on the maintenance, propagation and reception of this than of any other doctrine of revealed religion; *thirdly*, this is the only doctrine, which produces genuine holiness of heart and life.

Three points of the definition of justification quoted have been considered. Four others, viz.: the pardon of sin, the acceptance of the sinner in Christ, the imputation of Christ's righteousness, and the office of faith in justification, remain to be considered. Each of these is vastly important, and shall be distinctly treated. In the mean time let every one exalt the loving-kindness of him, who allows us to hope for full justification by the blood and righteousness of the great Redeemer. If ever glad tidings of great joy reached the ears of mortals, here it is: "Being justified by faith, we have peace with God, through our Lord Jesus Christ."

CHAPTER XXIV.

JUSTIFICATION.—THE PARDON OF SIN BY CHRIST'S BLOOD.

To holy angels *innocence* is a sweet word. But to humble, penitent sinners *forgiveness* is music and life. In itself the former is better than the latter, as uninterrupted health is better than recovery from sickness, unbroken friendship better than quarrels followed by reconciliations. Yet such is the wisdom of God in man's salvation that forgiveness has a sweetness and will be followed by glories, which never belonged to innocence. By the incarnation of Christ human nature is married to the divine, and is thus exalted to a seat on the throne of the universe. And as Christ has shown by three parables that it is common to men to rejoice more over one thing lost and recovered, than over ninety and nine things never lost, so we may for ever rejoice unspeakably more over a lost paradise regained, than we should have done over a paradise never lost. Surely the sweetest songs ever warbled, the most thrilling anthems ever sung, the loudest Alleluiahs ever thundered relate to redemption and forgiveness, to salvation and

> The Lamb, the Lamb, the loving Lamb,
> The Lamb, that died on Calvary.

Should such, however, be the result, it will not be because sin is not in its own nature ineffably mischievous and malignant; but solely because Jehovah is infinite in skill and love, bringing light out of darkness, joy out of sorrow, good out of evil. Marvellous is his loving-kindness. Plenteous is he in mercy. God alone is great.

Many words in Scripture point towards forgiveness, such as grace, mercy, peace with God, not imputing iniquity, taking away sin, bearing sin, making an end of transgression, covering sin, forgetting sin, not remembering iniquity, washing, cleansing and removing sin, casting it into the sea, or behind the back, scattering it like a cloud, burying it, blotting it out, pardoning it. When the scape-goat bore away the sins laid upon him to a land not inhabited, he only did in a figure what Jesus does in fulfilment of this and many other types. In the Old Testament the word often rendered atonement is literally "covering," or covering up. As we bury our dead out of *our* sight, so God buries the sins of believers out of *his* sight. In old times accounts were often kept on tables of wax, and when a debt was paid or forgiven, the account was blotted out by rubbing a smooth surface over it. So God cancels our debts, blots out the handwriting that was against us, not because we have paid what we owed or any part of it, but because he pities us and is rich in mercy towards us. When a master does not wish to notice the errors of a servant, he turns his head another way. So God hides his face from our sins, and refuses to "behold iniquity in Jacob," or to "see perverseness in Israel." Num. xxiii. 21. Yea God hides our sins themselves, not from his omniscience, for that is impossible, but from his punitive justice. "In those days, and in that time, saith the

Lord, the iniquity of Israel shall be sought for, and there shall be none; and the sins of Judah, and they shall not be found: for I will pardon them whom I reserve." Jer. l. 20. As a man ceases to brood over an offence, which he has forgiven, and does not wish to cherish a remembrance of it, so says God: "Their sins and iniquities will I remember no more." Heb. x. 17. And as a thing, which might do a child harm, is put far from it, so God's people sing: "As far as the east is from the west, so far hath he removed our transgressions from us." Psa. ciii. 12. The Scripture fully informs us that our hope of pardon is in God alone. "To the Lord our God belong mercies and forgivenesses, though we have rebelled against him." Dan. ix. 9. It no less distinctly lets us know that in pardoning us God is self-moved to so gracious an act: "I, even I, am he that blotteth out thy transgressions *for mine own sake*, and will not remember thy sins." Isa. xliii. 25. The forgiveness of sins is *free*. It is "without money and without price." We can do nothing to merit it, or prepare ourselves for it. To deserve forgiveness is a solecism in language, an absurdity in law, a heresy in doctrine, and an impossibility in practice.

When God pardons, he pardons all sins, original sin and actual sin, sins of omission and of commission, secret and open sins, sins of thought, word and deed. One unpardoned sin would destroy a soul for ever. A single transgression can rouse an enlightened conscience to the wildest fury. And "every sin deserves the wrath and curse of God both in this life, and in that which is to come." Yet to those, who believe in Jesus, all is freely forgiven. Full pardon, or none at all, is what God designs to give. This suits human necessities. Nor is this gift ever revoked by God. When he forgives, he forgives for ever. He, who is once pardoned, never again comes under the curse of the law. Upon new provocations men sometimes revive old controversies. Not so God. Sin once pardoned by him is done with for ever. He has cast it behind his back and will not return to search for it. Forgiveness of sins that are past is a sure pledge that future sins shall not have a condemning power. God forgives no sin until it is committed, but he executes his unchanging purposes of love to his people and judicially forgives their sins as soon as committed. 2 Sam. xii. 13. This does not screen them from fatherly chastisement for their good and his glory; but they never come into penal condemnation. At no time are believers under the law as a covenant of works, but they are always under grace.

Christ is set upon the hill of Zion to grant repentance and remission of sins. The *moving* cause of forgiveness is his boundless love; but the *procuring* cause is his own most precious blood. "Without shedding of blood is no remission." "By his own blood he entered in once into the holy place, having obtained eternal redemption for us." "The blood of Christ, who through the eternal Spirit offered himself without spot to God, shall purge your conscience from dead works to serve the living God." We have "boldness to enter into the holiest by the blood of Jesus, by a new and living way, which he hath consecrated for us, through the veil, that is to say, his flesh." Heb. ix. 12, 14, 22, and x. 19, 20. "As for thee also, by the blood of thy covenant I have sent forth thy prisoners out of the pit wherein is no water." Zech. ix. 11. "This is my blood of the New Testament, which is shed for many for the remission of sins." Matt. xxvi. 28. "Being justified by his blood, we shall be saved from wrath through him." Rom. v. 9. "In whom we have redemption through his blood, the forgiveness of sins, according to the riches of his grace." "In Christ Jesus, ye, who sometime were far off, are made nigh by the blood of Christ." Eph. i. 7, and ii. 13. He has "made peace through the blood of his cross." Col. i. 20. "The blood of Christ his Son cleanseth us from all sin." 1 John i. 7. So that nothing but extreme ignorance or extraordinary wickedness can induce a poor sinner to venture near to God except through the blood of Christ. By his stripes we are healed. By his chastisement is our peace. By his sorrows come our joys. By his death is our life. As our Surety he pays all our debt. As the lamb of God he takes away the sins of the world. By his expiation we go free. No man is truly blessed till he has this blessing, the pardon of sin. It is the pledge and forerunner of all others. It is a fountain of life. It takes away the sting of death. Augustine says: "All my hope is in the death of my Lord. His death is my merit, my refuge, my salvation, my life and my resurrection. The mercy of the Lord is my merit; I am not without merit, so long as the Lord of mercies is not wanting. And if the mercies of the Lord be many, I abound in merits." Again, "the certainty of our whole confidence consists in the blood of Christ." The blood of sprinkling speaketh better things than the blood of Abel. That called for vengeance, this for peace. How highly the people of God prize this blessing of forgiveness may be learned from their history in all ages: "Blessed is he whose transgression is forgiven, and whose sin is covered. Blessed is the man to whom the Lord imputeth not iniquity." Psa. xxxii. 1, 2. In enumerating the benefits he had received, David puts this first. "Bless the Lord, O my soul, and forget not all his benefits: who forgiveth all thine iniquities." Psa. ciii. 2, 3. So the Church of God has always held. The Confession of France says: "We affirm, that Jesus Christ is our perfect and entire washing; in whose death we obtain full satisfaction; whereby we are delivered from all those sins, whereof we are guilty, and from which we could not be acquitted by any other remedy." That of England says: "Our only succour and refuge is to fly to the mercy of our Father by Jesus Christ, and assuredly to persuade our minds, that he is the obtainer of forgiveness for our sins; and that, by his blood, all our spots of sin be washed clean; that he hath pacified, and set at one, all things by the blood of his cross." That of Scotland: "We confess and avow, that there remaineth no other sacrifice for sin; (Heb. x. 26,) which if any affirm, we nothing doubt to avow, that they are blasphemous against Christ's death, and the everlasting purgation and satisfaction purchased to us by the same." That of Belgia: "We account all things as dung, in respect of the excellency of the knowledge of Christ Jesus our Lord, finding, in his wounds and stripes, all manner of comfort that can be desired. Wherefore, there is no need, that either we should wish for any other means, or devise any of our own brains, whereby we might be reconciled unto God, besides this one oblation once offered, by which all the faithful, which are sanctified, are consecrated, or perfected for ever." That of Augsburg teaches that Christ, "who was born of the virgin Mary, did truly suffer, was crucified, dead and buried, that he might reconcile his Father unto us, and might be a sacrifice, not only for the original sin, but also for all actual sins, of men."

It is worthy of special notice that the nearness of death makes the pardon of sin and the blood of Christ very precious to the souls of good men. The Rev. Dr. Cornelius on his death-bed said: "The impression has been on my mind for these last three days, that this is my final sickness; and I bless God that I can look forward to the change before me with composure and hope. I feel that I am a poor sinner; I need to be washed from *head to foot* in the blood of atonement (this last was uttered with the most affecting solemnity) —but I hope I may be saved through the blood of Christ. Within the last year and especially of late, the Lord Jesus Christ has been becoming more and more precious to my soul. I feel that I can commit my immortal all to him; and here I wish to bear my dying testimony that I go to the judgment, relying on nothing but the blood of Christ. *Without that* I should have no hope."

CHAPTER XXV.

JUSTIFICATION.—ACCEPTANCE IN CHRIST.

It is an error of some that they make our entire justification to consist in the pardon of sin. It is not here denied that by a well-known figure of speech remission, pardon and forgiveness, are each sometimes put for the whole of justification, just as fear, love and faith are each put for the whole of religion, and just as the cross of Christ is spoken of to signify the whole system of truths essentially connected with the cross. But precious as is the gift of pardon, and certainly as it is accompanied by acceptance in the Beloved, yet it is not itself such acceptance. Our case demands more than mere remission. Bare pardon would save us from hell. It could give us no title to heaven. It would bar the gates of death, but it would not open the gates of life. It breaks off our chains and opens our prison doors, but it does not beauteously array us, and send us forth in the garments of salvation. It destroys the fear and takes away the pains of hell, but gives not the hope of glory, nor secures the rewards of grace. Pardon turns the rebel loose, but it does not authorize him to sit at the table of the king. It secures to us remission; we want admission to the divine favour. Pardon brings us out of Egypt. Acceptance enfeoffs us in Canaan. Pardon causes us to cease to be heirs of hell. Acceptance makes us heirs of heaven. It is also freely granted that forgiveness and acceptance, remission and a title to eternal glory are never separated, though they are distinct and different; just as faith, hope and love are never separated, yet no man will contend that they are the same Christian virtues. As many as God pardons, he accepts in Christ, regenerates, sanctifies and glorifies. A *separate* link of this blessed chain is never found, yet each link is distinct. As this distinction is highly important, and the opposition to it sometimes violent and scornful, it may be well to give the views of those, whose names are of weight with nearly all good men. It is strange that such hatred of the precious truth of God should ever be indulged, but the friends of sound doctrine cannot abandon the defence of that, which is so precious. It is their life. Calvin says: "We simply explain justification to be an acceptance, by which God receives us into his favour, and esteems us as righteous persons; and we say it consists in the remission of sins and the imputation of the righteousness of Christ." Owen says: "Had we not been sinners, we should have had no need of the imputation of the righteousness of Christ to render us righteous before God. Being so, the first end for which it is imputed is the pardon of sin; without which we could not be righteous by the imputation of the most perfect righteousness. These things therefore are consistent, namely that the satisfaction of Christ should be imputed unto us for the pardon of sin, and the obedience of Christ be imputed unto us to render us righteous before God. And they are not only consistent, but neither of them singly were sufficient unto our justification." How precious such doctrine is, how faith lays hold of it as with both hands! Bishop Hopkins says: "It is not therefore, O my soul, a mere negative mercy that God intends thee in the pardon of thy sins: it is not merely the removing of the curse and wrath, which thy sins have deserved, though that alone can never be sufficiently admired. But the same hand, that plucks thee out of hell by pardoning grace and mercy, lifts thee up to heaven by what it gives thee together with thy pardon, even a right and title to the glorious inheritance of saints above."

It is very strange that some should deny that the elder Edwards maintained this view, when in his sermon on justification he gives it great prominence, and that in the early part of the discourse. His language is: "A person is said to be *justified*, when he is approved of God as free from the guilt of sin and its deserved punishment, and as having that righteousness belonging to him that entitles to the reward of life. That we should take the word in such a sense, and understand it as the judge's accepting a person as having both a negative and positive righteousness belonging to him, and looking on him therefore as not only free from any obligation to punishment, but also as just and righteous, and so entitled to a positive reward, is not only most agreeable to the etymology and natural import of the word, which signifies to pass one for righteous in judgment, but also manifestly agreeable to the force of the word as used in Scripture.

"Some suppose that nothing more is intended in Scripture by justification, than barely the remission of sins. If so, it is very strange, if we consider the nature of the case; for it is most evident and none will deny, that it is with respect to the rule or law of God we are under, that we are said in Scripture to be either justified or condemned. Now what is it to justify a person as the subject of a law or rule, but to judge him as standing right with regard to that rule? To justify a person in a particular case, is to approve of him as standing right, as subject to the law in that case; and to justify in general is to pass him in judgment, as standing right in a state correspondent to the law or rule in general; but certainly, in order to a person's being looked on as standing right with respect to the rule in general, or in a state corresponding with the law of God, more is needful than not having the guilt of sin; for whatever that law is, whether a new or an old one, doubtless something positive is needed in order to its being answered. We are no more justified by the voice of the law, or of him that judges according to it, by a mere pardon of sin, than Adam, our first surety, was justified by the law, at the first point of his existence, before he had fulfilled the obedience of the law, or had so much as any trial whether he would fulfil it or no. If Adam had finished his course of perfect obedience, he would have been justified; and certainly his justification would have implied something more than what is merely negative; he would have been approved of, as having fulfilled the righteousness of the law, and accordingly would have been adjudged to the reward of it. So Christ, our second surety, (in whose justification all, whose surety he is, are virtually justified) was not justified till he had done the work the Father had appointed him, and kept the Father's commandments through all trials; and then in his resurrection he was justified. When he had been put to death in the flesh, but quickened by the Spirit, (1 Pet. iii. 18,) then he that was manifest in the flesh was justified in the Spirit, (1 Tim. iii. 16); but God, when he justified him in raising him from the dead, did not only release him from his humiliation for sin, and acquit him from any further suffering or abasement for it, but admitted him to that eternal and immortal life, and to the beginning of that exaltation, which was the reward of what he had done. And indeed the justification of a believer is no other than his being admitted to communion in the justification of this head and surety of all believers; for as Christ suffered the punishment of sin, not as a private person, but as our surety; so when after this suffering he was raised from the dead, he was therein justified, not as a private person, but as the surety and representative of all that should believe in him. So that he was raised again not only for his own, but also for our justification, Rom. iv. 25; 'who was delivered for our offences, and raised for our justification.' And therefore it is that the apostle says as he does in Rom. viii. 34, 'Who is he that condemneth? It is Christ that died, yea rather, that is risen again.'"

This great writer says yet more on the subject, but surely enough has been quoted incontestably to prove that he held that pardon was not the whole of justification. If any man shall hereafter claim him on that side, he must either betray great ignorance, or criminal perverseness of mind.

The bitterness, with which the present defenders of orthodox views in this matter, are assailed must justify the making of an extract from Dr. Thomas Scott: "*The justification of a sinner* must imply something distinct from a total and final remission of the deserved punishment; namely a renewed title to the reward of righteousness, as complete and effective as he would have had if he had never sinned, but had perfectly performed, during the term of his probation, all the demands of the divine law. The remission of sins would indeed place him in such a state, that no charge would lie against him; but then he would have no title to the reward of righteousness, till he had obtained it by performing, for the appointed time, the whole obedience required of him; for he would merely be re-admitted to a state of probation, and his justification or condemnation could not be decided till that were terminated. But the *justification* of the pardoned sinner gives him a *present* title to the reward of righteousness, independent of his *future* conduct, as well as without respect to his *past* actions. This is evidently the scriptural idea of justification: it is uniformly represented as immediate and complete, when the sinner believes in the Lord Jesus Christ; and not as a contingent advantage to be waited for till death or judgment: and the arguments, which some learned men have adduced, to prove that *justification* means nothing else than *forgiveness of sins*, only show that the two distinct blessings are never separately conferred. David, for instance, says, 'Blessed is the man to whom the Lord imputeth not iniquity;' and Paul observes that in that passage, 'David describeth the blessedness of the man, unto whom God imputeth righteousness without works.' This does not prove, that 'not imputing sin,' and 'imputing righteousness' are synonymous terms: but merely, that where God does not *impute sin, he does* impute righteousness:

and that he confers the title to eternal life, on all those whom he rescues from eternal death. Indeed *exemption from eternal punishment, and a right to an actual and vast reward*, are such distinct things, that one cannot but wonder they should be so generally confounded as they are in theological discussions."

These extracts from Scott and Edwards have been purposely given at length, because they fairly and cogently argue the question, because these writers are remarkable for sound and clear discrimination, because they were eminently earnest and deeply experienced Christians, because above most they were Bible theologians, and because they justly have great weight with good and sober people in settling the opinions of the wavering. It would be easy to swell the testimonies to this precious truth to a great number. Take the following as the only additional witness now offered. The latter Confession of Helvetia says: "To justify, in the apostle's disputation concerning justification, doth signify to remit sins, to absolve from the fault and punishment thereof, to receive into favour, to pronounce a man just." Still our dependence is on God's precious word for all our doctrinal principles. There we find the remission and the reward both stated. Jesus Christ says, "Verily I say unto you, he that heareth my word, and believeth on him that sent me, hath everlasting life, and shall not come into condemnation; but is passed from death unto life." John v. 24. Here life and death, everlasting life and condemnation are opposite, and justification by faith is described, not merely as escape from death and condemnation, but as a passage already made from death unto life. In Acts xiii. 38, 39, are these words also: "Be it known unto you therefore, men and brethren, that through this man is preached unto you the forgiveness of sins; and by him all that believe are justified from all things, from which ye could not be justified by the law of Moses." So Christ sent Paul to preach to the gentiles, "that they might receive forgiveness of sins, AND inheritance among them which are sanctified." Acts xxvi. 18. Here both the blessings are distinctly stated as flowing from Christ. So in Rom. v. 1, 2, "Therefore being justified by faith, we have peace with God through our Lord Jesus Christ, by whom also we have access into this grace wherein we stand, and rejoice in hope of the glory of God." Surely, the second verse here is not mere tautology. By the pardon of sin "there is no condemnation" to the believer; by his acceptance in the Beloved, "he is made an heir according to the hope of eternal life." Rom. viii. 1; Titus iii. 7. If the distinction has not been made clear, and also well established, perhaps it is hardly necessary to spend more time upon it. Its importance may be seen by asking, what is the true state of believers? Are they merely a company of pardoned wretches? or are they a glorious family of adopted children? Are they merely turned out of prison to wander at large? or are they through Christ entitled to eternal glory? Do they stand before God's tribunal as a reprieved felon stands before his king? or have they "a right to the tree of life?" Rev. xxii. But we are already trenching upon the subject of the next chapter, viz: the imputed righteousness of Christ. May this and that be a blessing to many a child of God. O that God's people knew their privileges and rejoiced in them continually. And "whilst we carry a sense of grace in our conscience to comfort us, let us carry a sense of sin in our memory to humble us."

CHAPTER XXVI.

JUSTIFICATION—CHRIST'S RIGHTEOUSNESS IS IMPUTED TO BELIEVERS.

As our works are the works of sinners we must either stand before God, covered with the filthy rags of our own righteousness, or we must obtain some better righteousness than we are capable of working out for ourselves. We must either be justified by God without any cause, and this would be both connivance at sin and approbation of it, to assert which of God would be blasphemy; or by works in their nature imperfect and sinful, as all ours confessedly are, and that would be an admission that the law had once demanded too much; or by the all-perfect work and infinite merit of Jesus Christ. This last is God's published plan. Christ is "the LORD our righteousness." The end of his life on earth was that he might be the end of the law for righteousness to every one that believeth. His righteousness is not imparted, but imputed to us. It does not cure our corruption, but it covers our nakedness. It is not infused into us, but it is reckoned to us. It is not inherent in us, but it is set down to our account. We do not imbibe it, but we are invested with it. We are not imbued but endued with it. It does not give us a fitness for heaven, but a title to it. It is not Christ's work in us, but his work and sufferings for us, which give us an indefeasible title to the privileges of sons of God. To enter the kingdom of God without a right would make us stand before him as presumptuous intruders, called by Christ "thieves and robbers, who had climbed up some other way." To enter it with a title less perfect than the law requires would be exalting mercy at the expense of justice, and relaxing all the bonds of God's moral government. To enter it with a title based upon our own merits would be a public and uncontradicted denial of our guilt and ruin. But here is Jehovah's way. "The grace of God, and the gift by grace, which is by one man, Jesus Christ, hath abounded unto many." "They which receive abundance of grace and of the gift of righteousness, shall reign in life by one, Jesus Christ." "By the righteousness of one the free gift came upon all men unto justification of life." "By the obedience of one shall many be made righteous." "Our righteousness," says Calvin, "is not in ourselves but in Christ. 'As by one man's disobedience many were made sinners, so by the obedience of one shall many be made righteous.' What is placing our righteousness in the obedience of Christ, but asserting that we are accounted righteous only because his obedience is accepted for us as if it were our own?"

Such Scriptures and such reasonings settle to the satisfaction of the great mass of God's people the truth of the imputation of Christ's righteousness to his people. The righteousness by which a sinner stands accepted is called the righteousness of God, because it is in opposition to the righteousness of men, because God provided and approves it and none other, and because he puts great honour upon it. It is called the righteousness of Christ, because our Lord Jesus

Christ, being made under the law, was obedient to all its precepts, and suffered its dreadful penalty for us, and so himself brought in everlasting righteousness for us. It is called the righteousness of faith, because it is apprehended and appropriated by faith. It is not a righteousness secured by *working*, but by *believing*. "We are justified by faith." This righteousness is at least once called the righteousness of the law, because in its absolute perfection it is all that the moral law, spotless and eternal, demands for the justification of a sinner in the sight of God. It may well excite amazement that the doctrine of the imputation of Christ's righteousness should be so violently opposed as it sometimes is. Owen says: "In our day nothing in religion is more maligned, more reproached, more despised, than the imputation of righteousness unto us, or our imputed righteousness." Dr. Thomas Scott says, "the proud heart of man is prone to deny, or object to it, even with blasphemous enmity." And Dr. Archibald Alexander says: "No part of evangelical doctrine has met with a more determined opposition than the doctrine of imputation. It has been loaded with reproaches, as a doctrine the most unreasonable, the most dangerous, and the most impious. It is a remarkable circumstance, however, that all the objections, which have been made to it, are founded on a misapprehension or a misrepresentation of the true nature of imputation." It is said that a divine of our own country has been so far left to himself as to say publicly that "imputed righteousness is imputed nonsense." The motives of those, who revile this doctrine, will be judged by Him, who cannot err. No human tribunal is competent to pronounce upon them. But the pretended arguments brought against the doctrine of the imputation of Christ's merits to his people, as they have often been, so they should again and again be fully and fairly answered. He who defends, and he who assails, this doctrine are busied at a vital point of Christianity. Some have really held and taught the substance of this doctrine, and yet rejected the term, imputation. If any ask, why we should insist on the use of the term and not yield it to such persons and others, the answer is ready. *First*, we have the example of inspired men on our side. Psa. xxxii. 2, and 2 Cor. v. 9; Rom. iv. 6, 11, 23—25. If David and Paul use the word, why may not we also? If any man should propose to banish the word *redemption* from our theological vocabulary, what friend of truth would consent to it? *Imputed righteousness* is and ought to be just as dear to millions of God's people as *redemption*. *Secondly*, we could not get on well without this term. It conveys the very idea we wish to present in the pulpit and in our writings. If a man gives due notice that henceforth he will always call a hat a spade, it cannot fairly be said that he deceives any one by such a freak, but surely he will give trouble both to himself and his friends. Nor will he gain any good, unless he esteems the reputation of singularity such. And he may mislead some one. *Thirdly*, good theological terms are not easily obtained and agreed upon; and when they are settled they become out-posts to important truths, and should not be surrendered. The man, who asks that the people of the United States shall no more use the phrases, republican government, union, federative system, rights of the States, is either not honest, or he is very weak.

It is an old art of enemies to assault and of traitors to surrender the out-posts. *Fourthly*, this phrase has long been in use, is incorporated into many symbols of faith, into many manuals of Christian doctrine, and into nearly all bodies of divinity, and so ought not to be given up. Those who have objected to it have suggested no better, indeed none so good. The Swiss Reformers in the latter Confession of Helvetia say: "God imputeth the righteousness of Christ unto us for our own: so that now we are not only cleansed from our sin, and purged, and holy, but also endued with the righteousness of Christ. * * To speak properly, then; it is God alone that justifieth us, and that only for Christ, by not imputing unto us our sin, but imputing Christ's righteousness unto us." Rom. iv. 23—25. The Augsburg Confession says: "When therefore we do say, that 'we are justified by faith,' Rom. v. 1, this is our meaning: that we do obtain remission of sins, and imputation of righteousness, by mercy showed us for Christ's sake." The confession of France says: "Casting away all opinion of virtues and merits, we do altogether rest in the only obedience of Jesus Christ, which is imputed to us, both that all our sins may be covered, and that we may obtain grace before God." The Confession of Saxony says: "Christ himself is our righteousness, because that by his merit we have remission, and God doth impute his righteousness to us, and for him doth account us just." The Confession of Belgia says: "Christ himself is our righteousness, which imputeth all his merits unto us: faith is but the instrument, whereby we are coupled unto him." The Church of England says: "We are accounted righteous before God only for the merits of our Lord and Saviour Jesus Christ by faith; and not for our own works or deservings, wherefore, that we are justified by faith only, is a most wholesome doctrine and full of comfort." The Church of Ireland says: "We are accounted righteous before God, only for the merit of our Lord and Saviour Jesus Christ, applied by faith. And this righteousness, which we receive of God's mercy, and Christ's merits, embraced by faith, is taken, accepted, and allowed of God, for our perfect and full justification." The Confession of Wirtemburg says, that "man is made acceptable to God and accounted just before him for the only Son of God, our Lord Jesus Christ, through faith; and when we appear before the judgment-seat of God, we must not trust to the merit of any of those virtues, which we have, but only to the merit of our Lord Jesus Christ, whose merit is ours by faith." The Confession of Sueveland says: "This whole justification is to be ascribed to the good pleasure of God, and to the merit of Christ, and to be received by faith alone." John i. 12, 13, Eph. ii. 8—10. The Savoy, the Cambridge and the Boston Congregational Confessions, and the London and Philadelphia Baptist Confessions hold forth these very words: "Those, whom God effectually calleth, he also freely justifieth, not by infusing righteousness into them, but by pardoning their sins, and by accounting and accepting their persons as righteous; not for anything wrought in them, or done by them, but for Christ's sake alone; not by imputing faith itself, the act of believing, or any other evangelical obedience to them as their righteousness, but by imputing Christ's active obedience unto the whole law, and passive obedience in his* death, for their whole

* The Baptist has "sufferings and" before "death."

and sole righteousness; they receiving, and resting on him and his righteousness by faith." It is well known that all branches of the Presbyterian Church in North America and in Great Britain and her colonies, with the exception of a few Arians in Ireland and a few Unitarians in England, who for some reason wear the Presbyterian name, use almost verbatim the same formula on this subject.

The Heidelberg Catechism thus speaks:

"56. What believest thou concerning the forgiveness of sins?

"That God, for the sake of Christ's satisfaction, will no more remember my sins, neither my corrupt nature, against which I have to struggle all my life long, but will graciously impute to me the righteousness of Christ, that I may never be condemned before the tribunal of God.

"59. But what doth it profit thee that thou believest all this?

"That I am righteous in Christ, before God, and an heir of eternal life.

"60. How art thou righteous before God?

"Only by a true faith in Jesus Christ; so that, though my conscience accuse me that I have grossly transgressed all the commands of God, and kept none of them, and am still inclined to all evil; notwithstanding God, without any merit of mine, but only of mere grace, grants and imputes to me the perfect satisfaction, righteousness, and holiness of Christ; even so, as if I never had had, nor committed any sin; yea, as if I had fully accomplished all that obedience which Christ hath accomplished for me; inasmuch as I embrace such benefit with a believing heart.

"61. Why sayest thou that thou art righteous by faith only?

"Not that I am acceptable to God on account of the worthiness of my faith, but only because the satisfaction, righteousness, and holiness of Christ is my righteousness before God, and that I cannot receive and apply the same to myself any other way than by faith only."

The Welch Calvinistic Methodists' Confession says: "Justification is an act of the grace of God, judging and proclaiming man to be righteous, through imputing to him the righteousness of Christ, which is received by the sinner through faith." "Justification includes in itself a forgiveness to the transgressor of all his iniquities, so that he shall not die on their account; an exaltation of the person to the favour of God; and a bestowing on him a lawful right to enjoy never-ending happiness."

We are made the righteousness of God in Christ, in the same sense in which he was made sin for us. As his receiving the curse for us did not defile his soul, or make him personally ill-deserving, so our receiving the blessing does not make us pure or personally meritorious. We are made righteous in Christ in the same way, in which we are made sinners in Adam. In neither case is there an identity of person. In neither case do the personal acts or qualities of these our representatives become our acts or qualities. In both cases are we counted, reckoned, regarded, held and treated in law as if they were ours. As Christ did none of the acts which were imputed to him for expiation, so we have done none of the acts, which are imputed to us for justification.

Men sometimes say, How can we be justified by a righteousness not our own? It is freely admitted that our justifying righteousness is not inherently ours. Nor is it in any sense so ours that we can proudly boast of it, and so deny that in ourselves we are perishing sinners. Nor is our justifying righteousness ours by any hereditary right, nor until God imputes it to us, and we receive it by faith. But if the objectors mean that when we believe in the Lord Jesus Christ, and God imputes his righteousness to us, it does not become ours in the eye of the law, then they do contradict God's word and the sense of God's people in all ages. How is he "*Jehovah our righteousness*," (Jer. xxiii. 6,) if his merits in no sense become ours? If these objectors are right, what sense is there in such passages of Scripture as those already quoted from the fifth chapter of Romans? or what is the meaning of these words: "Christ is the end of the law for righteousness to every one that believeth?" Rom. x. 4; or of this, "Christ is of God made unto us righteousness?" 1 Cor. i. 30; or of this, "He hath made him to be sin for us, who knew no sin, that we might be made the righteousness of God in him?" 2 Cor. v. 21. See also Rom. iv. 5, 6, and Gal. iii. 6, 9, 22. Augustine says: "There is a righteousness of God, which is made ours, when it is given unto us. It is called the righteousness of God, lest man should think that he had a righteousness of himself." Cowper says: "The righteousness of Christ is ours, and ours by as great a right, as any other thing which we possess; to wit, by the free gift of God; for it hath pleased him to give a garment to us, who are naked, and to give us, who had none of our own, a righteousness answerable to justice." Dr. A. Alexander says: "Whatever Christ has done or suffered for our salvation, in order that it may be available to us, must in some way become *ours.*" Again: "When God imputes the righteousness of Christ to a sinner, he actually bestows it upon him for all the purposes of his complete justification." The doctrine commonly held by the Church of God is, that what Christ has done and suffered for his people becomes actually and legally theirs, in the sight of God, in virtue of their union with him. So that we do not, we dare not teach that a man is justified by a righteousness in no sense his own. The great difference between saints and sinners in the matter of justification is, that the former are partakers of the righteousness of Christ, and the latter are not. No man has a title to anything better than this, that God gave it to him. This is our title to life, to reason, to our souls, to immortality. This is the believer's claim to the infinite merits of Christ.

Ridgley says that, "there are some who oppose this doctrine, by calling it a putative righteousness, the shadow or appearance of that, which has in it no reality, or our being accounted what we are not, whereby a wrong judgment is passed on persons and things. However, we are not to deny it because it is thus misrepresented, and thereby unfairly opposed. It is certain there are such words used in Scripture, and often applied to this doctrine, which without any ambiguity or strain on the sense thereof, may be translated, to reckon, to account, or to place a thing done by another to our account; or, as we express it, to impute." * * "This is the most perverse sense which can be put on words, or is a setting this doctrine in such a light as no one takes it in, who pleads for it." The truth is that the judgment of God is always according to truth; and the doctrine maintained is not that God regards us as having done acts, which were performed by Christ, nor that Jehovah has any false estimate of us whatever, nor that God *reputes* us as being in ourselves worthy, when the fact is that we are in ourselves wholly unworthy, nor that anything respecting our case has been ignored by the Almighty. But it is simply that God looks upon believers in Christ as one with the Saviour, that Christ's righteousness is counted, reckoned to them for righteousness, or that as their surety he meets all the demands of the law on them as transgressors, and makes over to them his perfect obedience as ground of their acceptance with God.

It is sometimes said that the doctrine of imputed righteousness sets aside the fulfilment of the law. But this is surely a mistake. Paul says, that God sent his Son to the very end "that the righteousness of the law might be fulfilled in us." And Dr. Gill well says that "though righteousness does not come by our obedience to the law, yet it does by Christ's obedience to it. Though by the deeds of the law as performed by man, no flesh shall be justified, yet by the deeds of the law as performed by Christ, all the elect are justified." So that now "if we confess our sins, God is faithful and JUST to forgive us our sins, and to cleanse us from all unrighteousness." 1 John i. 9. On any other scheme than that, which is here contended for, what sense is there in the word, *just*, in the text last quoted? If the import of the objection is that the doctrine is unfriendly to the promotion of holiness among men, the answers are ready. In Romans vi. 1, 2, Paul meets this objection thus: "What shall we say then? Shall we continue in sin that grace may abound? God forbid; how shall we, that are dead to sin, live any longer therein?" In that and the next chapter he says much more to the same effect. Besides, the whole gospel plan goes on the supposition that the strongest motive, which can incline man's heart to holiness, is love. Now "love is the fulfilling of the law." "We love him because he first loved us." "The love of Christ constraineth us, because we thus judge that if one died for all, then were all dead, and that he died for all, that they which live should not henceforth live unto themselves, but unto him that died for them." And the facts are all on one side. It would be impossible to find in any age an eminently holy man, who did not openly declare that his hope was in God's mercy, not in his own doings, in the righteousness of Christ, not in his own deservings. There was as much agreement among the Reformed churches, for more than two hundred years from the days of Luther and Calvin, in receiving this doctrine, as that of the divinity of Christ, or the personality of the Holy Ghost.

Some say, if we are justified on the ground of the merits of Christ, where are the grace and mercy of the gospel? The answer is that God's rich grace and abundant mercy shine forth in the whole work of salvation from first to last. The whole devising, execution, application and crowning of redemption flow from God's boundless grace, and infinite, eternal, and unchangeable love. Grace is not connivance at sin. Mercy is not contempt of law. The grace of Christ vindicates the justice and government of God, while it brings salvation to the guilty. Hear the language of the Baptist and Congregational Confessions, which have been already quoted in this chapter: "Christ by his obedience and death did fully discharge the debt of all those that are justified, and did by the sacrifice of himself, in the blood of his cross, undergoing in their stead the penalty due unto them, make a proper, real and full satisfaction to God's justice in their behalf; yet inasmuch as he was given by the Father for them, and his obedience and satisfaction accepted in their stead, and both freely, not for anything in them, their justification is only of free grace, that both the exact justice and rich grace of God might be glorified in the justification of sinners." The Presbyterian Confession has nearly the same words. To the question, "if our justification be thus purchased by the perfect obedience and satisfaction of Christ, how is it of free grace?" the Rev. Thomas Boston replies, "Very well; for 1. God accepted of a surety, when he might have held by the sinner himself, and insisted that the soul that sinned might die. Rom. v. 8. * * God did this freely. 2. God himself provided the Surety. John iii. 16. * * The Father gives the Son, and the Son assumes man's nature and pays the debt. What is there here but riches of grace to the justified sinner? 3. God demands nothing of us [in payment] for it. It is a rich purchase, a dear purchase, the price of blood; but the righteousness and justification are given to us most freely through faith. That is, we have it, for '*take-and-have.*' And the very hand, wherewith we receive it, namely faith, is the free gift of God unto us. Eph. ii. 8. So that most evident it is that we are justified freely by his grace." Calvin says: "It betrays ignorance to oppose the merit of

Christ to the mercy of God. For it is a common maxim, that between two things, of which one succeeds or is subordinate to the other, there can be no opposition. There is no reason therefore why the justification of men should not be gratuitous from the mere mercy of God, and why at the same time the merit of Christ should not intervene, which is subservient to the mercy of God." Thus the doctrine has been explained, it has been proven from Scripture, it has been shown to be interwoven with our best formulas of doctrine, and objections to it have been answered. In the next chapter some additional testimonies in its favour will be given.

CHAPTER XXVII.

JUSTIFICATION. — IMPUTED RIGHTEOUSNESS. — ADDITIONAL TESTIMONIES.

THERE is hardly anything more gratifying to the pious mind than to discover an agreement between its own conclusions and those of great and good men, who have lived in former generations. They may indeed have been mistaken, and so they are no *standard* to us; yet when their number is large, when they lived in different ages and countries, and yet were led by honest inquiry and much prayer to the same results, and when their well-earned reputation for piety, love of truth and diligence in study, create a strong presumption in favour of their united testimony, a good man will very carefully examine the grounds of his conclusions before he will refuse to adopt their sentiments, especially where they have all put much honour on God's holy word. In other chapters of this work many such witnesses have been adduced. But this chapter will consist *chiefly* of the views of others on the subject in hand. The language of God's people often varies considerably, but the sense of the following quotations is clearly confirmatory of our doctrine. Having already noticed the views of the writers of the first five centuries, the first now given is that of Gregory. He says: "Our righteous Advocate shall defend us in the day of judgment, because we know and accuse ourselves to be unrighteous. Therefore let us not trust to our tears, nor to our actions, but to the alleging of our Advocate."

Calvin remarking on Rom. v. 19, says: "The meaning is, that as by the sin of Adam we were alienated from God, and devoted to destruction, so by the obedience of Christ we are received into favour, as righteous persons. Nor does the future tense of the verb exclude present righteousness; as appears from the context. For he had before said, "The free gift is of many offences unto justification." Again, "if righteousness consist in an observance of the law, who can deny that Christ merited favour for us, when by bearing this burden himself he reconciles us to God, just as though we were complete observers of the law ourselves."

Bishop Latimer says: "When we believe in Christ, it is like as if we had no sins. For he changeth with us. He taketh our sins and wickedness from us, and giveth unto us his holiness, righteousness, justice, fulfilling of the law, and so consequently everlasting life. So that we be like as if we had done no sin at all; for his righteousness standeth us in good stead, as though we of our own selves had fulfilled the law."

Bishop Hooper says: "We must only trust to the merits of Christ, which satisfied the extreme jot and uttermost point of the law for us. And this his justice and perfection he imputeth and communicateth with us by faith."

Richard Hooker says: "Although in ourselves we be altogether sinful and unrighteous, yet even the man which is impious in himself, full of iniquity, full of sin, him being found in Christ through faith, and

20

having his sin remitted through repentance, him God beholdeth with a gracious eye, putteth away his sin by not imputing it, taketh quite away the punishment due thereunto by pardoning it, and accepteth him in Jesus Christ as perfectly righteous, as if he had fulfilled all that was commanded him in the law; shall I say more perfectly righteous than if himself had fulfilled the whole law? I must take heed what I say: but the apostle saith, 'God made him to be sin for us, who knew no sin, that we might be made the righteousness of God in him.' Such we are in the sight of God the Father, as is the very Son of God himself. Let it be counted folly or frenzy, or fury, whatsoever, it is our comfort and our wisdom; we care for no knowledge in the world but this, that man hath sinned and God hath suffered; that God hath made himself the Son of man, and that men are made the righteousness of God."

Grotius says: "Whereas we have said that Christ hath brought forth or procured two things for us, freedom from punishment and a reward, the ancient church attributes the one of them unto his satisfaction, the other unto his merit. Satisfaction consists in the translation of sins, merit in the imputation of his most perfect obedience performed for us."

Bates says: "There are but two ways of appearing before the righteous and supreme Judge: 1. In innocence and sinless obedience: or, 2. by the righteousness of Christ. The one is by the law, the other by grace. And these two can never be compounded; for he that pleads innocence, in that disclaims favour; and he that sues for favour acknowledges guilt. Now the first cannot be performed by us. For entire obedience to the law supposes the integrity of our natures, there being a moral impossibility that the faculties once corrupted should act regularly; but man is stained with original sin from his conception. And the form of the law runs universally, 'cursed is every one that continueth not in all things, written in the book of the law to do them.' In these scales one evil work preponderates a thousand good. If a man were guilty of but one single error, his entire obedience afterwards could not save him; for that being always due to the law, the payment of it cannot discount for the former debt. So that we cannot in any degree be justified by the law; for there is no middle between transgressing and not transgressing it. He that breaks one article in a covenant cuts off his claim to any benefit from it. * * Whoever presumes to appear before God's judgment-seat in his own righteousness shall be covered with confusion.

"2. By the righteousness of Christ. This alone absolves from the guilt of sin, saves from hell and can endure the trial of God's tribunal. This the apostle prized as his invaluable treasure, in comparison of which all other things are but dross and dung. * * That which is ordained, and rewarded in the person of our Redeemer, God cannot but accept. Now this righteousness is meritoriously imputed only to believers. * * As all sins are mortal in respect of their guilt, but death is not actually inflicted for them, upon the account of the grace of the new covenant; so all sins are venial in respect of the satisfaction made by Christ; but they are not actually pardoned, till the performing of the condition, to which pardon is annexed. Faith transfers the guilt from the sinner to the sacrifice."

Leighton says: "This is the great glad tidings, that we are made righteous by Christ; it is not a righteousness wrought by us, but given to us, and put upon us. This carnal reason cannot comprehend, and being proud, therefore rejects and argues against it, saying, *How can this thing be?* But faith closes with it, and rejoices in it. Without either doing or suffering, the sinner is acquitted, and justified, and stands as guiltless of breach, yea, as having fulfilled the whole law. And happy they that thus fasten upon this righteousness, that they may lift up their faces with gladness and boldness before God; whereas the most industrious, self-saving justiciary, though in other men's eyes and his own, possibly for the present, he makes a glittering show, yet when he shall come to be examined of God, and tried according to the law, shall be covered with shame, and confounded in his folly and guiltiness."

Owen says: "There is an imputation of mere grace and favour. And this is, when that which antecedently unto the imputation was no way ours, not inherent in us, not performed by us, which we had no right nor title unto, is granted unto us, made ours, so as that we are judged of, and dealt with according unto it. This is that imputation in both branches of it, negative in the non-imputation of sin, and positive in the imputation of righteousness, which the apostle so vehemently pleads for, and so frequently asserteth. Rom. iv. For he both affirms the thing itself, and declares that it is of mere grace, without respect unto anything within ourselves. And if this kind of imputation cannot be fully exemplified in any other instance, but this alone, whereof we treat, it is because the foundation of it in the mediation of Christ is singular, and that which there is nothing to parallel in any other case." "The imputation we plead for is not a judging or esteeming of them to be righteous, who truly and really are not so." In imputation God "makes an effectual grant and donation of a true, real, perfect righteousness, even that of Christ himself unto all that do believe, and accounting it as theirs, on his own gracious act, both absolves them from sin, and granteth them right and title unto eternal life. In this imputation, the thing itself is first imputed unto us, and not any of the effects of it, but they are made ours by virtue of that imputation." "To say the righteousness of Christ is not imputed unto us, only its effects are so, is really to overthrow all imputation."

Charnock says: "All the world stands guilty before God; cannot present God with a righteousness of their own commensurate to the law; not one act any man can do can bear proportion to it; all strength to do anything suitable to it was lost in Adam. Since no righteousness of our own can justify, it must be the righteousness of the Son of God, which must be imputed to us in the same manner our sins were imputed to him; as it is accepted by God for us, so it is accounted by God to us. 2 Cor. v. 21. Sin was in us, but charged upon Christ; righteousness is in Christ, and imputed to us."

Tuckney says: "We are *made the righteousness of God* in Christ in the same way that he *was made sin* for us, that is, by imputation."

Ryland says: "Justification by Christ's imputed righteousness is the centre arch of that bridge, by which we pass out of time into a blissful eternity."

John Willison when near death ejaculated: "I am living on the righteousness of Christ, yea dying in the Lord. * * It is not past experiences or manifestations I depend upon; it is Christ, a present, all-sufficient Saviour, and perfect righteousness in him, I look to. All my attainments are but loss and dung besides him."

Bunyan said: "There is no other way for sinners to be justified from the curse of the law, in the sight of God, than by the imputation of that righteousness long ago performed by, and still residing with the person of Jesus Christ."

The author of the sermon on justification in the "Morning Exercises" published in 1675 says: "To be justified is to be freely accepted of God as righteous, so as to have pardon and title to life, upon the account of Christ's righteousness. We cannot be accepted as righteous till we be acquitted from guilt." "There are these severals considerable about the imputing this righteousness; first, substitution; Christ satisfied in our stead, i. e. he tendered that which was due from us. Secondly, acceptance; the Father accepted what Christ performed in our stead, as performed on our behalf. Thirdly, participation; we have the fruits and advantages of his undertaking, no less than if we ourselves had satisfied."

Stedman says: "The first blessing that I shall mention as depending upon union with Jesus Christ is *the justification of a sinner in the sight of God*, upon the account of Christ's righteousness imputed to him; whereby the guilt of sin is removed, and the person of the sinner accepted as righteous with the God of heaven." "*The only matter of man's righteousness* since the fall of *Adam*, wherein he can appear with comfort before the justice of God, and *consequently* whereby alone he can be justified in his sight, *is the obedience and sufferings of Jesus Christ*, the righteousness of the Mediator."

Wilcox says: "If thou ever sawest Christ, thou sawest him a rock higher than self-righteousness, Satan and sin, and this rock doth follow thee; and there will be a continual dropping of honey and grace, out of this rock, to satisfy thee."

Crisp says: "These are the sure mercies of David, when a man receives the things of Christ, only because Christ gives them; and not in regard of any action of ours, as the ground of taking them. Christ is not more rich in himself than he is liberal to contribute of his treasures. He makes his people sharers to the uttermost of all that he has."

Bengel says: "The law presseth on a man, till he flees to Christ; then it says, Thou hast gotten a refuge. I forbear to follow thee. Thou art wise. Thou art safe."

Glascock says: "The grand design of all false religion is to patch up a righteousness for the justification of the sinner before God. The Christian religion teaches us to seek justification before God by the imputation of Christ's righteousness to us upon our believing on him. The denial of a believer's justification, by the imputation of Christ's righteousness to him, stabs the very heart of Christianity, and destroys all true revealed religion."

Philip Henry cried: "Lord, clothe me with thy righteousness, which is a comely, costly, lasting, everlasting garment."

Richard Taylor says: "Christ will only be a *strength* to them that trust in him for *righteousness;* they, that will not have him for righteousness, shall not have him for their strength, to enable them to resist temptations, to mortify sin and corruption, and to bring forth the fruits of holiness."

During the last century there arose a philanthropic Englishman, whose deeds of mercy have resounded throughout the civilized world. "He visited," says Burke, "all Europe—not to survey the sumptuousness of palaces, or the stateliness of temples, not to make accurate measurements of the remains of ancient grandeur, nor to form a scale of the curiosity of modern art; not to collect medals, or collate manuscripts: —but to dive into the depths of dungeons; to plunge into the infection of hospitals; to survey the mansions of sorrow and pain; to take the gauge and dimensions of misery, depression, and contempt; to remember the forgotten, to attend to the neglected, to visit the forsaken, and to compare and collate the distresses of all men in all countries. His plan is original; and it is as full of genius as it is of humanity. It was a voyage of discovery; a circumnavigation of charity. Already the benefit of his labour is felt in every country: I hope he will anticipate his final reward, by seeing all its effects fully realized in his own." Now would it not be instructive, if we could penetrate the hidden recesses of Howard's thoughts, and find out what gave him this heavenly zeal? He himself has told us in one of the most solemn acts of his life. The inscription, which he directed to be put on his tomb, besides his name and some dates, was this: "Christ is my hope."

Hervey says: "Had I all the faith of the patriarchs, all the zeal of the prophets, all the good works of the apostles, all the holy sufferings of the martyrs, and all the glowing devotion of the seraphs; I would disclaim the whole, in point of dependence, and count all but dross and dung, when set in competition with the infinitely precious death, and infinitely meritorious righteousness of the Lord Jesus Christ."

Dr. Thomas Scott, remarking on Rom. x. 4, says: "This 'righteousness of God is without the law,' being entirely independent of our personal obedience, either before or after justification; it becomes ours 'by faith in Christ Jesus;' and in the next chapter we read of 'righteousness *imputed* without works.' Is it not then plain that 'the righteousness of God is *unto all* that believe,' by *imputation?* Thus likewise it is '*upon all* that believe:' for they 'have put on Christ;' God now looking on them, there appears nothing but Christ; they are as it were covered all over with him, as a man with the clothes he has put on. Hence in the next verse it is said, they 'are all one in Christ Jesus,' as if there were but one person. These are the words in which Mr. *Locke* delivers his exposition of this text."

The Rev. Alexander Hill says: "Considered in themselves believers are guilty and deserve to suffer, but by means of the imputation of Christ's righteousness, they are completely acquitted from the punishment due to their sins, because it was endured for them by the Lord Jesus, and they acquire a right to eternal life, because it was purchased for them by his obedience." He also says that this is the catholic opinion.

Dr. Chalmers says: "I trust I shall never lose my hold of the fulness and peace, which lie in the doctrine of Christ's imputed righteousness." Later in life he says: "O my God, enable me to lay hold of the righteousness of Christ as my righteousness. . . . Never am I in a better frame than when dwelling in simple faith on Christ's offered righteousness, and making it the object of my acceptation. O Lord, I pray for more and more of the clearness and enlargement of this view, and grant me the Spirit of adoption."

Indeed so uniform has been the love of Christians of all ages and nations to the doctrine of salvation by the imputed righteousness of Christ, that it is hardly less for a wonder than for a lamentation that any in our day should express doubts on the subject. Christ's righteousness meets the greatest want of an enlightened conscience. It is the strength of all holy joy on earth. It is the life of a believer's soul. In the last day the shouts of grace, grace unto it, shall be heard from all the redeemed as the topstone shall be laid on the living temple, the Church. To Christ, who has paid the ransom for us, God's faithfulness and justice bind him to give all whom in covenant he had promised, yea, finally to give him the heathen for his inheritance and the uttermost parts of the earth for a possession. But to sinners saved, all is grace, unmerited favour, because it comes to them through the imputed righteousness of our Lord Jesus Christ. And all this is but the fulfilment of the prophecy of Isaiah (chap. xlv. 24, 25): "Surely shall one say, In the Lord have I RIGHTEOUSNESS and strength;" and "In the Lord shall all the seed of Israel be JUSTIFIED and shall glory." Even "he that hath clean hands, and a pure heart, who hath not lifted up his soul unto vanity, nor sworn deceitfully" shall not be saved by his own merits, but "he shall receive the blessing from the Lord, and RIGHTEOUSNESS *from the God of his salvation.*" Psa. xxiv. 4, 5. Indeed the capital error of multitudes in every age has been that "they, being ignorant of God's righteousness, and going about to establish their own righteousness, have not submitted themselves unto the righteousness of God." Rom. x. 3. Here, just here myriads have lost their all. Reader, let it not be so with you.

It has been already stated that some persons, who have objected to the phrase, *imputed righteousness*, have yet held the substance of what was taught by that doctrine. Owen expresses the judgment that it is "impossible that any man should be justified before God any other way, but by the imputation of the righteousness of Christ," and says this was a common sentiment among the orthodox. Yet he as readily says that "they do not think or judge that all those are excluded from salvation, who cannot apprehend, or do deny the doctrine of the imputation of the righteousness of Christ, as by them declared." "To believe the doctrine of it, or not to believe it, as thus or thus explained, is one thing; and to enjoy the thing, or not to enjoy it, is another. I no way doubt, but that many men do receive more grace from God than they understand, or will own." "Men may be really saved by that grace which doctrinally they do deny; and they may be justified by the imputation of that righteousness which in opinion they deny to be imputed." Such views relieve the mind not only of uncharitableness, but also of anguish respecting some, who have difficulties on the subject. It is well known that the venerable Dr. Dwight at one time wrote against the doctrine of imputation of righteousness; but it is delightful to find that when he had recovered from a long and dangerous illness, he poured out his thoughts before his pupils in these words: "Those acts of my life concerning which I entertained the best hopes which I was permitted to entertain, those, which appeared to me the least exceptionable, were nothing, and less than nothing. The mercy of God as exercised through the all-sufficient and glorious righteousness of the Redeemer, yielded me the only foundation of hope for good beyond the grave. During the long continuation of my disease, as I was always, except when in paroxysms of suffering, in circumstances entirely fitted for solemn contemplation, I had ample opportunity to survey this most interesting of all subjects on every side. As the result of all my investigations, let me assure you, and that from the neighbourhood of the eternal world, *confidence in the righteousness of Christ* is the only foundation furnished by earth, or heaven, upon which, when you are about to leave this world, you can safely rest the everlasting life of your souls. To trust upon anything else will be to *feed upon the wind and sup up the east wind.* You will then be at the door of eternity; will be hastening to the presence of your Judge; will be just ready to give up your account of the *deeds done in the body;* will be preparing to hear the final sentence of acquittal or condemnation; and will stand at the gate of heaven or of hell. In these amazing circumstances you will infinitely need, let me persuade you to believe and to feel that you will infinitely need, a firm foundation on which you may stand, and from which you will never be removed. There is no other such foundation but the *Rock of Ages*. Then you will believe, then you will feel that there is no other." How precious is such truth! There is ground of hope for a sinner in the righteousness of Christ. How solemn the testimony here borne to its vital importance! And neither the wit of man, nor the wisdom of God has pointed out any method by which that righteousness may become ours "to all the ends of a complete justification," unless God in mercy will impute it to us.

Such language from President Dwight reminds one of that of President Davies describing his thoughts during an illness. He says: "In my sickness, I found the unspeakable importance of a Mediator, in a religion of sinners. O! I could have given you the word of a dying man for it, that Jesus, *that* Jesus whom you preach, is indeed a necessary and an all-sufficient Saviour. Indeed he is the only support for a departing soul. *None but Christ, none but Christ.* Had I as many good works as Abraham or Paul, I would not have dared build my hopes on such a quicksand, but only on this firm eternal Rock." Indeed to dying believers Christ's righteousness is very, very precious. The Rev. W. H. Hewitson dying said: "The righteousness of Christ is my stay. That sustained me in Madeira in the midst of persecution and difficulties; it has sustained me through all my ministry; and it sustains me now." Indeed Christ is all and in all to his departing followers. It is not long since a pious native Christian in India was asked, on her dying bed, what was the state of her mind. She replied, "Happy, happy!" Then laying her hand on the Bengalee Bible she said, "I have Christ *here*;" then pressing it to her heart she said, "And Christ *here;*" then pointing toward heaven she added, "And Christ *there.*" Thrice blessed soul. In whatever part of the universe she might be, Christ was with her. He was formed in her the hope of glory. "There is none like Jesus."

What say you to these things? Is Christ all your hope? Are you building on this sure, this only foundation? In coming before God dare you make mention of any but his righteousness, even of his only? Let every man take heed that he be not found naked, or clothed in rags and shame. Hold fast the merits of the Redeemer and you are safe. Let them go and you are undone. His blood alone atones. His righteousness alone justifies.

CHAPTER XXVIII.

THE OFFICE OF FAITH IN JUSTIFICATION.

THE Scriptures abound with assertions that our justification is by faith. Thus Habakkuk says: "The just shall live by faith." Chap. ii. 4. Some would read the passage thus, "The just by faith shall live." There is no solid ground of objection to this rendering, for it really asserts but the same thing now taught by it. We are at no loss for the sense of this passage; for we have an inspired interpretation of it given by Paul. Indeed it seems to have been a very favourite text with him. He quotes it in Rom. i. 17, Gal. iii. 11, Heb. x. 38. But we may go further back than the days of Habakkuk, even to the time of Abraham. Of him we read: "And he believed in the Lord and he counted it to him for righteousness." Gen. xv. 6. This passage is no less celebrated than that already quoted. It is also divinely interpreted by the inspiration of God in Rom. iv. 1—6, Gal. iii. 6—14. Upon the first part of Romans iv. Beza well says: "From this single example of Abraham, as deservedly selected from among all the fathers, the apostle intended to draw a conclusion, which would necessarily take in all believers. And that he might do this fairly, he intimates at the very entrance of the question, that he did not propose Abraham as one of the number of believers, but as the father of the Church; that he might properly reason from the father to his children, the foundation of which he lays in the thirteenth verse. * * In whatever way Abraham, the father of believers was justified, in the same must all his children (that is all believers) be justified; but Abraham was not justified, and made the father of the faithful, by any of his own works, either preceding or following his faith in Christ, as promised to him; but merely by faith in Christ, or the merit of Christ by faith imputed to him for righteousness. Therefore all his children become his children and are justified, not by their works, either preceding or following their faith; but by faith alone in the same Christ, who was at length to come; * * and thus they are at present justified, and shall be to the end of the world." And so "they which be of faith shall be blessed with faithful Abraham." Gal. iii. 9. Indeed the Scriptures are very explicit on this point: "A man is not justified by the works of the law, but by the faith of Jesus Christ." Gal. ii. 16. "Being justified by faith, we have peace with God through our Lord Jesus Christ." Rom. v. 1. "The law was our schoolmaster to bring us to Christ, that we might be justified by faith." Gal. iii. 24. "Thou standest by faith." Rom. xi. 20. "God shall justify the circumcision by faith, and the uncircumcision through faith." Rom. iii. 30. Many other texts are no less clear.

But what is the meaning of the expression "we are justified by faith?" How are we justified by faith? Why are we never said to be justified by other Christian graces? Humility is an excellent grace, much commended in Scripture, and putting us where we ought to be, in the dust. Meekness bears with pity and forgiveness outrageous wrongs heaped upon us, and so makes us like Christ, who was brought as a lamb to the slaughter, and as a sheep before her shearers is dumb, so he opened not his mouth. Hope is an anchor to the soul, both sure and steadfast, and being lively, animates the soul in all times of trial. Charity with her broad mantle covers the faults of others, fills the world with the fame of her deeds, and never faileth. Penitence sits at the feet of Jesus and bathes them with its tears. The fear of the Lord is a fountain of life to depart from the snares of death. Excellent as all these graces are, yet it is nowhere said in Scripture that a man is justified by fear, by charity, by penitence, by hope, by meekness, or by humility. But he is often said to be justified by faith. God does not put this honour upon faith because it is greater than other graces, for it is not. 1 Cor. xiii. 13. Love is greater. So are all graces, which shall flourish for ever. But the reason why faith justifies is because it receives Christ. In the language of the Bible, to receive Christ is to believe on him. "To as many as received him to them gave he power to become the sons of God, even to as many as believed on his name." John i. 12. The hand of the beggar receives the loaf, which charity offers him, and so he is fed by his hand and not by another member of his body. To believe in Christ is in Scripture said to be "looking to him." Isa. xlv. 22, Heb. xii. 2. Now although he, who looks, may have all his other senses, and in other respects they may be of eminent use to him, yet he sees only with his eyes. Faith is the vision of the new-born soul. It looks back thousands of years. "Through faith we understand that the worlds were made." Heb.

xi. 3. It looks forward also thousands of years "Abraham rejoiced to see my day and he saw it and was glad." John viii. 56. And as the dying Israelite looked to the brazen serpent and was healed, so do perishing sinners look by faith to Jesus and are saved. They look and live. Faith is a reliance upon testimony, and saving faith has special regard to the testimony of God concerning his Son. Even to men we extend our belief of their word in certain circumstances. But "if we receive the witness of men, the witness of God is greater: for this is the witness of God, which he hath testified of his Son. He that believeth on the Son of God hath the witness in himself; he that believeth not God hath made him a liar, because he believeth not the record that God gave of his Son. And this is the record, that God hath given to us eternal life; and this life is in his Son. He that hath the Son hath life; and he that hath not the Son of God hath not life." 1 John v. 9—12. So that he, who believes he has need of a Saviour and credits this testimony of God, does rest the whole weight of his salvation here and not elsewhere. He takes Christ as his sole, sufficient Redeemer. Faith justifies us only as it receives Jesus Christ as "the Lord our Righteousness." It takes the robe he has wrought and puts it on, and so hides the nakedness of the soul. The Westminster Confession says: "Justifying faith is a saving grace, wrought in the heart of a sinner, by the Spirit and word of God; whereby he, being convinced of his sin and misery, and of the disability of himself and all other creatures to recover him out of his lost condition, not only assenteth to the truth of the promise of the gospel, but receiveth and resteth upon

Christ and his righteousness therein held forth, for the pardon of sin, and for the accepting and accounting of his person righteous in the sight of God for salvation."

Bishop Hall says: "The spiritual hand whereby we receive the sweet offer of our Saviour is faith; which in short is no other than an affiance in the Mediator. Receive peace, and be happy; believe, and thou hast received."

Usher says: "Justifying faith consists in these two things, in having a mind to know Christ, and a will to rest upon him. Whosoever sees so much excellency in Christ, that thereby he is drawn to embrace him as the only Rock of salvation, that man truly believes to justification."

Others very well represent the office of faith when they say that by means of it a union is formed between Christ and believers. Thus Luther says: "Faith unites the soul with Christ as a spouse with her husband. Everything which Christ has, becomes the property of the believing soul; everything which the soul has, becomes the property of Christ. Christ possesses all blessings and eternal life—they are thenceforth the property of the soul. The soul has all its iniquities and sins: they become thenceforward the property of Christ. It is then that a blessed change commences: Christ, who is both God and man, Christ who has never sinned, and whose holiness is perfect, Christ the Almighty, and Eternal, taking to himself, by his nuptial ring of *faith*, all the sins of the believer, those sins are lost and abolished in him; for no sins dwell before his infinite righteousness. Thus, by faith, the believer's soul is delivered from sins, and clothed with the eternal righteousness of her bridegroom, Christ. O happy union! the rich, the noble, the holy Bridegroom takes in marriage his poor, guilty and despised spouse, delivers her from every evil, and enriches her with the most precious blessings. Christ, a King and a Priest, shares this honour and glory with all Christians. The Christian is a king, and consequently possesses all things; he is a priest, and consequently possesses God, and it is faith, not works, which brings him all this honour. A Christian is free from all things, above all things, faith giving him richly all things." Should any be startled at such expressions as "he possesses God," let them consider the import of these words: "Thou art my portion, O Lord." Psa. cxix. 57; "God is our refuge and strength." Psa. xlvi. 1; "I am the Lord thy God," and many such expressions of Scripture. On the other hand how many scores of times does God call the saints, "*my* people," "the lot of mine inheritance," "my redeemed," "my love," &c. "All grace flows from Christ united to the soul, as all life flows from the soul united to the body." This union between Christ and believers shall never be broken. It is in perpetuity as to all its blessed consequences.

From all that has been said, it is very evident that there is no *merit* in our believing, though by believing we become interested in the merits of Christ. If faith itself, the act of believing, were the ground of our acceptance, it would certainly be works, even the work of faith. And as no man's faith is absolutely perfect, we should then have justification by a work full of imperfection. Faith is indeed the instrument, but not the ground; the means, but not the cause of our justification. If faith itself were the *ground* of our acceptance, it would be our saviour, and it would be entitled to all the glory of our salvation. And as faith is an act of the soul, each man would then be entitled to the full honour of his own salvation; and instead of boasting being excluded, as Paul says (Rom. iii. 27,) all heaven would be filled with it, and each man would have a right to say that he came thither by his own act, merit and virtue. And where then would be the glory of Christ? His reward would consist in nothing. Those, who should be saved, would owe him nothing. They would have saved themselves. To be justified by faith itself as the ground of acceptance would surely be to be "justified by works of righteousness, which we had done," and Paul says this is impossible.

The faith, by which a soul is united to Christ, is itself the gift of God, and a gift, which never could have been bestowed but for the finished work of Christ. That it is a gift from God is declared in Matt. xvi. 16, 17, in John i. 13, in Rom. xii. 3, in Eph. ii. 8, in Phil. i. 29, and in many other places. The Saviour is expressly called "the author and finisher of our faith." Heb. xii. 1. Again it is expressly ascribed to God's Spirit: "The fruit of the Spirit is faith." Gal. v. 22. How then could itself be any just ground of acquitting the guilty, and of taking the undeserving into the favour of God? Faith makes no satisfaction for sin. Faith even when genuine is not in any case perfect and blameless. Should we have no better righteousness than this in which to appear before God, his holy eye would behold rents in every part of it. So that the Scriptures ascribe even our believing to the amazing kindness of God. In Acts xviii. 27, men are in so many words said to have "believed through grace."

These general views of the subject are common to all evangelical Christians. The Augsburg Confession says: "Christ is given for a Mediator to us, and this honour is not to be transferred unto our works. When therefore we do say that 'we are justified by faith,' we do not mean that we are just for the worthiness of that virtue; but this is our meaning: that we do obtain remission of sins and imputation of righteousness by mercy shown us for Christ's sake. But now this mercy cannot be received but by faith. * * When Paul saith, 'Faith is reckoned for righteousness,' he speaketh of a trust and confidence of mercy, promised for Christ's sake; and his meaning is, that men are pronounced righteous, that is, reconciled, through mercy promised for Christ's sake, whom we must receive by faith. Now the novelty of this figurative speech of Paul, 'We are justified by faith,' will not offend holy minds, if they understand that it is spoken properly of mercy, and that herein mercy is adorned with true and due praises. For what can be more acceptable to an afflicted and fearful conscience in great griefs, than to hear that this is the commandment of God, and the voice of the Bridegroom, Christ Jesus, that they should undoubtedly believe, that remission of sins, or reconciliation, is given unto them, not for their own worthiness, but freely, through mercy, for Christ's sake, that the benefit might be certain."

The Latter Confession of Helvetia says: "Because faith doth apprehend Christ our righteousness, and doth attribute all to the praise of God in Christ, in this respect justification is attributed to faith chiefly because of Christ, whom it receiveth, and not because it is a work of ours. For it is the gift of God. Now, that we do receive Christ by faith, the Lord showeth at large, in the sixth chapter of John, where he putteth eating for believing, and believing for eating. For as by eating we receive meat, so by believing we are made partakers of Christ."

The Confession of Bohemia speaking "of true justification of faith" says: "This faith properly is an assent of a willing heart to the whole truth delivered in the gospel, whereby man is enlightened in his mind and soul, that he may rightly acknowledge and receive for his only Saviour, his God, and Lord Jesus Christ, and upon him, as on a true rock, he may build his whole salvation, love, follow and enjoy him, and repose all his hope and confidence in him." "But the lively and never dying spring of justification is in our Lord Jesus Christ alone, by those his saving works, that is, which give salvation."

The Confession of Belgia says: "True faith doth embrace Jesus Christ, with all his merits, doth challenge him unto itself, as proper and peculiar, and doth seek for nothing besides him." "He, who by faith possesseth Jesus Christ, hath also perfect salvation." "Yet to speak properly, we do not mean that faith by itself, or of itself, doth justify us, which is but only as an instrument, whereby we apprehend Christ, who is our righteousness. Christ therefore himself is our righteousness, which imputeth all his merits unto us." The London and Philadelphia Baptist Confessions, the Confessions of the Savoy, Cambridge and Boston, and the Confessions of Presbyterian Churches generally in Great Britain and America agree in saying, "Faith receiving and resting on Christ and his righteousness, is the alone instrument of justification; yet is not alone in the person justified, but is ever accompanied with all other saving graces, and is no dead faith but worketh by love." Some of the old writers quaintly say, "We are justified by faith *sole*, but not *solitary*."

Leighton says: "True it is, that this faith purifies the heart, and works holiness, and all graces flow from it; but in this work of justifying the sinner, it is alone, and cannot admit of any mixture, as Luther's resemblance is, 'Faith is as the bride with Christ in the bed-chamber alone, but when she cometh forth, hath the attendance and train of her graces with her.'"

The Synod of Dort says: "To as many as truly believe, and through the death of Christ are delivered and saved from sin and condemnation, this benefit comes from the sole grace of God, which he owes to no man, given them in Christ from eternity."

The Welch Calvinistic Methodists' Confession says: "It would be as improper to attribute the righteousness of Christ to faith [itself], as to attribute the light of the sun to the medium through which it is transmitted to us."

Further testimonies are needless. How clear and harmonious is God's way of saving sinners! And how safe is it to follow him in all things! Holiness no less than bliss follows a true faith. "Reliance is the essence of faith. Christ is the object, the word is the food, and obedience the proof; so that true faith is a depending upon Christ for salvation in the way of obedience, as he is offered in the word." Well may all give thanks for such a gift. It is the earnest of salvation.

"Peace be to the brethren, and love with faith from God our Father and the Lord Jesus Christ."

CHAPTER XXIX.

WHY GOOD WORKS ARE NECESSARY.

THE Church of Christ has uniformly insisted upon good works as being pleasing and honourable to God, as being the evidences of faith and the fruits of love, and as being profitable to our neighbour. The Scriptures are as careful to insist that good works be performed, as they are to warn us against trusting in them for justification before God. They are often commanded in the plainest terms. "Depart from evil and do good." Psa. xxxiv. 14. "Trust in the Lord and do good." Psa. xxxvii. 3. "Let your light so shine before men, that they may see your good works, and glorify your Father which is in heaven." Matt. v. 16. "Dearly beloved, I beseech you as strangers and pilgrims, abstain from fleshly lusts, which war against the soul; having your conversation honest among the gentiles: that whereas they speak against you as evildoers, they may by your good works, which they shall behold, glorify God in the day of visitation." 1 Pet. ii. 11, 12. "Herein is my Father glorified, that ye bear much fruit, so shall ye be my disciples." John xv. 8. "Walk worthy of the Lord unto all pleasing, being fruitful in every good work." Tit. iii. 1. "These things I will that thou affirm constantly, that they who have believed in God, might be careful to maintain good works. These things are good and profitable unto men." Tit. iii. 8. "Let ours also learn to maintain good works for necessary uses." Tit. iii. 14.

These are but specimens of scores of texts of Scripture, which assert the necessity of good works in all, who would glorify God, be useful to their generation, or evince a true Christian character. There is no substitute for a life of holiness.

Nothing is a good work unless it is something commanded by God. Human inventions may please men, win the applause of the ignorant, and build up in us a vain self-confidence. But "who hath required this at your hand?" is a terrible challenge from God to all who follow such devices. It was a great complaint of God against some, "this people draw near me with their mouth, and with their lips do honour me, but have removed their heart far from me, and their fear toward me is taught by the precepts of men." Isa. xxix. 13. And Christ said of some; "In vain do they worship me, teaching for doctrines the commandments of men." Matt. xv. 9.

The symbols of the various Churches of Christ are remarkably clear and harmonious on the subject of works. Here is the testimony of the Confession of Sueveland: "We are so far from rejecting good works, that we do utterly deny that any man can fully be saved except that he be thus far brought by the Spirit of Christ, that he find no want at all in him, touching those good works whereunto God hath created him." A declaration this parallel to these, "Without faith it is impossible to please God," and "Without holiness no man shall see the Lord." The Confession of Wirtemburg says "that good works, commanded of God, are necessarily to be done." The Confession of

Saxony says: "Obedience, and the righteousness of a good conscience, must be begun in this life; and this obedience, although it be very far from that perfection, which the law requireth, is nevertheless, in the regenerate, acceptable to God, for the Mediator's sake: who maketh request for us, and by his merit doth cover our great and unspeakable miseries." The Confession of Scotland says, "That God hath given to man his holy law, in which not only are forbidden all such works as displease and offend his godly majesty, but also, are commanded all such as please him, and as he hath promised to reward. Exod. xx. 1—17. Deut. v. 1—21. And these works be of two sorts. The one are done to the honour of God, the other to the profit of our neighbours." The Confession of England says, "Though we say we have no shelter at all in our own works and deeds, but appoint all the means of our salvation to be in Christ alone; yet say we not, that for this cause men ought to live loosely and dissolutely: nor that it is enough for a Christian to be baptized only, and to believe; as though there were nothing else required at his hand. For true faith is lively, and can in no wise be idle. Thus therefore teach we the people: that God hath called us, not to follow riot and wantonness, but as St. Paul saith, 'unto good works, to walk in them;' Ephes. ii. 10; that we are delivered from the power of darkness, (Col. i. 13); to the end that we should serve the living God, (Heb. ix. 14); to cut away all the remnants of sin, and to work out our salvation with fear and trembling, (Phil. ii. 12); that it may appear that the Spirit of sanctification is in our bodies, and that Christ himself dwelleth in our bodies." The Confession of France says: "So far is faith from extinguishing the desire to live well and holily, that it doth rather increase and kindle it in us: whereupon good works do necessarily follow." The Confession of Bohemia having quoted at length 2 Pet. i. 5—8, 2 Cor. iii. 10, 2 Pet. i. 11, 12, Luke vi. 36, 38, and xii. 33, and xiv. 13, 14, says, "By these it is plain and manifest that those works which proceed of faith, do please God, and are rewarded with abundant grace: to wit, with the recompense of all kind of good things and blessings, both in this life and in the life to come." The Heidelberg Catechism under the head of Thankfulness thus speaks:

"86. Since then we are delivered from our misery, merely of grace through Christ, without any merit of ours, why must we still do good works?

"Because that Christ, having redeemed us and delivered us by his blood, also renews us by his Holy Spirit, after his own image; so that we may testify, by the whole of our conduct our gratitude to God for his blessings, and that he may be praised by us; also, that every one may be assured in himself of his faith, by the fruits thereof; and that by our godly conversation others may be gained to Christ.

"87. Cannot they then be saved, who, continuing in their wicked and ungrateful lives, are not converted to God?

"By no means; for the holy Scripture declares that no unchaste person, idolater, adulterer, thief, covetous man, drunkard, slanderer, robber, or any such like, shall inherit the kingdom of God.

"88. In how many parts doth the true conversion of man consist?

"In two parts; in the mortification of the old, and in the quickening of the new man.

"89. What is the mortification of the old man?

"It is a sincere sorrow of heart, that we have provoked God by our sins; and more and more to hate and flee from them.

"90. What is the quickening of the new man?

"It is a sincere joy of heart in God, through Christ, and with love and delight to live according to the will of God in all good works.

"91. But what are good works?

"Only those which proceed from a true faith, are performed according to the law of God, and to his glory, and not such as are founded on our imagination or the institutions of men."

The Confession of Basle says: "The faithful do work, not to satisfy for their sins, but only that they may in some sort show themselves thankful unto God our Lord for the great benefits bestowed upon us in Christ." The former Confession of Helvetia says, "This is indeed the only true worship of God: to wit, a faith most fruitful of good works, and yet not putting any confidence in works." The latter Confession of Helvetia says, "We condemn all those, who do contemn good works, and do babble that they are needless, and not to be regarded." Again, "Works do necessarily proceed from faith." The Church of England says that "good works are the fruits of faith and follow after justification," and that "they are pleasing and acceptable to God in Christ, and do spring out necessarily of a true and lively faith, insomuch that by them a lively faith may be as evidently known, as a tree is discerned by the fruit." The Church of Ireland uses almost the very same words and in the same connection. The Westminster Confession says, "The persons of believers being accepted through Christ, their good works also are accepted in him; not as though they were in this life wholly unblamable and unreprovable in God's sight, but that he, looking upon them in his Son, is pleased to accept and reward that which is sincere, although accompanied with many weaknesses and imperfections." So that unless men intend to abandon themselves to wickedness, despise God's authority, and fly in the face of the testimony of all true Christians, they must lead lives of holiness and obedience. Indeed the uniform teaching of Scripture is that while no man shall be saved for the merit of his works, yet men shall be judged and treated according to their works. The wicked deserve all that shall come upon them by want of good works and their performance of evil works. The righteous do not indeed *deserve* any good thing, yet of his mercy and grace God will at last reward them, as though they deserved much. Thus we read: "The work of a man will God render unto him, and cause every man to find according to his ways." Job xxxiv. 11. "Thou renderest to every man according to his work." Psa. lxii. 12. "Say ye to the righteous, that it shall be well with him: for they shall eat the fruit of their doings. Woe unto the wicked! it shall be ill with him; for the reward of his hands shall be given him." Isa. iii. 10, 11. "I the Lord search the heart, I try the reins, even to give every man according to his ways, and according to the fruit of his doings." Jer. xvii. 10. "The Son of man shall come in the glory of his Father, with his angels; and then he shall reward every man according to his works." Matt. xvi. 27. God "will render to every man according to his deeds."

Rom. ii. 6. See also 2 Cor. v. 10; Col. vi. 7; Eph. vi. 8; 1 Pet. i. 17; Rev. ii. 23, and xx. 12, and xxii. 12. So that the doctrine is clear. He that soweth sparingly shall reap also sparingly, while he that sows bountifully shall reap also bountifully. He, who cared comparatively little for the cause of Christ, and did but little for it, shall have a comparatively small reward, while he who gave up all and lived and died for Christ shall be very glorious. "One star differeth from another star in glory. So also is the resurrection from the dead." To render mistake on this doctrine impossible let it never be forgotten that the works of believers will not be the cause but only the occasion of their many rich blessings; the measure but not the merit of their reward.

Nor is there anything in this contrary to the doctrine of gratuitous salvation; for these very works themselves are the fruit of God's mercy and love. He works in us both to will and to do of his good pleasure, and then kindly takes occasion from our obedience to measure out to us, of his own love and bounty, richer and vaster blessings still. That our works themselves are from God the Bible everywhere teaches. "From me is thy fruit found." Hos. xiv. 8. "Lord, thou wilt ordain peace for us: for thou also hast wrought all our works in us." Isa. xxvi. 12. "God is able to make all grace abound toward you; that ye, always having all sufficiency in all things, may abound to every good work." 2 Cor. ix. 8. In fact Jesus Christ "gave himself for us that he might redeem us from all iniquity, and purify unto himself a peculiar people, zealous of good works." Titus ii. 14. "Faith if it hath not works is dead, being alone." James ii. 17. And here precisely is what the apostle James meant when he said we are justified by works. His meaning is that we are justified in making our profession of faith, we establish our sincerity and consistency, we prove to all the world and to God himself that we are what we profess to be and ought to be, when our lives show forth the glory of God. Christian brethren, let us not be weary in well-doing, for in due time we shall reap if we faint not. Let us abound unto every good word and work. How dishonourable to religion it would be, if it were otherwise. Is not all religion an entire failure, if it does not bring us into conformity to God? "Grace is an immortal seed, cast into an immortal soil, that brings forth immortal fruit."

CHAPTER XXX.

REGENERATION.

FROM first to last salvation is all of grace. Paul says: "We ourselves were sometimes foolish, disobedient, deceived, serving divers lusts and pleasures, living in malice and envy, hateful, and hating one another. But after that the kindness and love of God our Saviour toward man appeared, not by works of righteousness, which we have done, but according to his mercy he saved us, by the washing of regeneration, and renewing of the Holy Ghost, which he shed on us abundantly, through Jesus Christ our Saviour." Tit. iii. 3—6. So that it is clearly by the grace and mediation of our Lord Jesus Christ that the Holy Spirit is sent down to renew our natures, and to accomplish in us the new birth. Pardon saves a sinner from the curse of the law and the lake of fire; acceptance through Christ gives him a title to heaven; but in regeneration the dominion of sin begins to be destroyed, and the soul begins to be fitted for the Master's use. The new birth is a great mystery, yet it is much insisted on in Scripture. "The washing of regeneration" is as necessary as washing in the blood of Christ. "The renewing of the Holy Ghost" is as essential as the "justification of life." Within the space of four verses our Lord thrice declares how necessary it is to salvation. Hear him: "Verily, verily, I say unto thee, except a man be born again, he cannot see the kingdom of God;" "Except a man be born of water, and of the Spirit, he cannot enter into the kingdom of God;" "Marvel not that I said unto thee, Ye must be born again." John iii. 3, 5, 7. The fallow ground must be broken up or the good seed will not take root in our hearts. The wild olive must undergo the operation of engrafting with the good olive, or it will remain worthless. All the Scriptures teach as much. Christ regarded it as by no means marvellous that a vile sinner must undergo a great spiritual change, before he could be fit for the service of God.

Perhaps there is not a more driveling error than that which teaches that baptism with water is the regeneration, which Jesus Christ and his apostles insist upon. When men can confound the "washing of regeneration" with the washing with water, they are fully prepared to follow, in fact they are already following, in the footsteps of those, who confounded "that circumcision, which is outward in the flesh," with that circumcision, which is "of the heart, in the spirit, and not in the letter; whose praise is not of men, but of God." Perhaps, too, no error is more mischievous than this. It is monstrous that such error and folly should be taught in lands where God's word is in general use.

To baptism some add an outward reformation and insist that this should be admitted as sufficient. Supposing this to be the meaning of Christ and his apostles, it is impossible to defend them from the charge of using very mysterious language to convey so simple an idea. But such a belief is never entertained by those, who have a becoming respect for God's word.

It will therefore claim no more attention at this time.

Sound divines have very remarkably agreed in telling us what regeneration is. Dr. Witherspoon says: "A new birth implies an universal change. It must be of the whole man, not in some particular, but in all without exception." And he shows at length that it is not PARTIAL, EXTERNAL, IMPERFECT, but that it is UNIVERSAL, INWARD, ESSENTIAL, COMPLETE, and SUPERNATURAL.

Charnock says: "REGENERATION IS A MIGHTY AND POWERFUL CHANGE, WROUGHT IN THE SOUL BY THE EFFICACIOUS WORKING OF THE HOLY SPIRIT, WHEREIN A VITAL PRINCIPLE, A NEW HABIT, THE LAW OF GOD, AND A DIVINE NATURE ARE PUT INTO AND FRAMED IN THE HEART, ENABLING IT TO ACT HOLILY AND PLEASINGLY TO GOD, AND TO GROW UP THEREIN TO ETERNAL GLORY."

Dr. Thomas Scott quotes with approbation another definition, but does not give his author. He says: "Regeneration may be defined—'A change wrought by the power of the Holy Spirit, in the understanding, will and affections of a sinner, which is the commencement of a *new kind of life*, and which gives another direction to his judgment, desires, pursuits, and conduct."

Although this change is called by various names, yet the doctrine of Scripture respecting it is uniform. Sometimes it is called a holy calling, a creation, a new creation, a translation, a circumcision of the heart, a resurrection; but whatever be the name, the thing signified is everywhere spoken of in very solemn terms and as a rich fruit of God's grace. Thus says Paul, "It pleased God, who separated me from my mother's womb, and called me by his grace, to reveal his Son in me." Gal. i. 15, 16. Again: God "hath saved us and called us with a holy calling, not according to our works but according to his own purpose and grace, which was given us in Christ Jesus before the world began." 2 Tim. i. 9. Again Peter says that "the God of all grace hath called us unto his eternal glory by Christ Jesus." 1 Pet. v. 10.

Nor have the purest churches ever doubted the necessity of this change. They also remarkably agree concerning its nature. The Westminster Assembly teaches that "God is pleased in his appointed and accepted time, effectually to call his people by his word and Spirit out of that state of sin and death, in which they are by nature, to grace and salvation by Jesus Christ; enlightening their minds spiritually and savingly to understand the things of God; taking away their heart of stone, and giving them a heart of flesh; renewing their wills, and, by his almighty power, determining them to that, which is good, and effectually drawing them to Jesus Christ; yet so as they come most freely, being made willing by his grace." The Latter Confession of Helvetia says, "In regeneration the understanding is illuminated by the Holy Ghost, that it may understand both the mysteries and will of God. And the will itself is not only changed by the Spirit, but is also endued with faculties, that, of its own accord, it may will and do good," and quotes in proof, Rom. viii. 4; Jer. xxxi. 33; Ezek. xxxvi. 27; John viii. 36; Phil. i. 6, 29; and ii. 13. The Synod of Dort says, "This regenerating grace of God work eth not upon men as if they were stocks and stones, nor doth it abolish the will and properties of their will, or violently constrain it, but doth spiritually revive it, heal it, rectify it, and powerfully yet gently bend it: so that where formerly the rebellion of the flesh, and stubbornness did domineer without control, now a willing and sincere obedience to the Spirit begins to reign; in which change the true and spiritual rescue and freedom of our will doth consist. And surely, unless the wonderful Worker of all goodness should deal with us in this sort, there were no hope left for man to arise from his lapse by his free-will, through which, when standing, he threw himself headlong into destruction." The truth is that if we give up regeneration, the last hope that a sinner may ever again be either holy or happy is gone for ever. The Church of Ireland holds that "All God's elect are in their time inseparably united unto Christ, by the effectual and vital influence of the Holy Ghost, derived from him, as from the head, unto every true member of his mystical body. And being thus made one with Christ they are truly regenerated, and made partakers of him and all his benefits." Indeed nothing could more distress one, who rightly considered his lost estate, than to have the hope, which springs from the doctrine of regeneration, destroyed or seriously shaken. In other words God does in regeneration but graciously respond to an urgent demand of every enlightened conscience. Every man, who has ever had his eyes opened to see his own wretchedness and vileness, will agree to the saying of Usher: "It is not a little reforming will save the man, no, nor all the morality of the world, nor all the common graces of God's Spirit, nor the outward change of the life: they will not do, unless we are quickened and have a new life wrought in us."

In his old age, when he could no longer see to read, John Newton heard some one repeat this text, "By the grace of God I am what I am." He remained silent a short time and then, as if speaking to himself, he said: "I am not what I *ought* to be. Ah! how imperfect and deficient! I am not what I *wish* to be. I abhor that which is evil, and I would cleave to that which is good. I am not what I *hope* to be. Soon, soon I shall put off mortality, and with mortality all sin and imperfection. Though I am not what I *ought* to be, what I *wish* to be, and what I *hope* to be, yet I can truly say, I am not what I once was, a slave to sin and Satan; I can heartily join with the apostle and acknowledge, '*By the grace of God I am what I am.*'"

God's people are born three times, once into this world, once into a state of grace, and once into glory. They and the finally impenitent have the first and none but the first birth in common. It brings the same to all. "That which is born of the flesh is flesh." This natural birth is a great wonder. Devout men have always so regarded it. David says, "Thou art he that took me out of my mother's bowels; my praise shall be continually of thee." Warm should be the heart and thankful should be the song of her, who is made the joyful mother of a living healthy child. To how many is the womb the grave. The wonder is that it is not so to more. Every good man is ready to say, "I bless God that ever I was born."

"Those born once only, die twice. They die a temporal, and they die an eternal death. But those who are born twice, die only once; for over them the second death has no power."

Our second birth brings us into a state of grace. It is one of the richest of God's covenanted mercies. When one is born anew, a fatal blow is given to Satan's kingdom in the heart; for "that which is born of the Spirit is spirit." This is a work of amazing energy. It was for good cause that the Synod of Dort taught "that God, in regenerating a man, doth employ that omnipotent strength, whereby he may powerfully and infallibly bow and bend his will unto faith and conversion." Paul uses all the strong words he is master of to teach us that we are renewed by *power*, by amazing *energy*. He prayed that his Ephesians might know "what is the exceeding greatness of his power to us-ward who believe, according to the working of his mighty power, which he wrought in Christ when he raised him from the dead." Eph. i. 18, 19. We know of no greater power than that which accomplished the resurrection of the Lord Jesus Christ. Yet the same power converts the soul. Augustine says: "To justify a sinner, to new create him from a wicked person to a righteous man, is a greater act, than to make such a new heaven and earth as is already made." Dr. Nevins says, "Some think it easy to save a soul, to bend a will, to change a heart. But it is God's greatest work. Creation is not so hard. It is the most wonderful species of resurrection. With men it is impossible, with God it is possible. In saving a soul he puts forth a mightier energy than in making many worlds." In his Views in Theology Dr. Beecher admits that "the power of God in regeneration is represented as among the greatest displays of his omnipotence ever made, or to be made in the history of the universe. When the fair creation rose fresh in beauty from the hand of God, the morning stars sang together, and all the sons of God shouted for joy; but sweeter songs will celebrate and louder shouts will attend the consummation of redemption by the power of God's Spirit; and such brighter glories of God, and illustrations of his power will be manifested to principalities and powers by the Church, as will cause the light of his glory in physical creation to go out and be forgotten, as the stars fade and are lost amid the splendours of the sun." Mr. Hervey says, "Without the powerful agency of the blessed Spirit to enlighten our understandings, and to apply the doctrine of the Bible to our hearts, we shall be, even with the word of light and life in our hands, somewhat like blind Bartimeus, sitting amidst the heat of day; or like the withered arm, with invaluable treasure before it." Upheld in being by God's power and left to the freedom of his own will, man easily destroyed himself; but omnipotence alone can save him. In physical, as in spiritual things, destruction is easy, and restoration difficult. A child may in an hour burn down an edifice, which it took a hundred men a year to erect. One stroke of the sword may sunder from the body a limb, which all the surgeons on earth cannot restore to its position and its functions. A man may easily take his own life, but no finite power can restore it. The first Adam though earthy could ruin all whom he represented. But the second Adam must needs be the Lord from heaven, as his work was to save the lost.

Thus the Church of God has always held. The Savoy Confession well says, "Although the Gospel be the only outward means of revealing Christ and of saving grace, and is, as such, abundantly sufficient thereunto; yet that men, who are dead in trespasses, may be born again, quickened, or regenerated, there is moreover necessary an effectual, irresistible work of the Holy Spirit upon the whole soul, for producing in them a new spiritual life, without which no other means are sufficient for their conversion unto God." Our second birth is the result of the almighty energy of God's Holy Spirit.

Regeneration is no less the fruit of matchless kindness. So teach the Scriptures. "God, who is rich in mercy, for his great love wherewith he loved us, even when we were dead in sins, hath quickened us together with Christ." This is the way the Bible everywhere speaks. It holds no other language. Gurnall well observes that, "It is a greater act of grace, for God to work conversion in a sinner, than to crown that conversion with glory. It is more gracious and condescending in a prince to marry a poor damsel, than having married her to clothe her like a princess. He was free to do the first, or not; but the relation to her pleads strongly for the other. God might have chosen whether he would have given thee grace, or no; but, having done this, thy relation to him, and his covenant with thee in his Son, do oblige him to add more and more, until he hath fitted thee as a bride for himself in glory."

This love of Christ shown in regeneration is exercised in a sovereign way. "Of his own will begat he us." They who receive Christ Jesus are "born, not of blood, nor of the will of the flesh, nor of the will of man, but of God." The vessels to honour and those to dishonour are made "of the same lump." By nature there is no difference between the elect and the non-elect. Paul was as bloody a persecutor as Domitian; Zaccheus as unconscionable and greedy a worldling, as the rich man, who lifted up his eyes in hell; and the thief, who cried, Lord, remember me, as guilty and felonious as he, who perished, reviling the dying Saviour. Manasseh was for half a century wholly corrupt and hardened, covered with sins and crimes, yet he was saved; while the young ruler, who was so amiable as to draw forth the natural affections of Christ, persisted in his covetousness, and rejected Christ.

This new birth is sometimes called a "translation." As Enoch and Elijah were taken out of this world and borne to heaven, so in its renewal, the soul is "translated out of darkness into the kingdom of God's dear Son." "Outer darkness" excepted, there is none worse than that, out of which the soul is brought in the day of its turning unto God. The kingdom, into which it is translated, is righteousness, peace and joy in the Holy Ghost. Sinful nature is thus slain, while grace is enthroned and sways her peaceful sceptre over the will and affections. This new birth we must all undergo or be for ever undone. "All hangs upon this hinge. If this be not done, ye are undone—undone eternally. All your profession, civility, privileges, gifts, duties are cyphers, and signify nothing, unless regeneration be the figure put before them." This great change is a passing from death unto life. Nor can that transition ever be made in any other way. Better to have been born a heathen, a beast or a monster, yea, better never to have been born at all, than not to be born again. I have known many to celebrate every year the day of their birth; but the day of one's second birth is far more worthy of annual celebration. Flavel says: "What a distinguishing and seasonable mercy was ushered in by providence in the day of your conversion! It brought you to the means of salvation in a good hour. At that very point of time when the *angel* troubled the waters you were brought to the *pool*. John v. 4. Now the accepted day was come, the Spirit was in the ordinance or providence that converted you, and you were set in the way of it. It may be you had heard many hundred sermons before, but nothing would strike till now, because the hour was not come. * * There were many others under that sermon, that received no such mercy. * * As 'there were many lepers in Israel in the days of Eliseus; but to none of them was the prophet sent, save unto Naaman the Syrian,' (Luke iv. 27,) so there were many poor unconverted souls besides you under the word that day, and it may be that unto none of them was salvation sent that day but to you. O blessed providence, that set you in the way of mercy at that time! * * * For consider,

"1. Of all mercies, this comes through most and greatest difficulties. Eph. i. 19, 20.

"2. This is a spiritual mercy, excelling in dignity of nature all others more than *gold* excels the *dirt* under your feet. Rev. iii. 18. One such gift is worth thousands of other mercies.

"3. This is a mercy immediately flowing out of the fountain of God's *electing love*, a mercy never dropt into any but an elect vessel. 1 Thess. i. 4, 5.

"4. This is a mercy that infallibly secures salvation; for as we may argue from conversion to election, looking back; so from conversion to salvation looking forward. Heb. vi. 9.

"5. *Lastly*. This is an eternal mercy, that which will stick by you when father, mother, wife, children, estate, honour, health, and life shall fail thee. John iv. 14."

In due time the regenerate experience their third birth, which is into glory, but of this more hereafter. The first of these births is natural, the second and third are supernatural; the first is carnal, the others are spiritual; the first inclines to sin ("they go astray so soon as they are born"); the second inclines to holiness ("he that is born of God sinneth not"); the third for ever perfects both holiness and happiness; ("we shall be like him, for we shall see him as he is"). Each of these births proves that God is almighty, wise and good. Yet the manner of their occurrence is not very clear to us. The transition from nothing to something, from death to life, from earth to heaven will perhaps ever be somewhat obscure. "Thou knowest not the way of the Spirit, nor how the bones do grow in the womb of her that is with child." "The wind bloweth where it listeth, and thou hearest the sound thereof, but canst not tell whence it cometh, nor whither it goeth; so is every one that is born of the Spirit." Each of these births has its sorrows. We come into the world with a cry. We forsake sin and turn to God, mourning as for a first-born son, or as the people wept at Hadadrimmon in the valley of Megiddon, when their good king, Josiah, was slain. We leave this world with a groan. Yet of the righteous it is always true that "the day of one's death is better than the day of one's birth." We cannot be too grateful for either of these births; but the pious heart loves to dwell on the first as the beginning of natural life, on the second as the beginning of spiritual life, and on the third as the beginning of everlasting life. Neither of these births is the cause of the other, but God is the author of them all. To him belongs all the glory of our being, of our well-being, of our unfading bliss. In our spiritual regeneration the grace of God, the Father, Son, and Holy Ghost, is very illustrious. Redemption devised by God, and purchased by Christ, is in the new birth applied by the Spirit.

One of the most admirable effects of divine grace in regeneration is the victory gained over the strongest evil inclinations. Many a time the bitterest foes have by the power of the new birth become the warmest friends of truth and righteousness. As David displayed his prowess by slaying Goliath, so the grace of God gains the victory over champion sins. The jailor at Philippi practised gratuitous cruelty towards his prisoners, but as soon as his heart was changed, he washed their stripes. In particular does the new birth bring a sinner out of himself, and lead him to exalt the Saviour, and glorify God with all his powers. So that the soul rests in God, is satisfied with him as its chief good, and glories even in shame and reproach for the advancement of his cause.

"Blessed be the God and Father of our Lord Jesus Christ, which, according to his abundant mercy, hath begotten us again unto a lively hope by the resurrection of Jesus Christ from the dead, to an inheritance incorruptible, undefiled, and that fadeth not away, reserved in heaven for you."

CHAPTER XXXI.

SANCTIFICATION.

It is by the grace of our Lord Jesus Christ that the work of purifying our natures is carried on to completion. "Without holiness no man shall see the Lord." Only "the pure in heart shall see God." Holiness in man is conformity to God. The beginning of it is in regeneration. The measure of it is the law of God. The author of it is the Spirit of God. The source of it is the mediation of Christ. The necessity of it is laid in God's spotless holiness and in man's wicked enmity and utter helplessness. The end of it is eternal life.

"Be ye holy, for I am holy" never proceeded from a false God. Indeed the heathen never used a word, which to their minds signified what we mean by sanctification. Their holiness was outward, official, ceremonial. Gospel holiness is inward, personal, spiritual—of the heart. It is true of all men that "out of the heart are the issues of life." As is the heart so is the word, or the deed. As is the motive so is the man. Men cannot bring themselves to be thankful for an act, however advantageous to them, if they know it was not so designed. But they often feel grateful for kind intentions, which resulted in no good to them. God and good men often take the will for the deed; but God never takes the deed for the will, and man never does it but through ignorance. Jehovah makes one demand on old and young, prince and peasant, saint and sinner, and that is for holiness of heart. Nor will he relax this demand to save a soul from hell. To abate aught of his requirements would be to deny himself. He always has said and ever must say, "My son, give me thy heart." So reasonable a command ought promptly to be obeyed.

The Westminster Assembly give this definition: "Sanctification is a work of God's grace, whereby they, whom God hath, before the foundation of the world, chosen to be holy, are, in time, through the powerful operation of his Spirit, applying the death and resurrection of Christ unto them, renewed in the whole man after the image of God; having the seeds of repentance unto life, and all other saving graces, put into their hearts, and those graces so stirred up, increased and strengthened, as that they more and more die unto sin, and rise unto newness of life." The great difference between the two houses which Solomon built was, that he himself dwelt in one, and God in the other. The great difference between a saint and a sinner is, that God inhabits the former, and Satan the latter. To Christians Paul says: "Ye are the temple of the living God; as God hath said, I will dwell in them and walk in them, and I will be their God, and they shall be my people." Again, "His Spirit dwelleth in you." It is indeed wonderful that the tabernacle of God should be "with men," but it is still more marvellous that it should be *in* men. O the condescending greatness of Jehovah! The Holy Ghost is greatly honoured in all the Scriptures. There he is called the Spirit of God, the Spirit of Jehovah, the Spirit of Christ, the Spirit of adoption, the Spirit of wisdom, the Spirit of understanding, the Spirit of counsel, the Spirit of might, the Spirit of knowledge, the Spirit of the fear of the Lord, the Spirit of grace, the Spirit of supplication, the Spirit of glory, the Spirit of judgment, the Spirit of promise, the Spirit of prophecy, the Spirit of truth, the Spirit of holiness, the Holy Spirit, the Comforter. He purifies the heart. He stirs us up to fervent prayer. He makes us to hunger and thirst after the knowledge and image of God. He abides with the Church for ever. He, whose heart is thus inhabited, shall indeed be prepared "unto glory." The influence of the Holy Spirit is necessary to help us on continually. An occasional impulse is not enough. "The ship in full sail keeps on her way for a short distance after her canvass is taken in; but if the propelling power is not renewed, she moves slowly, then stops, and then is drifted backward by the tide." The soul needs help from above all the day long. And how delightful it is to find inspired men teaching this doctrine, not in a cold logic, nor in angry disputations, but with raptures of delight. Hear Paul; "We are bound to give thanks always to God for you, brethren, beloved of the Lord, because God hath from the beginning chosen you to salvation, through sanctification of the Spirit and belief of the truth." And Peter addresses the people of God as "elect according to the foreknowledge of God the Father, through sanctification of the Spirit, unto obedience and sprinkling of the blood of Jesus." So that our fellowship is with the Father and the Son by the Spirit. "It is not the sages, but the saints that are the excellent of the earth." They are "called with a holy calling." The Holy Ghost thoroughly cleanses their natures. The Confession of Scotland thus sums up the leading truths respecting the Spirit of God: "Faith, and the assurance of the same, proceed not from flesh and blood; that is to say, from no natural powers within us; but is the inspiration of the Holy Ghost; Matt. xvi. 17; John xiv. 26; xv. 26; and xvi. 13; whom we confess, equal with the Father and with the Son; Acts v. 3, 4, who sanctifieth us, and bringeth us into all verity by his own operation; without whom we should remain for ever enemies to God, and ignorant of his Son Christ Jesus. For of nature we are so dead, so blind, and so perverse, that neither can we feel when we are pricked, see the light when it shineth, nor assent to the will of God when it is revealed, unless the Spirit of the Lord quicken that which is dead, remove the darkness from our minds, and bow our stubborn hearts to the obedience of his blessed will. And so, as we confess that God the Father created us, when we were not, Psa. c. 3; as his Son our Lord Jesus redeemed us, when we were enemies to him, Rom. v. 10; so also do we confess, that the Holy Ghost doth sanctify and regenerate us, without all respect of any merit, proceeding from us, be it before, or be it after our regeneration. Rom. v. 8. To speak this one thing yet in more plain words: as we willingly spoil [strip] ourselves of all honour and glory of our own creation and redemption, so do we also of our regeneration and sanctification; for of ourselves we are not sufficient to think one good thought; 2 Cor. iii. 5; but he, who hath begun the work in us, is only he that continueth in us the same, (Phil. i. 6,) to the praise and glory of his undeserved grace." Eph. i. 6.

The question is sometimes asked, What is the difference between regeneration and sanctification? The answer is that they are not different in their author, who is the Holy Spirit; nor in the means used, which is God's truth; nor in the fruit produced, which is conformity to God. They differ only as the completion of a work differs from its commencement. Regeneration is the beginning of sanctification. Sanctification is the carrying out of regeneration to its end. Regeneration is an *act* of God's Spirit. Sanctification is a *work* of God's Spirit, consequent upon that act. Regeneration is the tender blade. Sanctification is its growth until it is the full-ripe corn. In regeneration we become "new-born babes;" in sanctification we attain the stature of full-grown men in Christ Jesus. Although sanctification is not perfected in this life, yet it is finished at the death of all the saints.

Another question of great importance is, What is the difference between justification and sanctification? The answer is that they do not differ in their importance. Both are essential to salvation. Without either we must perish. Indeed God has inseparably joined them together. Christ Jesus is always made sanctification to those, to whom he is made righteousness. Nor do they differ in their source, which is the free grace and infinite love of God. Nor do they differ because one of them is accomplished by faith and the other without it. For it is often said that we are justified by faith, and it is as distinctly said that our hearts are purified by faith. Faith is the instrument of justification. It is the root of sanctification. In justification sin is pardoned, in sanctification it is slain. In the former we obtain forgiveness and acceptance; in the latter we attain the victory over corruption, and obtain rectitude of nature. Justification is an act of God complete at once and for ever. Sanctification is a work of God begun in regeneration, conducted through life and completed at death. The former is equal and perfect in all; the latter is not equal in all, nor perfect in any till they lay aside the flesh. In justification God imputes to us the righteousness of Christ; in sanctification he infuses grace, and enables us to exercise it. Justification always precedes sanctification. Sanctification always comes after justification. A late writer says, "Justification and sanctification differ, 1st. in their *causes*. Justification comes by the righteousness of *Christ;* sanctification by the agency of the *Holy Ghost*. 2d. In their *effects*. The effect of justification consists in our external restoration to the favour of God, and the bestowment on us of a covenant title to eternal life; that of sanctification, in the removal of our inbred corruption, and the renewal of the divine image in the soul. 3d. In their *locality*. Justification is an act of God, done amid the solemnities of his court in *Heaven;* sanctification is a work of the Holy Spirit, wrought on the dispositions of our inner man on *earth*. 4th. In *time* and *degree*. Justification lies at the *beginning* of the Christian life, and, except in its consequences, does not extend beyond it, but is instantaneous and complete upon our first exercise of cordial faith. Sanctification begins where justification ends, runs throughout the Christian life, and is partial and progressive, from measure to measure, until it reaches its perfection in glory. In short, justification is God's act *for* us, through the righteousness of his Son; sanctification is his work *in* us, by the power of his *Spirit*. The former is our *title* to Heaven; the latter is our *education* for Heaven. In the one God acts *alone*; in the other he brings us to co-operate *with him*. To thrust ourselves into the former would rob God of his glory; to keep ourselves out of the latter would perpetuate our incapacity for bliss." So long as churches preserve this distinction clear and entire, its influence for good will be manifest. In some respects men may widely differ on doctrinal points, but if right here, you will find them rallying around the vital truths of Christianity in a manner very pleasing. Mr. Wesley says that sanctification "is, indeed, the immediate fruit of justification; but, nevertheless, is a distinct gift of God, and of a totally different nature. The one implies what God does *for us* through his Son; the other, what God works *in us* by his Spirit. So that, although some rare instances may be found, wherein the terms *justified* and *justification* are used in so wide a sense as to include sanctification also, yet in general use they are sufficiently distinguished from each other, both by Paul and the other inspired writers." Other writers have also supposed that *justification* is sometimes used in Scripture to include *sanctification*. If so it is only by synecdoche. Nor is justification ever specially referred to the Holy Spirit as its author, but sanctification of the soul is often said to be through the Spirit. Nor does that saying of Paul (1 Cor. vi. 11) when rightly interpreted contravene this statement. His words are: "And such were some of you; but ye are washed, but ye are sanctified, but ye are justified in the name of the Lord Jesus, and by the Spirit of our God." The peculiarity of this and some other texts is that the first and last clauses of the sentence belong to each other, while the second and third belong to each other. Thus the real meaning is "ye are washed, ye are sanctified by the Spirit of our God, and ye are justified in the name of the Lord Jesus." We have a text of the same construction in the sermon on the mount: "Give not that which is holy unto the dogs, neither cast ye your pearls before swine, lest they trample them under their feet, and turn again and rend you." Matt. vii. 6. All critics know that the *rending* here spoken of is ascribed to the dogs and the trampling to the swine, as if it read, "Give not that, which is holy unto the dogs lest they turn again and rend you, nor cast ye your pearls before swine lest they trample them under their feet." This form of construction it is well known can be found in the classics of all ancient nations. So that Paul does not confound justification and sanctification, nor put one for the other, as some have erroneously supposed, yet it is a blessed truth that these gifts of God are never separated. Whoever has one has both. The prophet David in Psa. xxxii. 1, 2, and the apostle Paul in Rom. viii. 1, have both clearly taught us that the pardoned are without guile, and that the justified walk after the Spirit. He who would *separate* things which God has thus joined together, does wickedly; while to *distinguish* between them is an important duty and of great influence for good.

CHAPTER XXXII.

SANCTIFICATION, CONTINUED.

THERE is a great mystery in sanctification. It is a mystery for the love it displays, for the power it manifests, for the method it employs, and for the work it accomplishes. "We all with open face beholding as in a glass the glory of the Lord are changed into the same image from glory to glory, even as by the Spirit of the Lord." When Moses looked upon that bright effulgence in the mount, he gradually caught some of the same glory, so that his face shone. When we behold the image of the invisible God, as it is presented in the person and character of Christ, we too are made like it, not indeed by a mere natural effect, but "by the Spirit of the Lord." Likeness to God alone is holiness. Growth in this likeness is growth in grace. It is all by Jesus Christ.

It is true that "the best of men are men at the best," and so are far from being perfect as their Father in heaven is perfect. "There is no man that sinneth not." Yea, "there is not a just man upon earth, that doeth good, and sinneth not." But the righteous man is not a willing captive of sin, whereas the unrenewed man rejoiceth in iniquity. The child of God is becoming more and more like God. The wicked wax worse and worse. The saint longs for God's salvation. The sinner sleeps not except he has done some mischief.

The heart of a believer is the best part about him. If he could have things as he would, he never would sin any more. The life of an unconverted man is commonly not near so bad as his heart. He is restrained in many ways from acting out the worst that is in him. The holy man blushes at a sinful thought. The wicked man loves to have vain thoughts lodge within him. It is the business of a good man's life to please God and perfect holiness. It is the business of a sinner's life to please himself and commit sin. The work of purifying the heart shall be finished in due time, and all the righteous shall be satisfied, when they awake, with the likeness of God, fully drawn upon their souls.

If we are called to be saints, we are not called to serve any but the Lord Christ. Holiness may be out of fashion here, but not in heaven. It is infinitely better to be "a peculiar people, zealous of good works," than "a people, laden with iniquity." When a prince was about to travel, he asked his tutor for some maxims, by which to govern his behaviour, and received this: "Remember that thou art the son of a king." Let all Christians remember that they are the sons and daughters of the Lord Almighty," and "if sons, then heirs, heirs of God, and joint heirs with Jesus Christ." With what force and point the exhortation comes to such, "Be ye not conformed to this world, but be ye transformed by the renewing of your mind." Children of the Highest, never forget that "ye cannot serve two masters." "Walk not after the flesh but after the Spirit." "They that walk after the Spirit do mind the things of the Spirit." If you entertain any view of gospel grace, which encourages you to lead a sinful or even a careless life, you have grossly perverted the gospel. Truth never generates licentiousness. Actual participation in Christ's righteousness is always manifested by the possession of his image and temper.

It is sad proof of a wicked heart when a professor of Christ's gospel attempts to live as near as possible to the line separating sin from holiness. Let him eschew and abhor evil. Excess in many things is easy, but no man fears or hates sin too much. So far as we know, it is the only thing which God hates. There are many filthy reptiles, unclean beasts and venomous serpents from which we instinctively turn away; yet God's tender mercies are over all of these. He opens his hand and supplies the wants of every living thing. To the end which he proposed in their creation, they are well adapted. But sin is in its own nature and tendency only evil. God abhors it. It dishonours him, it grieves him, it vexes him. It is the only thing which does dishonour or offend him. He is angry with the wicked every day. When one of Christ's people sins, it is wounding our Saviour "in the house of his friends."

An alleged work of grace on the heart, which gives no outward signs and leaves the life wicked, is good for nothing. True holiness is not dormant but active, not merely a negation of evil, but the positiveness of good. For a while Joseph and Nicodemus may be timid, but when the great question is raised by the crucifixion, we find them open and bold disciples. The fruit of a holy nature is a holy life. Justin Martyr said: "God will admit none into his presence but such as can persuade him by their good works that they love him." If "God's husbandry" brings forth the same fruits and flowers and plants as grow in the wild mountains of error, how is it better than they? Surely "love, joy, peace, long-suffering, gentleness, goodness, faith, meekness, temperance," are very different and very distinguishable from the works of the flesh. In some measure these graces belong to all, who are born from above, and grow with the increase of holiness in their hearts. Nor is there on earth a more interesting sight than a child of God warring with the flesh, resisting the devil, overcoming the world, working the works of God, fighting the good fight, and laying hold on eternal life. Such "shall do exploits," and at last sit down with Christ on his throne, as he also overcame, and is set down with his Father on his throne.

The great test of personal piety is personal holiness. It is better to have the evidence of a meek, forgiving temper, of a serious, devout spirit, of a tender, grateful heart, of a chaste, pious conversation, of a consistent, holy life, in favour of our acceptance with God, than it would be to have an angel bring down from heaven the book of life, and show us our names written therein. *This* might astound, it might for a while delight us; but then we should probably soon become presumptuous, or fall into doubts, under the impression that we had been deluded. But a life of holiness is not only in the general reliable, it is in fact infallible evidence that we are God's people. Nothing can set it aside. Human character is like a web of cloth made up of a great number of small threads, any one of which is not very important or conspicuous, but all together make up the piece. He who thinks a fine selvedge at the last end will make his cloth salable or valuable will be deceived. "Patient continuance in well-doing" constitutes the true test of excellence.

Public and great occasions may furnish opportunities for wonderful displays of what men can sometimes do; but they will commonly amount to little more than sad failures, unless the grace of God has been sufficient to enable a man to behave wisely in little things.

When the world comes in with violence, will it not spoil all our pleasant things, unless there be one stronger still? Who can look without trembling at a feeble creature, unguarded, unrestrained, unsupported by the grace of God, as the world makes its successive attacks upon him? In the Bay of Fundy, where the tide rises to the height of from forty to sixty feet, and comes in with a tremendous roar, due warning is given. Yet with every precaution many vessels are lost. But when a tide of worldliness rolls in on the soul, its greatest swells are commonly noiseless, give no alarm, and seem to threaten nothing. Divine grace, not human power, must give us the victory over the world. Sometimes our inbred corruptions seem to defy all our vigilance and power. Our foes within us are lively, many and subtle. Then there are principalities and powers, and spiritual wickednesses in high places. These are the terror and the torment of the saints in every age. Who shall withstand them? Who shall cause us to triumph over them? None but God. He is mighty. He can make us conquerors and more than conquerors. In the words, "My grace is sufficient for thee," is found the last hope of sinking human nature. Our Rock is Christ. There never was any other. Nothing is too hard for him. Which side he is on is sure to conquer. By him holy men of old "subdued kingdoms, wrought righteousness, obtained promises, stopped the mouths of lions, quenched the violence of fire, escaped the edge of the sword, out of weakness were made strong, waxed valiant in fight, turned to flight the armies of the aliens," &c. What has not divine grace done? No deeds of fortitude or of heroism can compare with the achievements of the saints. Divine grace makes the feeble like David, and the house of David like the angel of God. It is stronger than passion, than the flesh, than the world, than fallen angels, than death and hell. Marvellous is the grace of God in all its displays and in all its effects. "Though ye have lien among the pots, yet shall ye be as the wings of a dove covered with silver, and her feathers with yellow gold." O that all, who name the name of Christ, knew what this meaneth: "The Spirit is life because of righteousness."

CHAPTER XXXIII.

RELATIVE DUTIES.

A PIOUS minister, in preaching to his people immediately preceding a communion season, invariably spoke of the performance of relative duties as a necessary proof of the sincerity of a religious profession. He was right. Bad parents, bad children, bad husbands, bad wives, bad masters, bad servants, bad rulers, bad subjects cannot be good Christians. On all these points the Scriptures speak explicitly: "Parents, bring up your children in the nurture and admonition of the Lord, not provoking them to anger lest they be discouraged;" "Children, obey your parents in the Lord;" "Husbands, love your wives, and be not bitter against them;" "Wives, obey your husbands;" "And ye masters, do the things that are just and equal;" "Servants, be obedient to them that are your masters according to the flesh, with fear and trembling;" "Let every soul be subject unto the higher powers;" "Render to all their dues;" these are but specimens of the stringent and clear teachings of God's word. Particularly has God put high honour upon the family relation and guarded it at every point. It was formed in paradise, and has been continued ever since with many divine sanctions. The proper duties of it are pointed out in the ten commandments. Jesus Christ personally set an example of domestic subordination in his childhood and youth, and of filial piety when he was dying. It is worthy of note that in the most thoroughly doctrinal epistles of the New Testament, the apostles find room for pressing these duties. Nor is there a more striking difference between heathenism and Christianity, or between the pure and the corrupt forms of Christianity, than in their respective influence on families and on social life in general.

The reasons urged in God's word for the careful performance of relative duties are many, and striking. They are such as these: "For that is right;" "That he, who is of the contrary part, may be ashamed, having no evil thing to say of you;" "That ye may put to silence the ignorance of foolish men;" "That if any obey not the word, they may be won by the conversation of the wives, while they behold your chaste conversation, coupled with fear;" "That the name of God and his doctrine be not blasphemed;" "That they may adorn the doctrine of God our Saviour in all things;" "If any provide not for his own, and specially for those of his own house, he hath denied the faith and is worse than an infidel." Such reasonings cannot be answered, though their force may be evaded. No good man will try to diminish their power over him.

The virulence and malignity of communism are seen in nothing more plainly than in its various and violent assaults on the family institution. The folly of the high priests of this dreadful form of wickedness has commonly been made very manifest. The wild confusion, which has reigned over their practical endeavours, has in most cases resulted in speedy disorganization. Order supposes subordination; and without this all attempts to improve men or manners are idle. When one sees the waves dashing against the rock of Gibraltar, he fears not that it will be carried away. So when men foam out their own shame and fury against institutions, which find their necessity in human nature, their sanction in God's revealed will, and their foundation in his unvarying ordinances, the result is not doubtful. When a spirit, leading men to canvass all opinions and to unsettle everything, first appears in each generation, the timid cry out: "What are we coming to?" The ignorant gaze and gape as though they were about to see wonders; the rash raise a shout and cry, "Here is wisdom;" but the wise calmly set themselves to look at the foundations of things, and soon perceive the rock of truth, after which they are no more afraid with any amazement. "Those who attempt to level never equalize." They destroy, but they build not.

Domestic virtue requires the elements of truth, justice, uniformity, condescension, candour, gentleness and kindness from superiors; respect, love, obedience, honour from inferiors; truth, justice, tenderness and brotherly kindness from equals. A family thus regulated will be an emblem of the family named in heaven —an emblem, faint indeed, but clear enough to make a good man say: "It is good to be here." The very last place on earth, where the fires of virtue and piety burn, is the domestic hearth. A profession of even the true religion, when not accompanied by a cheerful and habitual performance of relative duties, is nothing worth. Heaven is not a den of outlaws. If we love not our brother whom we have seen, how can we love God whom we have not seen? The merciful shall obtain mercy; the cruel shall reap the fruit of their own doings; the meek shall inherit the earth, but violent men shall not live out half their days. Tyrants and rebels are alike rejected.

As truth is always in order to godliness, so it will produce its fruits under all circumstances. The rules of right are few and simple. He may read that runs. Yet how little are they heeded except where impressed by religious sanctions and inwrought in the soul by the power of God's Spirit. *Then* they are mighty. Who can but admire the effects produced in a Christian household by such maxims and precepts as these?

1. Be humble. "Only by pride cometh contention."

2. "Keep thy tongue from evil, and thy lips from speaking guile."

3. Find your own happiness in trying to make others happy.

4. Mind your own business. Meddle not. Be not officious.

5. Beware of a fretful, suspicious, or censorious temper.

6. Overcome evil with good. Bless and curse not.

7. "Love is the fulfilling of the law."

8. Endeavour daily to add something to the common stock of useful knowledge in your family.

9. Do not magnify the trials or afflictions of life.

10. Beware of sloth. There is no greater enemy of peace and happiness.

11. Make it your business to serve God.

12. Keep out of debt. "Owe no man anything." Duns breed bad tempers and mean dispositions.

13. "Remember the Sabbath-day to keep it holy." There is no happy family, that forgets that precept.

14. Keep the end of life in view. This will repress many vain wishes and chasten immoderate desires.

15. Let your prayers be frequent and fervent.

16. Never listen to scandal nor backbiting.

17. Set the Lord always before you. Seek his glory. Do and suffer his will with readiness.

18. Let Christ be all and in all. He is everything to us poor sinners. He is the chiefest among ten thousand and altogether lovely.

19. Grieve not for things, which cannot be helped.

20. Trust in the Lord for ever.

There is something peculiarly pleasing in the manifestations of the grace of Christ to a truly pious family, however humble their condition in life. Hitherto the Lord has gathered a far richer harvest of praise from the dwellings of the poor than from the palaces of kings. Not that humble souls in any rank of life are excluded, but it is so hard for the great to lie down in the dust, that most of them are offended in Christ.

CHAPTER XXXIV.

TEMPTATION.—HOW TO TREAT IT.

THOUGH it is not profane, yet it is foolish to speak lightly of the devil. He is not a sacred but he is a dangerous person. Thoughts of levity concerning him are quite out of place. They throw us off our guard, make us secure, lead us to sloth and carelessness, and thus to sin. He who is our adversary, and has slain his thousands and tens of thousands, is never more sure of his prey than when there is least fear of him. He began his work of revolt in heaven, afterwards invaded Eden, assaulted the Son of God himself with the greatest violence and rancor, and will always be busy till he is chained down in the pit.

His ways are various. Sometimes he appears as an angel of light. He has cordials for wounded consciences. He speaks much of mercy. He delights in corrupting the truth. His great object is to keep men from embracing Christ. He has much to do with good men and religious ordinances. He never misses a sermon. He knows that men can go to hell in the pew of a church as well as in the box of a theatre. If they will rest in forms and be satisfied with the ordinances of God without the God of the ordinances, if they will go about to establish their own righteousness, and not submit to the righteousness of Christ, he will encourage them, and help them to be joyful. He frequents our closets and there practises the same arts.

Again, he will turn accuser. He will tell men it is too late to repent, and that it is vain for them to hope for mercy. He will roar like a lion. He delights in terrifying souls from Christ. He would scare all away from the cross. He has no pity. He is wholly malignant and unprincipled. To dishonour God, destroy souls, fill earth with woe and hell with the damned, is his trade and his delight. The keener the anguish, the more pitiless the remorse and the deeper the guilt of man, the more is Satan gratified. He does all he can to make earth like hell, men like devils, and saints like sinners. He delights in seeing all wickedness raging and rioting on earth. He is the God of the men of this world. He commands and they obey. He is the prince of the power of the air, the spirit that now worketh in the children of disobedience. His empire is built on usurpation and fraud, cruelty and crime, blood and rebellion.

Christ came to destroy the reign of devils, nor will he rest till his enemies are put down. The most terrible blow Satan's empire ever received was in the death of Christ. In compassing that, Satan missed his mark. The resurrection, ascension to heaven, and session at the right hand of power showed the end of Christ's death and his Sonship with God. By all these Christ has bruised Satan under him. By pouring out the Holy Spirit, Christ continually weakens the power of the enemy. Satan rages, and hates, and lies, and murders the saints; but his kingdom must fall. The kingdoms of the world shall become the kingdoms of the Lord, and of his Christ. Glorious things are spoken of Zion, and they shall all be fulfilled. Yet these very things awaken the malice of the arch enemy. Finding he cannot rule, he tempts and annoys the children of God. He is their great foe. He studies their tempers, and adapts his temptations to their age, office and inclination. He commonly attacks them in the weakest point. He worries those whom he cannot destroy. If he cannot prevent their getting a crown, he will at least labour that it shall not be a bright one. There is no deeper distress of mind on earth than is sometimes felt by men sorely tempted by thoughts of unbelief, despair, blasphemy, or other sins.

A few words of counsel are here offered to the tempted.

1. Resist the devil, and he shall flee from you. Fight on. Be not terrified, nor faint at his assaults. He is not almighty.

2. Do not attempt to out-wit and out-reason your adversary; but like Christ, quote the word of God upon him. The metal of that sword is too high and its edge too keen for him. He hates to hear, "It is written," or "Thus saith the Lord."

3. Lay firm hold on the promises made to the tempted, and be strong in the Lord. "He will not suffer you to be tempted above that ye are able to bear." "With the temptation he will provide a way of escape." The promises when believed are fatal to Satan's suggestions. "My grace is sufficient for thee," rendered harmless all the buffetings of Satan in the case of Paul. Know God's word. Beware of ignorance.

4. Be much on your guard in times of high religious privilege and enjoyment. Pirates let empty vessels

pass without molestation, but attack those which are well freighted. "If thou comest to serve the Lord, prepare thyself for temptation."

5. Be on your guard in the day of fear and sadness. Satan loves to terrify those already affrighted, and to oppress those already sorrowful. Encourage yourself in the Lord your God.

6. "When a Christian is about some notable enterprise for God's glory, then will Satan lie like a serpent in the way, or as an adder in the path, to bite the horse's heels that the rider may fall backward." In all new and difficult circumstances be vigilant.

7. If formerly you have fallen under the power of any evil, take heed that you fall not again. One lapse often paves the way for another.

8. Beware of attempting to comprehend things beyond your reach, to understand things unintelligible, or to know things not revealed. "There are three kinds of straits, wherein Satan attempts to entrap believers, nice questions, obscure scriptures, and dark providences."

9. Be humble. Humility is a defence better than all gifts besides. "All temptations are laid in self-righteousness and self-excellency. God pursues thee by setting Satan upon thee, as Laban pursued Jacob for his images. These must be torn from thee, how unwilling soever thou art. These hinder Christ from coming in." Humility cannot be too profound. "With the lowly is wisdom."

10. If you have been led astray in the least, hasten your return to God. Stay not away because you have sinned much or little. The message is the same to all who have erred. "O Israel, return unto the Lord thy

God; for thou hast fallen by thine iniquity. Take with you words, and turn to the LORD."

11. If you have been able to repel the assaults of the wicked one, be encouraged but not rendered careless. "Be not high-minded but fear." "Let him that thinketh he standeth take heed lest he fall." "Satan's opportunity is a soul off its guard," said Hewitson. "The saint's sleeping time is the devil's tempting time," says Gurnall. Haweis says: "As not ignorant of his devices, we should especially beware of security. *Let not him that putteth on the armour boast as he who putteth it off.* When the cold turf covers our head, *then the wicked will cease from troubling, and the weary have perfect rest;* but here every step we take we are among lions, and must stand on our watch-tower, fearing always, and working out our salvation with that trembling and care which alone can secure it. A holy jealousy is the great preservative against falling away. The moment we begin to slumber, our watchful adversary is ready to take advantage against us; but *blessed is the man whom his Lord when he cometh shall find watching.*"

12. Be greatly on your guard in solitude, or when called to perform duty alone, and without the aid and encouragement of others. Watch closely then your thoughts and ways. "Two are better than one; because they have a good reward for their labour. For if they fall, the one will lift up his fellow; but woe to him that is alone when he falleth; for he hath not another to help him up." Ecc. iv. 9, 10. It seems to have been when Eve was alone that she was tempted and overcome, and so she was *first in the transgression.* Satan knew what an advantage solitude would give him

in plying the blessed Master with his wicked suggestions when he was in the wilderness. Doubtless our Lord felt this at that time. It is certain he felt his solitude in his last temptation, when "he cometh unto his disciples, and findeth them asleep, and saith unto Peter, What! could ye not watch with me one hour?"

13. When you find yourself quite fascinated with any temporal plans, pursuits or pleasures, set a double guard against temptation.

> "We should suspect some danger nigh,
> Where we possess delight."

The Bible urges moderation and the suppression of inordinate affection by the most solemn considerations, such as that "the Judge standeth before the door;" "The Lord is at hand."

14. Be prepared for temptations at all times. Satan invades our most sacred retirements. He follows us everywhere. He is the "lion of the evening." He may assault you even when dying a Christian death. When great John Knox was near his end, he lay with his eyes closed for a while, but sighed deeply. Being asked the cause, he said: "I have formerly, during my frail life, sustained many contests and many assaults of Satan, but at present that roaring lion has assailed me most furiously, and put forth all his strength to devour and make an end of me at once. Often before hath he placed my sins before my eyes, often tempted me to despair, often attempted to ensnare me by the allurements of the world; but these weapons being broken by the sword of the Spirit, the word of God, he could not prevail. Now he has attacked me in another way. The cunning serpent has laboured to persuade me that I have merited heaven and eternal

blessedness by the faithful discharge of my ministry. But, blessed be God, who has enabled me to beat down and quench his fiery darts by suggesting to me such passages of Scripture as these: '*What hast thou, that thou hast not received? By the grace of God I am what I am; not I, but the grace of God in me.*' Being thus vanquished, he left me."

15. Beware of idleness. Be diligent in business. Keep your mind employed in something profitable, and your hands engaged in something lawful. "Our idle days are the devil's busy ones," says Bishop Hall.

16. Our great refuge in temptation is the throne of grace, sprinkled with atoning blood. In vain will we watch unless we pray. In vain will we pray, if we plead any goodness of our own. Let us make mention of Christ's righteousness, even of his only. "There are no saving views of God but in Christ, and there are no gracious views God hath of men but in Christ. If we look on God out of Christ, we are dazzled with an overwhelming, confounding majesty; if God look on us out of Christ, he seeth hateful and hated sinners." Nothing but the blood of Christ can quench the fire of God's wrath, the fire of lust, or the fiery darts of Satan. That blood can be found at the throne of grace, and nowhere else. Hold fast also all God's word says of Christ's intercession. It is life from the dead to the tempted. "Simon, Simon, Satan hath desired to have you, that he may sift you as wheat; but I have prayed for thee, that thy faith fail not." Luke xxii. 31, 32. "Seeing that we have a great High Priest, that is passed into the heavens, Jesus the Son of God, let us hold fast our profession. For we have not a High Priest which cannot be touched with

the feeling of our infirmities; but was in all points tempted like as we are, yet without sin. Let us therefore come boldly unto the throne of grace, that we may obtain mercy, and find grace to help in time of need." Heb. iv. 14—16. "And I heard a loud voice saying in heaven, Now is come salvation, and strength, and the kingdom of our God, and the power of his Christ; for the accuser of our brethren is cast down, which accused them before our God day and night. And they overcame by the blood of the Lamb, and by the word of their testimony; and they loved not their lives unto the death." Rev. xii. 10, 11. Are you content, are you resolved to walk in their footsteps? If so, you too shall soon overcome.

CHAPTER XXXV.

THE POWER OF DIVINE GRACE TO CONSOLE.

THE gospel is called the power of God, and the wisdom of God. Nor is it losing any of its efficacy. In the hands of the Holy Spirit it works wonders. The secret of its power is chiefly in its grace. By revealing love it begets love. "Responsibility prevents crimes and makes all attempts against law dangerous." But love goes much further. It never ceases to desire to serve and please. It is ingenious in devising methods of service. It is full of alacrity, life and energy. It never counts the cost, and is patient of endurance; even as "Jacob served seven years for Rachel, and they seemed unto him but a few days, for the love he had to her." Important as are the principles of natural religion, it is an honour peculiar to revealed truth, that it converts the soul. It not only converts men; it guides and cheers, purifies and elevates their minds. It throws floods of light on the darkness that surrounds us, and makes us sweetly submissive to God's will and authority. Who does not need such help? There is no sober mind on earth, which, like the sundial, notes only the unclouded hours. We all have our days of darkness. "Man, that is born of a woman, is of few days, and full of trouble." "Who has not lost a friend?" Who has not wept over departed joys, blighted hopes, and darkened prospects? At times nature casts a dark pall over all her face, providence assumes a threatening aspect, fears rise up like mountains in our path, and trouble comes in like waves of the sea, or falls like water-spouts from heaven. At such a time, God's Spirit can pour light and joy into our hearts, and give us songs in the house of our pilgrimage. But if so, he will put great honour upon the Bible. "Remember the word unto thy servant, upon which thou hast caused me to hope. This is my comfort in my affliction: for thy word hath quickened me." Psa. cxix. 49, 50. Solid peace to the troubled mind must be based in the pardon of sin and the favour of God. The gospel calls the poor and needy, the weary and heavy-laden, the sad and sorrowful, and leads them to Christ, and through his blood and righteousness gives comfort, which can be found nowhere else. Even a little divine knowledge firmly believed will do great things for us in the day of calamity, while a soul without acquaintance with God is shut up to misery.

Marcus Fabius Quintilian was a great critic, advocate and orator. He was the friend of Pliny, and received the favour of the emperors. He died at Rome A. D. 60. His great work is his "Institutes of the Orator." The introduction to the sixth book of this treatise relates the loss of his wife and children, and especially the recent death of a promising son. What are his thoughts on an occasion so full of interest? He complains of the "bitterness of fortune," and says that this was "the second wound that was struck deep to afflict me, now a childless father! What then shall I do? or on what shall I any more employ the unhappy talents, which the gods seem to reprove? It was my misfortune to be borne down by a like stroke, when I set about writing the book, which I gave to the public, 'On the Causes of the Corruption of Eloquence.' Why then did I not cast into the fire that accursed work? Why did not I commit it, with that little unhappy learning I might have, to the flames of the funeral pile kindled so untimely to consume my bowels? * * What good parent would pardon me, if I again engaged in study? Who would not detest my insensibility, if I made any other use of my voice, than to vent complaints against the injustice of the gods, who have made me survive all that was dearest to me in the world; if I did not proclaim aloud that there is no providence in the regulation of human affairs? * * There reigns a secret envy, jealous of our happiness, which pleases itself in nipping the bud of our hopes. * * If my life be my crime, it shall also be my punishment. * * I can brave fortune; it has brought my vexations to their height, and in this I find a doleful but just security." Who can without a shudder of horror read such effusions of rage, pride, sullenness and impiety? A human soul, thus stung, rebellious and maddened, is one of the saddest spectacles ever beheld on earth. A wild bull caught in a net, and filling the forest with his roaring, is a Hebrew emblem of a man thus minded. In the day of calamity how gloomy is heathenism, how cheerless is philosophy! Neither brings any solace to the stricken heart.

On the other hand a little light from heaven is a blessing. The man of Uz was also a great orator.

"Unto him men gave ear, and waited, and kept silence at his counsel." After his words "they spoke not again, and they waited for him as for the rain." He was held in the highest veneration. "When the young men saw him, they hid themselves." In his presence "the aged arose and stood up. The princes refrained talking, and laid their hands on their mouth. The nobles held their peace, and their tongue cleaved to the roof of their jaws." He was also the greatest captain of his age. "He dwelt as king in the army. He brake the jaws of the wicked, and plucked the spoil out of his teeth." He was also a great philanthropist. "When the ear heard him then it blessed him; and when the eye saw him, it gave witness to him; because he delivered the poor that cried, and the fatherless, and him that had none to help him. * * He caused the widow's heart to sing for joy; he was eyes to the blind, and feet to the lame. He was a father to the poor: and the cause, which he knew not, he searched out." He was also the richest man in the East. "He washed his steps with butter, and the rock poured him out rivers of oil." For a long time he enjoyed this prosperity and said, "I shall die in my nest, and multiply my days as the sand." "His root was spread out by the waters, and the dew lay all night upon his branch. His glory was fresh in him, and his bow was renewed in his hand." He had seven thousand sheep, three thousand camels, five hundred yoke of oxen, and a great number of servants. He had also ten children, seven sons and three daughters. Yet in one day all were taken from him. He was bereft indeed, and with crushing suddenness. Suspicion instantly wrapped him in her poisoned mantle, and neglect from his servants, and scorn from the abjects speedily followed. "Then Job arose, and rent his mantle, and shaved his head, and fell down upon the ground, and worshipped, and said, Naked came I out of my mother's womb, and naked shall I return thither: The LORD gave, and the LORD hath taken away; blessed be the name of the LORD. In all this Job sinned not, nor charged God foolishly." Job i. 20—22. It is commonly believed that Job lived before any part of God's word was written, though not before many important truths had been revealed to the fathers. He had some light, though not the full light of the gospel. He also embraced the truth as far as he knew it. Behold the difference between the proud Roman and the humble Arabian, the former without God in the world, the latter saying, "I will trust him though he slay me." Quintilian lived in the days of Christ and his apostles, and might have heard Paul preach, and might have known the truth as it is in Jesus. In one sentence of his work he is thought by some to have made a scornful allusion to the Christians. Strange that a man should blaspheme his own gods, and yet see no need of a better religion. Without the light of truth, life is without happiness, and death is without hope. A false religion is a horrible engine of torture. But the gospel freely offers precious blessings to all the sons of men, and especially to the children of sorrow. So that all, who heartily embrace it, may even "rejoice in tribulation." How strange it is that any should oppose the spread of the gospel. How can one defend himself from the charge of malignancy, when he would withhold from the wretched of his race the cup of divine consolations? Let those, who tell of the happiness of the heathen, henceforth keep silence. "Their sorrows shall be multiplied that hasten after another god." Their idols "have mouths but they speak not; eyes have they, but they see not; they have ears but they hear not; noses have they, but they smell not; they have hands, but they handle not; feet, but they walk not; neither speak they through their throat. They that make them are like unto them; so is every one that trusteth in them." There is but one only living and true God; and Jesus Christ is his Son. His mediation alone can bring salvation. His word is truth. His blood is the sole efficacious sacrifice for sin. His gospel is glad tidings of great joy to all, that hear the joyful sound. Blessed are they, all they, and only they, who have made Jehovah their refuge, and hope and portion. This must be done with the heart. The Holy Ghost must illumine the darkened understanding, else we shall be like the bat and the owl, which see not at noon. The divine Spirit alone can so reveal to us the fulness and excellency of Christ, as to enable us to "glory in tribulation." Oh that all the wretched would come and with joy draw water out of the wells of salvation. Jesus came "to appoint unto them that mourn in Zion, to give them beauty for ashes, the oil of joy for mourning, the garment of praise for the spirit of heaviness." "Happy is he that hath the God of Jacob for his help, whose hope is in the LORD his God: which made heaven, and earth, the sea, and all that therein is; which executeth judgment for the oppressed; which giveth food to the hungry. The LORD loveth the prisoners. The LORD openeth the eyes of the blind; the LORD raiseth them that are bowed down; the LORD loveth the righteous; the LORD pre serveth the strangers; he relieveth the fatherless and widow; but the way of the wicked he turneth upside down. The LORD shall reign for ever, even thy God, O Zion, unto all generations. Praise ye the LORD."

CHAPTER XXXVI.

AFFLICTIONS OF THE RIGHTEOUS—SAYINGS—PROMISES.

It has long excited surprise that God's people should in all ages quietly bear the ills of life. Sinners have fainted at seeing or hearing of sufferings, in which the patient publicly and loudly gloried. The grace of Christ is very delightfully manifested in taking away the evil of affliction, in giving support under it, in bringing good out of it, and in granting a final victory over it. Perhaps there is on earth no saint, who believes that he could have made his present attainments with less affliction than has fallen to his lot. Nor is there any good man, who has fully escaped from any trial, however grievous, who does not look back with gratitude to the mercy manifested both in sending and in sanctifying it to his good. Indeed from the earliest times down to the present, such strange things have been said and done under and after the sorest afflictions, as can be accounted for in no way irrespective of the amazing kindness of the Lord Jesus. Scripture, Church History, and Religious Biography abound in what the wicked commonly esteem paradoxes on this subject. Instead of framing any formal argument, or indulging in any exhortation on the subject, some of these immortal sentences are set down for the use of all concerned. Let us first look at a few found in God's word: "Shall we receive good at the hand of the Lord, and shall we not receive evil?"—*Job.* "Our God has punished us less than our iniquities deserve."—*Ezra.* "I was dumb, I opened not my mouth; because thou didst it." "It is good for me that I have been afflicted; that I might learn thy statutes." "Before I was afflicted I went astray: but now have I kept thy word."—*David.* "I will look unto the Lord; I will wait for the God of my salvation; my God will hear me." "The Lord doth not afflict willingly, nor grieve the children of men." "Wherefore should a living man complain, a man for the punishment of his sins?"—*Jeremiah.* "Rejoice not against me, O mine enemy; when I fall, I shall arise; when I sit in darkness, the Lord shall be a light unto me."—*Micah.* "Although the fig-tree shall not blossom, neither shall fruit be in the vines; the labour of the olive shall fail, and the fields shall yield no meat; the flock shall be cut off from the fold, and there shall be no herd in the stalls, yet I will rejoice in the Lord, I will joy in the God of my salvation."—*Habakkuk.* "All that the Father giveth me shall come to me; and him that cometh to me I will in no wise cast out." "Peace I leave with you, my peace I give unto you; not as the world giveth, give I unto you. Let not your heart be troubled, neither let it be afraid."—*Jesus Christ.* "We know that all things work together for good to them that love God, to them who are the called according to his purpose." "Our light affliction, which is but for a moment, worketh for us a far more exceeding and eternal weight of glory." "If we suffer with him, we shall also reign with him." —*Paul.*

The secret of these triumphs of faith is disclosed in two precious passages of Scripture, each of which shows the connection of all these things with Jesus Christ. The first is in Rev. iii. 19, where the Son of God says, "As many as I love, I rebuke and chasten." If any word in this sentence should be emphatic, perhaps it is the pronoun, *I*. The other passage is in Isa. lxiii. 9: "In all their affliction he was afflicted, and the angel of his presence saved them; in his love and in his pity he redeemed them; and he bare them, and carried them all the days of old." "The angel of his presence" is unquestionably the same that Malachi calls the Angel or "Messenger of the covenant." The grace of Christ always was the stay of the Church. He has chosen his people in the furnace of affliction. In short God fulfils to them those faithful promises, "When thou passest through the waters, I will be with thee, and through the rivers, they shall not overflow thee; when thou walkest through the fire, thou shalt not be burned; neither shall the flame kindle upon thee." Isa. xliii. 2. "I will not leave you comfortless; I will come to you." John xiv. 18. "Even the very hairs of your head are all numbered." Luke xii. 7. "As thy days, so shall thy strength be." Deut. xxxiii. 25.

Not only do we find the Scriptures full of such things as have just been quoted, but even since the close of the sacred canon the Church of God has been full of precious sayings suited to encourage the most sorrowing. Here is a short and very imperfect selection of such thoughts, given merely as a specimen of the common sentiments of God's people respecting affliction. It will be readily seen that they are drawn from the word of God.

"God had one Son on earth without sin, but never one without affliction."—*Augustine.*

"Afflictions are the theology of Christians."—*Luther.*

"Without adversity grace withers."—*Mason.*

"God may cast down but he will never cast off true believers."—*Case.*

"Sanctified afflictions are spiritual promotions."—*Dodd.*

"Time is short; and, if your cross is heavy, you have not far to carry it."—*Anon.*

"Afflictions are blessings to us, when we can bless God for afflictions."—*Dyer.*

"Christian, hath not God taught thee, by his word and Spirit, how to read the short-hand of his providence? Dost thou not know that the saints' afflictions stand for blessings?"—*Gurnall.*

"*No righteous man would,* in his right mind, be *willing to make an exchange* of his smartest afflictions for a wicked man's prosperity, with all the circumstances attending it. It cannot therefore be bad with the righteous in the worst condition."—*Charnock.*

"This winter-weather shall be useful to destroy and rot those rank weeds, which the summer of prosperity bred."—*Flavel.*

"The school of the cross is the school of light."—*Anon.*

"God's people have often been carried to heaven in the fiery chariot of affliction."—*Mrs. Savage.*

"Winter leads the sap down into the roots, while summer calls it up into the branches, and displays it in the blossoms and fruit."—*Jay.*

"The tree of the cross being cast into the waters

of affliction has rendered them wholesome and medicinal."—*Owen.*

"Our departed Christian friends cannot descend to share with us in our sorrows; but by holy contemplation we may daily ascend, and partake with them in their joys."—*Howe.*

"In times of affliction we commonly meet with the sweetest experiences of the love of God."—*Bunyan.*

"As no temporal blessing is good enough to be a sign of eternal *election;* so no temporal affliction is bad enough to be an evidence of reprobation."—*Arrowsmith.*

"What unthankfulness is it to forget our consolations, and to look only upon matter of grievance; to think so much upon two or three crosses as to forget an hundred blessings."—*Sibbs.*

"Every man has a heaven and a hell. Earth is the sinner's heaven; his hell is to come. The godly have their hell upon earth, when they are vexed with temptations and afflictions by Satan and his accomplices, their heaven is above in endless happiness. If it be ill with me on earth, it is well that my torment is so short and easy; I cannot be so unreasonable as to expect two heavens."—*Bishop Hall.*

"All is well that ends everlastingly well."—*Anon.*

"It is a blessed thing for the afflicted to wait God's time and determination."—*Lightfoot.*

"When temporal evils are effectual means to promote our everlasting happiness, the amiableness and excellency of the end changes their nature, and makes these calamities that in themselves are intolerable to become light and easy."—*Anon.*

"Crosses and afflictions are God's call to examine our hearts and our lives."—*Richardson.*

"Too much honey doth turn to gall, and too much joy, even spiritual, would make us wantons. Happier a great deal is that man's case, whose soul by inward desolation is humbled, than he whose heart is through abundance of spiritual delight lifted up and exalted above measure. Better it is sometimes to go down into the pit with him, who beholding darkness, and bewailing the loss of inward joy and consolation, crieth from the bottom of the lowest hell, *My God, my God, why hast thou forsaken me?* than continually to walk arm in arm with angels, to sit as it were in Abraham's bosom, and to have no thought, no cogitation, but, *I thank my God it is not with me as it is with other men.*"—*Hooker.*

"Through Christ's satisfaction for sin, the very nature of affliction is changed, with regard to believers. As death, which was, at first, the wages of sin, is now become a bed of rest (Isa. lvii. 2); so afflictions are not the rod of God's anger, but the gentle physic of a tender father."—*Crisp.*

"That is always best for us, which is best for our souls."—*P. Henry.*

"Afflictions are sent to stir up prayer. If they have that effect, and, when we are afflicted, we pray more, and pray better, than before, we may hope that God will hear our prayer, and give ear to our cry; for the prayer, which, by his providence, he gives occasion for, and which, by his Spirit of grace, he indites, shall not return void."—*M. Henry.*

"If we have the kingdom at last, it is no great matter what we suffer by the way."—*Manton.*

"To the poor, humble, and despised believer the kingdom of heaven exclusively belongs; there his best desires will be eternally satisfied, his tears will be changed for triumphant songs of joy, and 'his reward will be great' in the blessed society of the holy prophets and apostles; and in that of the incarnate Son of God, who passed the same way to his glory."—*Dr. Thomas Scott.*

"No cloud can overshadow a true Christian but his faith may discern a rainbow in it."—*Anon.*

"He, who is prepared in whatsoever state he is therewith to be content, has learned effectually the art of being happy, and possesses the alchymic stone, which will change every metal into gold."—*Dwight.*

"I have never met with a single instance of adversity which I have not afterwards seen to be for my good." "I have never heard a Christian on his deathbed complaining of his afflictions."—*Dr. Alexander Proudfit.*

"All the sufferings of the believer are not hell, but they are all the hell he shall suffer."—*Mason.*

"Christians ought neither to expect nor wish to have suffering with Christ, disconnected with their being glorified with him. The former is a preparation for the latter. Rom. viii. 17."—*Hodge.*

"Oh, what must Christ be in himself, when he sweetens heaven, sweetens Scriptures, sweetens ordinances, sweetens earth, and even sweetens trials!"—*J. Brown of Haddington.*

"It is happy for us if we have suffered enough to make us desire a better country, that is a heavenly; but surely all the painful experiences we have hitherto met with have not been more than sufficient to bring us into this waiting posture."—*John Newton.*

"God denies a Christian nothing, but with a design to give him something better."—*Cecil.*

"If the blessed Jesus, who had no sin of his own, bore the wrath of his heavenly Father for a world of sinners, how willingly ought I to endure all the pain I suffer, if my dying example might be but the means of the salvation of one soul."—*David Rice of Ky.*

"There is really much more real satisfaction to be found in a crucified than in an idolized world."—*Witherspoon.*

> "Wherefore will not God
> E'en now, from ills on others brought, exempt
> The offspring of regenerating grace,
> The children of his love? Imperfect yet,
> They need the chastening of eternal care,
> To save them from the wily blandishments
> Of error, and to win their hearts away
> From the polluting, ruining joys of earth."
> [*Carlos Wilcox.*

One thing is a source of unspeakable comfort to God's people in all their tribulation. It is that God will in fact never leave them, nor forsake them. Their wants shall be all supplied. That great witness for Christ, Cyprian, says: "Indeed it is impossible that a good man should be in want of his daily bread. It is expressly promised, 'the Lord will not suffer the soul of the righteous to famish.' And again it is written: 'I have been young, and now am old; yet have I not seen the righteous forsaken, nor his seed begging bread.' And our Lord has thus encouraged our dependence upon him in the following words: 'Take no thought, saying, What shall we eat? or, what shall we drink? or wherewithal shall we be clothed? (for after all these things do the gentiles seek) for your Heavenly Father knoweth that ye have need of all these things.

But seek ye first the kingdom of God and his righteousness, and all these things shall be added unto you.' We see that he promises that every thing else of this kind and nature shall be added to those, who seek the kingdom of God and his righteousness. For since all things are God's, he who hath God will have all things with him, if he on his part be not wanting in his duty to God." Whatever will be to our advantage, if we shall act virtuously, is not only just but benevolent. And if any thing more be wanting here it is: "Many are the afflictions of the righteous: but the Lord delivereth him out of them all." Psa. xxxiv. 19.

CHAPTER XXXVII.

THE RIGHTEOUS SHALL HOLD ON HIS WAY.

THE regenerate have many fears. They know the power, cunning, and malice of their enemies to be great. They are also conscious of much weakness and corruption. In themselves they have no might. So far as fears lead men to watch and pray in faith and hope, they are useful. But where they beget discouragement, or diminish confidence in God, they are sinful and mischievous. One apprehension of the pious is that sin may regain its dominion over them, and at last all their hopes of heaven be disappointed. They often have great fears about their final acceptance. Even when they cannot deny that God has done great things for them, they sometimes fear that yet there may be some deception in their case, and so all their hopes be blasted. To such the truth should be often and clearly presented, that those who have been really born again shall neither totally nor finally fall away from the favour of God and the power of his grace, but shall surely hold on their way unto death, and be for ever saved. The assurance of final victory warranted by Scripture is not in any degree built upon natural courage, or firmness, or goodness, or strength of mind, or of resolution. None more readily than the friends of this doctrine admit that "because of the remains of indwelling sin, and moreover, also, because of the temptations of the world and of Satan, the converted could not continue in a gracious state, if they were left to their own strength." Nor is it denied or doubted that truly converted persons may be left by God to fall into grievous sins, from which if they were not rescued by pardoning and restoring mercy, they could not be saved. The two memorable cases of David and Peter settle this point. Sin has as fearful a malignity in the case of a child of God as in that of the openly profane. If it does not utterly and eternally destroy, it is God's grace that makes the difference between one case and another. The Scriptures thus provide: "If his children forsake my law, and walk not in my judgments; if they break my statutes, and keep not my commandments; then will I visit their transgressions with the rod, and their iniquity with stripes. Nevertheless my loving-kindness will I not utterly take from him, nor suffer my faithfulness to fail." Psa. lxxxix. 30—33. "Though a good man fall, he shall not be utterly cast down; for the Lord upholdeth him with his hand." Psa. xxxvii. 24.

And yet it is true that all who are justified shall at last be glorified. So the Scriptures clearly teach. "The righteous shall hold on his way, and he that hath clean hands shall wax stronger and stronger." Job xvii. 9. "This God is our God for ever and ever; he will be our guide even unto death." Psa. xlviii. 14. "Being confident of this very thing, that he which hath begun a good work in you, will perform it until the day of Jesus Christ." Phil. i. 6. "I give unto my sheep eternal life, and they shall never perish, neither shall any pluck them out of my hand. My Father, which gave them me, is greater than all; and none is able to pluck them out of my Father's hand." John x. 28, 29. "Because I live, ye shall live also." John xiv. 19. "Having loved his own, which were in the world, he loved them to the end." John xiii. 1. "Although my house be not so with God, yet he hath made with me an everlasting covenant, ordered in all things and sure. For this is all my salvation, and all my desire." 2 Sam. xxiii. 5. "The Lord will perfect that which concerneth me." Psa. cxxxviii. 8. "With everlasting kindness will I have mercy on thee, saith the LORD thy Redeemer." Isa. liv. 8. "Whosoever is born of God doth not commit sin, for his seed remaineth in him, and he cannot sin, because he is born of God." 1 John iii. 9. "Ye are kept by the power of God through faith unto salvation." 1 Pet. i. 5. "The foundation of God standeth sure, having this seal, The Lord knoweth them that are his." 2 Tim. ii. 19. "By one offering he hath for ever perfected them that are sanctified." Heb. x. 14. See also John xvii. 11, 24; Heb. vii. 25, and ix. 12—15; Luke xxii. 32. From these and similar passages of Scripture we can but infer the certainty of the final salvation of all believers, and we base the doctrine as the Scriptures do upon the nature of the covenant of grace, upon the promised aid of God's Spirit, upon the efficacy of Christ's blood, upon the prevalency of Christ's intercession, upon the incorruptible nature of the divine seed within us, and upon the unchangeableness of God's love and counsels.

On this subject there is a very powerful and conclusive species of argument several times resorted to by Paul: "If when we were enemies, we were reconciled to God by the death of his Son; much more, being reconciled, we shall be saved by his life." Rom. v. 10.

Again: "He that spared not his own Son, but delivered him up for us all, how shall he not with him also freely give us all things?" Rom. viii. 32. The pious Charnock very forcibly presents the true spirit of such reasoning, when he says: "If God has made thee (of a great sinner) the object of his mercy, thou mayest be assured of the continuance of his love. He pardoned thee when thou wast an enemy; will he leave thee now that thou art his friend? He loved thee when thou hadst rased out in a great measure his image and picture, which he had set in thy soul; will he hate thee now, since he has restored that image, and drawn it with fresh colours? He justified thee when thou wast ungodly; and will he cast thee off, since he hath been at such pains about thee, and written in thee a counterpart of his own divine nature in the work of grace? Were his bowels first moved when thou hadst no grace; and will they not sound louder when thou hast grace? Thou hadst a rich present of his grace sent thee when thou couldst not pay for it; and will he not much more give thee whatever is needful when thou callest upon him? He was found of thee when thou didst not seek him; and will he hide himself from thee, when thou art inquiring after him? God considered before he began with thee, what charge thou wouldst stand him in, both of merit in Christ, and of grace in thee; so that the grace he hath given thee is not only a mercy to thee, but an obligation on himself, since his credit is engaged to complete it. Thou hast more unanswerable arguments to plead before him than thou hadst, viz., his Son, his truth, his promise, his grace, his name, wherein before thou hadst not the least interest. To what purpose hath God called thee and washed thee, if he did not intend to supply thee with as much grace as shall bring thee to glory? Hath God given thee Christ, and will he detain [withhold] anything else?" God never begins to build without knowing that he is able to finish.

Paul's reasoning from such premises is of precisely the same description. Here it is: "Who shall lay anything to the charge of God's elect? It is God that justifieth. Who is he that condemneth? It is Christ that died, yea rather that is risen again, who is ever at the right hand of God, who also maketh intercession for us. Who shall separate us from the love of Christ? Shall tribulation, or distress, or persecution, or famine, or nakedness, or peril, or sword? * * Nay in all these things we are more than conquerors, through him that loved us. For I am persuaded that neither death, nor life, nor angels, nor principalities, nor powers, nor things present, nor things to come, nor height, nor depth, nor any other creature, shall be able to separate us from the love of God, which is in Christ Jesus." Rom. viii. 33—39.

And what an illustrious display of almightiness is here! "Perhaps it is a greater energy of divine power, which keeps the Christian from day to day, from year to year,—praying, hoping, running, believing—against all hindrances—which maintains him a living martyr—than that which bears him up for an hour in sacrificing himself at the stake." To be girded with omnipotence will make any one triumphant. To surround any man with walls of fire will secure to the feeblest safety and deliverance. If Christ dying could procure us a pardon, if Christ rising could secure for us justification, surely Christ interceding can supply us with strength,

Christ reigning can give us the victory, and Christ sitting in judgment can and will give us a final and glorious acquittal. Fairer, stronger reasoning can nowhere be found.

"He that hath the Son hath life, and he that hath not the Son of God hath not life." 1 John v. 12. On this an old writer well says: "If he, who once has the Son, may cease to love the Son, though it be for a moment, he ceases for that moment to have life. But the life of them which have the Son of God, is everlasting in the world to come. But because as Christ being raised from the dead, died no more, death hath no more power over him; so justified man being allied to God in Jesus Christ our Lord, doth as necessarily from that time forward always live, as Christ, by whom he hath life, liveth always." The same writer says: "The faith of God's people, when it is at the strongest, is but weak; yet even then, when at the weakest, it is so strong, that utterly it never faileth, it never perisheth altogether, no not in them who think it extinguished in themselves." Some persons, who make a great show of zeal for old English divines, will turn away from such doctrine, although these are the very words of Richard Hooker. Indeed he uses if possible still stronger language: "'I know whom I have believed.' I am not ignorant whose precious blood has been shed for me. I have a Shepherd full of kindness, full of love, and full of power: unto him I commit myself. His own finger hath engraven this sentence on the tables of my heart: 'Satan hath desired to winnow thee as wheat, but I have prayed that thy faith fail not.' Therefore the assurance of my hope I will labour to keep as a jewel unto the end, and by labour, through the gracious mediation of his prayer, I shall keep it." Dr. Scott, in his Force of Truth, having quoted this paragraph, says: "With such words in my mouth, and such assurance in my heart, I wish to live, and hope to die."

Such has long been the doctrine of the church of God, excepting only the Remonstrants of the Low Countries and their followers in this and other lands. The Synod of Dort records the historical verity concerning this doctrine, in saying: "The spouse of Christ hath always most tenderly loved it, as a treasure of inestimable value, and hath constantly defended it, which indeed that she may still do, God will provide." Again: "The Synod judges these doctrines to be agreeable to the Confessions of the Reformed Churches."

Some object to the doctrine: 1. That numerous persons make a great show of piety, and by and by fall quite away. This is true; but John (1 John ii. 19) explains their conduct: "They went out from us, but they were not of us; for if they had been of us, they would no doubt have continued with us: but they went out, that they might be made manifest that they were not all of us."

2. Some object that such doctrine renders means unnecessary. But no church so holds the doctrine. The Synod of Dort says that "by hearing, reading, meditation, by exhortations, threatenings, promises, and moreover by the use of the sacraments, God preserves, continues and perfects his work in us."

3. There is therefore no force in the objection that this doctrine teaches that every converted man will be saved, *let him live never so wicked a life.* For the doctrine is that a holy heart will produce a holy life, and

that God's grace will maintain within us the love of holiness, and recover us if we fall. "I will make an everlasting covenant with them, that I will not turn away from them, to do them good; but I will put my fear in their hearts, that they shall not depart from me." Jer. xxxii. 40.

Therefore let us lay fast hold of God's covenant, and plead with him for full salvation and final victory. Prayer is a necessary means of being preserved unto life eternal. Therefore cry: Keep me as the apple of thine eye; hide me under the the shadow of thy wings. Keep me from the snare laid for me. Keep me from the hour of temptation. Hold thou me up, and I shall be safe. Preserve thou my soul, O my God; save thy servant that trusteth in thee. Make me meet to be a partaker of the inheritance of the saints in light. And in all the trials of life be courageous. Remember who hath said, "I will never leave thee, nor forsake thee." If you are a sinner, you are not a greater one than he who said, "The Lord shall deliver me from every evil work, and will preserve me unto his heavenly kingdom."

Well did Jude know what he was saying, when he closed his epistle with that triumphant doxology: "Now unto him that is able to keep you from falling, and to present you faultless before the presence of his glory with exceeding joy; to the only wise God our Saviour, be glory and majesty, dominion and power, both now and ever. Amen."

CHAPTER XXXVIII.

THE ABBREVIATION OF HUMAN LIFE.

THE New York Observer of the 6th of March, 1851, contained obituary notices of ten persons, the aggregate of whose ages was more than *eight hundred and eighty-five* years. The youngest of the ten was *seventy-nine* years old. The average of their ages was over *eighty-eight* years. The aggregate number of years attained by them, over *threescore* and *ten*, was *one hundred* and *eighty-five*, being an average of *eighteen* years and a *half* over the time usually allotted to man. Of these persons seven were males, and three females. The habits of all are not particularly stated, but so far as they are noticed, they seem to have been simple and temperate.

In reflecting on such a record, one of our first thoughts is, How long they lived! Both the average and the aggregate of their lives surprise us. Such a record shows that in the divine plan respecting human life there has been no considerable change since the days of Moses. The *minimum* of human life will probably not be lower till the end of the world. And as these ten persons are confessedly rare exceptions to the usual course of things, we have no reason to suppose that the *maximum* of human life will hereafter be greater than it is at present. The increased virtue of mankind would no doubt considerably raise the *average* of human life, but the *maximum* will not materially vary in future ages.

But when we compare the present with the first ages of the world, our thoughts take quite a different turn. Adam lived *nine hundred* and *thirty*, or nearly *forty-five* years longer than all the ten, of whom notice has been taken. Seth lived *nine hundred* and *twelve* years, Enos *nine hundred* and *five*, Canaan *nine hundred* and *ten*, Mahaleel *eight hundred* and *ninety-five*, Jared *nine hundred* and *sixty-two*, Enoch *three hundred* and *sixty-five*, Methuselah *nine hundred* and *sixty-nine*, Lamech *seven hundred* and *seventy-seven*, and Noah *nine hundred* and *fifty* years. The aggregate of the ages of these ten men was *eight thousand five hundred* and *seventy-five* years. Had Enoch not been translated till he was as old as the youngest of the other *nine*, the aggregate of the ages of these ten antediluvians would have been more than ten times as great as that of the ten first mentioned. Compared with the life of man before the flood, how short are our days! If any ask the reason of this change, let them know that it is the sovereign will of God, who holds all second causes and all human affairs under his control. To infer from this difference in human life that we and the men before the flood belong not to the same race, is as illogical as to argue that a child dying a year old is not of the same race with its parents, who live half a century. The whale is said to live a *thousand* years, the elephant *four hundred*, the swan *two hundred*, the terrapin *one hundred* and *fifty*, the eagle *one hundred*, and the ass *eighty*. But human life is still shorter. Man has more enemies, dangers stand thicker around him. *Seventy* years only are appointed to him.

Let us not repine at this state of things. As this world ever since the fall of Adam has been under the mediatorial government of Jesus Christ, whatever has been done to the race has been merciful. The abbreviation of human life was unquestionably a kindness to the world. When men lived nearly a *thousand* years, human wickedness became intolerable. Except when renewed by God's grace, human nature is the same in all ages; and if the wicked lived *nine hundred* years, earth would again be like hell. Even now we find blasphemers and murderers in their 'teens. Men are often deeply practised in crime, and fearfully hardened in atheism before they have lived out half their days. Men have committed more murders than they were years old. If men should live as long as the patriarchs before the flood, and wickedness should grow, as it now does, personal hostilities would be dreadful, and family feuds and national quarrels would find no termination. How could the world endure for seven or eight centuries the tread of a Claverhouse, a Jeffreys, a Duke of Alva, an Alaric, a Nero, or an Alexander? In one century the scholars of vice would acquire such proficiency as to make their names terrible. Though life is short, it is long enough to answer all the highest ends of existence. All adult persons have more time than they profitably employ. Those, who waste their lives in vanity and wickedness, have no right to complain of the brevity of their existence. From him, who misuses what is given him, may justly be withheld all further bounties. And the righteous "would not live alway." They seek a better country, even a heavenly. They have a desire to depart and be with Christ, which is far better than any earthly inheritance.

God often takes first those whom he loves best. Abel left the world, it is thought, at the age of *one hundred* and *twenty years*, while his fratricidal brother lived through centuries of guilt and remorse. Enoch seems to have been the most pious of the ten mentioned in Genesis v., yet he did not remain on earth half so long as the shortest lived of the other nine. "Were the world less miserable, it would be no loss to die and go to heaven; nor can it ever be gain to live and treasure up wrath by sin."

Still unless we can lay hold on the higher truths of religion, it is painful to dwell on the brevity of our earthly existence. Of all persons born into the world, one-third do not live two years, and one half do not see seven years. Of the residue, more than half die before they are forty-five years old. But here and there one lives to be old. The habitable earth and the sea also have become vast grave-yards.

If life be so short let us defer no duty. Let there be a time for everything, and everything in its time. In Christian countries most men fail by wicked delays. Around that rock lie the bleached bones of myriads, who intended to live to God, but never did. Inch by inch their lives were stolen from them, and at the end all they could say was, "The harvest is past, the summer is ended, and we are not saved." A disposition to put off preparation for death would be greatly strengthened by a knowledge that we had centuries before us. From Gen. v. 12, 22, some infer that Enoch was not truly pious, or at least not eminently so till he was *sixty-five* years old. However this may be we all know the strong propensity in men to say, "There is time enough yet." Beware of this dangerous practice. The next hour may usher any one of us into eternity.

Nor is an early death an evil to him who is prepared. He thereby escapes much suffering. He is taken away from the evil to come. Tacitus, in his life of Agricola, seems pleased that he did not live to see the Senate intimidated by soldiers, courts of law shut up, and rapine and slaughter prevalent. "O Agricola, thou art happy, not only by the excellence of thy life, but by thy opportune death!" Agricola died at the age of *fifty-six* years. If a heathen could comfort himself for the death of so honoured a father-in-law by such a consideration, how much more may we be cheered by knowing that our departed pious friends no more see, or hear, or feel those things, which were they alive, must vex their righteous souls from day to day. Let us not be over anxious for long life. The failure of hope, the decline of usefulness, the neglect of juniors, the memory of past joys, the presence of many pains and infirmities burden nearly all the very aged. Their senses are blunted, their strength is not firm, their fears have the ascendency, the almond-tree flourishes, the grasshopper is a burden, and desire fails.

Our advancing years bring increased responsibility. He, who has lived thirty-five years has had five full years of Sabbaths. He, who is *seventy* years old, has had ten solid years of holy time. Frequent interviews with distressed souls and dying people have painfully impressed the writer's mind that there are two sins which have a fearful burden and sting in them. The first is the slighting of gospel grace and mercy. The other is the neglect or abuse of holy time. Most dying sinners seem to desire longer time only that they may spend it as they should have done their holy Sabbaths.

Let us not waste our time in idle regrets on the shortness of life, but let us work while it is day." "THE NIGHT COMETH WHEN NO MAN CAN WORK." "It is good to be zealously affected always in a good thing." Let us do even a little at a time. Despise not the day of small things. "It is not great talents God blesses, so much as great likeness to Jesus." Holiness is a greater means of usefulness than extraordinary natural gifts, or vast learning. "A heated iron, though blunt, will pierce its way even where a much sharper instrument, if it be cold, cannot penetrate." One of the best models of zeal among fallible men is found in Nehemiah. A perfect pattern was Jesus Christ. The zeal of God's house consumed him.

Live and labour to be not only real but eminent Christians. Let us not sleep as do others. Heaven or hell will soon receive all that now live. Let your standard be the word of God and the example of Christ. Forget past attainments, and reach after greater things. Live as seeing Him, who is invisible. Never count that you have attained till you have got your crown. "He, who is contented with just enough grace to escape hell and get to heaven, and desires no more, may be sure he has none at all, and is far from the kingdom of God." Be not conformed to this world, but be transformed by the renewing of your mind. Fight the good fight of faith.

One reason, why some have so great a dread of the close of life, is that it is so rarely a theme of meditation. Men, who will not think, cannot understand.

Mere thoughts of dying will make no one holy, but they have often led men to seek salvation. I have read of a man, whose conversion was traced to those words so often repeated in Gen. v. "AND HE DIED." Live as you may, it will soon be said of you, "*and he died.*" Are you ready for death?

The grace of Christ is necessary to enable us to live well and to die well. His death was the death of death, because it was the death of sin. We may confidently plead with the Saviour for all needed help. He can make goodness and mercy follow us when living; and glory and honour meet us when dying. His grace can moderate our love of life, and take away our fear of death. He can teach us that this is not our rest. He can make us willing to be chastened of the Lord, that we may not be condemned with the world. He can do for us exceeding abundantly above all we can ask or think. He is the good Shepherd. In him we may safely trust and for ever rejoice. If this life is short, Christ's people shall the sooner be with him.

CHAPTER XXXIX.

THE BELIEVER'S VICTORY OVER DEATH.—THE MARTYRS.

As we can die but once, we should seek to die well. The honours which Christ and his gospel have won from the field of the last battle of the saints, have been vast, peculiar, and effective of much good. To glorify God in death is both a duty and a privilege. For this end we should labour and pray at all times. A happy death is a noble end of a well spent life. It crowns a consistent profession of piety with appropriate honours. It proves that God is still faithful. It evinces the tenderness of Christ to his chosen. It soothes the bitter anguish of loved and loving survivors. In itself and for the manifold blessings which follow in its train, it is every way desirable.

And yet how depressing to the spirits of many devout servants of God is the thought of lying down in the grave. That house is so narrow, so damp, and so dark, that they shrink from entering it. We naturally love and cherish our own bodies, and dread the pains of dissolution. Yet believers need not be dismayed at the prospect of exchanging worlds. Death is indeed our greatest, but he is our last enemy. He is the king of terrors and the terror of kings; but it is, and was, and ever shall be true, that

> "The chamber where the good man meets his fate,
> Is privileged beyond the common walks
> Of life—quite on the verge of heaven."

The wicked still have cause to say, "Let me die the death of the righteous, and let my last end be like his." Inspiration still cries: "Mark the perfect man, and behold the upright, for the end of that man is peace." The timid and desponding should lay fast hold of all the encouragements of God's word on this whole subject. In it we learn that "there remaineth a rest to the people of God." Heb. iv. 9. Jesus Christ himself said: "In my Father's house are many mansions: if it were not so, I would have told you. I go to prepare a place for you. And if I go and prepare a place for you, I will come again and receive you unto myself, that where I am there ye may be also." God's word abounds in strong consolations on this subject. Treasure them up. "Though death is the enemy of nature, it is the friend of grace." "Death is the day-break of eternity." Let us not foster our natural dread of pain. Sufficient unto the day is the evil thereof. Many die with very little bodily suffering. When our systems can bear no more, they will sink in death, and so we shall be at rest.

Dissolution and corruption are painful subjects, but our blessed Lord has hallowed the tomb with his own sacred body. Let us follow him even into the grave. Besides, he has taken away the sting of death, which is the guilt of sin, and so has for ever disarmed that enemy. Let no one afflict himself with needless fears of coming short of eternal life, simply because the prospect of death is not always pleasant. "Even a strong believer may be afraid to die. We are not in general fond of handling a serpent, or a viper, though his sting is drawn and we know it to be so." It powerfully tends to preserve human life and to prevent acts of self-destruction, and so is a great mercy to our race, that men should have a natural dread of death. Nor is this commonly taken quite away until God is about to set his chosen free from the bondage of the flesh. That is soon enough for all the best ends of the covenant of grace. Many have confirmed the testimony of Dr. Gill, who says: "Though a believer may have his darkness, doubts, and fears, and many conflicts of soul, while on his dying bed; yet usually these are all over and gone before his last moments come, and death does its office and work upon him. From the precious promises of God to be with his people, even until death; from the scriptural account of dying saints; and from the observations I have made during the course of my life, I am of opinion that, generally speaking, the people of God die comfortably; their spiritual enemies being made to be as still as a stone, while they pass through Jordan, or the stream of death." The prevailing sentiment of every Christian community is, that in death Christ shows great grace to his elect, and fulfils the promise, "As thy days, so shall thy strength be." Every child of God may embrace this good word, and pray like him who said: "Lord, I am called to work I never did: Oh, give me grace I never had." If men would more frequently visit the beds of dying Christians, they would better know the amazing mercy of Christ to departing saints. It is truly wonderful, and surpasses the love of women. And here it gives me great pleasure in a public and solemn manner to record my testimony for the glory of God, and the comfort of all his people, who may peruse these pages. It is this: that the tenderness of Christ to his sick and dying servants is great, and that in the hour of their last trial, he does not leave them, nor forsake them. For a long time I have visited, as I had opportunity, the sick and suffering people of God, without regard to age, sex, rank, complexion, or denomination. The result is that I have never known one who had made so credible a profession of love to Christ, as to secure the general confidence of Christians of the vicinage, left to die an undesirable death. Some endured great bodily pain, but God was with them. Some left the world in a state of unconsciousness, but their last moments of rationality were cheered by blessed rays of light from heaven. Early in their sickness some were sorely tempted, but the victory came at last. Some had been subject to mental derangement, but they were permitted to enter eternity without a cloud over their reason. Yet had they died maniacs, the promises would not have failed. Some were young in years, and in Christian experience; but the good Shepherd gathered them like lambs in his arms, and carried them in his bosom. Some were in middle life, and left helpless children behind them; but I have seen the dying mother kiss her little babe, and bid the world farewell with entire composure. The peace of God ruled her heart by Jesus Christ. Some were old, nervous, and, on other subjects, full of fancies; but Christ, the Rock, followed them to Canaan. What God has done for his people in days past, should encourage those who live at the present time. God's faithfulness to the departed should invigorate the faith and expel the fears of the waiting. God's people have left the world in various ways. Some have died violent and ignominious deaths, and some have died in their beds. Some have had long notice, and others hardly any. Some have died old, some in the midst of their days, and some in the morning of existence, yet they have commonly agreed in leaving an animating testimony to the power of Christ's grace to their departing spirits. The great advantages of good examples are that they express with clearness the duty to be done, that they show the possibility of doing it, and that they incite us to imitation. These advantages are fully realized in the examples of dying saints. The following sayings of God's people have been collected in the hope that they may encourage the faint, embolden the timid, confirm the strong, and animate all classes of real Christians. Most of them were uttered in a dying hour, and many of them were *last* words. Let us begin with the sayings of some of the martyrs.

Stephen said, "Lord Jesus, receive my spirit;" and "Lay not this sin to their charge."

Paul, the aged: "I am now ready to be offered, and the time of my departure is at hand. I have fought a good fight, I have finished my course, I have kept the faith; henceforth there is laid up for me a crown, which the Lord, the righteous Judge, shall give me at that day, and not to me only, but also to all them that love his appearing."

Polycarp: "O Father of thy beloved and blessed Son, Jesus Christ! O God of all principalities and of all creation! I bless thee that thou hast counted me worthy of this day, and this hour, to receive my portion in the number of thy martyrs, in the cup of Christ." "He that gave me strength to come to the fire, will give me patience to endure the flame without your tying me."

Ignatius: "I die willingly for God." "I am God's

wheat, and shall be ground by the teeth of the wild beasts, that I may be found the pure bread of God." "Now I begin to be a disciple." "It is better for me to die for Jesus Christ than to reign over the ends of the earth."

Cyprian: "Let him fear death, who must pass from this to the second death." "I thank God for freeing me from the prison of this body."

Justin Martyr, with six other Christians, stood before the prefect, who examined each one, and then turned to Justin, saying, "Hear thou, who hast the character of an orator, and imaginest thyself in possession of truth. If I scourge thee from head to foot, thinkest thou that thou shalt go to heaven?" Justin said: "Although I suffer what you threaten, yet I expect to enjoy the portion of all Christians; as I know that the divine grace and favour is laid up for all such, and shall be while the world endures." Rusticus asked: "Do you think that you shall go to heaven and receive a reward?" "I not only think so, but I know it, and have a certainty of it, which excludes all doubts," was the reply. Here the prefect insisted that they should all sacrifice to the gods. "No man," said Justin, "will desert true religion for the sake of error and impiety." Urbicus said: "Unless you comply, you shall be tormented without mercy." Justin replied: "We desire nothing more sincerely than to endure tortures for our Lord Jesus Christ, and be saved. Hence our happiness is promoted, and we shall have confidence before the awful tribunal of our Lord and Saviour, before which by divine appointment the whole world must appear." The others assented, and said: "Despatch quickly your purpose; we are Christians, and cannot sacrifice to idols." The sentence was, that they should be scourged, and then beheaded. They heard it with joy, and bore the scourging without a murmur, nay with ecstacy. They were then beheaded, and their bodies were decently interred by their friends.

John Huss: "In these flames, I offer to thee, O Christ, this soul of mine."

Jerome of Prague: "Kindle not the fire behind me, but before my face; for if I had been afraid of it, I had not come to this place, having had so many opportunities offered me to escape."

When Mrs. Jane Askew was offered her life at the stake, if she would recant, she said: "I came not hither to deny my Lord and Master."

Mrs. Joyce Lewis said: "As for death, I fear it not; for, when I behold the amiable countenance of Jesus Christ, my dear Saviour, the ugly face of death doth not much trouble me."

John Nisbet, the younger: "Now, farewell all true friends in Christ; farewell Christian relations; farewell sweet and holy Scriptures; farewell prayer and meditation; farewell sinning and suffering. Welcome heaven; welcome innumerable company of angels, and the church of the first-born, and the spirits of just men made perfect; welcome Father, Son, and Holy Ghost; welcome praises for evermore. Now, dear Father, receive my spirit, for it is thine; even so, come Lord Jesus."

Donald Cargill: "This is the most joyful day that ever I saw in my pilgrimage on earth. My joy is now begun, which I see shall never be interrupted. I see both *my* interest and *His* truth, and the sureness of the one, and the preciousness of the other. * * I have been a man of great sins, but he has been a God of great mercies. And now, through his mercies I have a conscience as sound and quiet, as if I had never sinned. It is long since I could have adventured on eternity, through God's mercy and Christ's merits, and now death is no more to me, but to cast myself into my Husband's arms, and to lie down with him."

Indeed so wonderfully has God been with the faithful martyrs in all ages, making them joyful in all their tribulation, that the effect has been truly astonishing. In the early ages it was often said, "The blood of the martyrs is the seed of the church." It is stated that at the close of the martyrdom of one young woman in Rome, five hundred persons were induced to offer themselves as victims to the rage of the persecutors. Similar effects have been noticed in modern times. Archbishop Tillotson says, he thinks it a true observation, "that catechizing and the history of the martyrs have been the two main pillars of the Protestant religion."

CHAPTER XL.

SAME SUBJECT.—OTHER EXAMPLES, ANCIENT AND MODERN.

SOME have feared that if there was nothing peculiarly trying in the form of their death, they should not have special assistance in their last moments. But the history of God's people shows how kind he has ever been to them in the final conflict. Here are a few out of thousands of cases, which might be cited.

When leaving the world Joseph said: "I die, and God shall surely visit you, and bring you out of this land."

Joshua: "Behold, this day I am going the way of all the earth, and you know in all your hearts and in all your souls, that not one thing hath failed of all the good things which the Lord your God spake concerning you."

Simeon: "Lord, now lettest thou thy servant depart in peace, according to thy word, for mine eyes have seen thy salvation."

Chrysostom: "Glory be to God for all events."

Luther thrice said: "Into thy hands I commit my spirit; God of truth, thou hast redeemed me."

Theodore Beza: "Lord, perfect that, which thou hast begun, that I suffer not shipwreck in the haven."

Thomas Holland: "Come, O come, Lord Jesus, thou bright Morning Star! Come, Lord Jesus, I desire to be dissolved and to be with thee."

Rutherford: "I have got the victory, and Christ is holding out both arms to embrace me."

Richard Baxter: "I have pains, there is no arguing against sense; but I have peace, I have peace. * * Almost well. * * The Lord teach you how to die."

Bunyan: "Weep not for me but for yourselves. I go to the Father of our Lord Jesus Christ, who no doubt will receive me though a sinner, through the mediation of our Lord Jesus Christ; where I hope we shall ere long meet to sing the new song, and remain happy for ever, in a world without end. Amen."

John Owen: "The long wished for day is come at last, in which I shall see the glory of Christ in another manner, than I ever have done, or was capable of doing in this world."

John Flavel: "I know that it will be well with me."

Philip Henry: "O make sure work for your souls, by getting an interest in Christ, while you are in health, for if I had that work to do now, what would become of me? But I bless God, I am satisfied. See to it that your work be not undone, when your time is done, lest you be undone for ever."

Matthew Henry: "This is my dying saying: A life spent in the service of God, and communion with him, is the most comfortable life any one can live in this world."

John Janeway: "Come, Lord Jesus, come quickly."

Richard Hooker: "I am at peace with all men, and God is at peace with me; from which blessed assurance I feel that inward joy, which the world can neither give nor take away."

Col. J. Blackader: "O the kindness and compassion of God, who knows our frame, that we are dust, and has no pleasure in afflicting his poor creatures. O may this [illness] be a rod to chase me to Christ; and the fruit of all to purge away sin."

Alexander Henderson: "I am near the end of my race, hasting home, and there was never a schoolboy more desirous to have the play, than I am to have leave of this world."

Bishop Hall: "If I die, the world will miss me but little, because it has plenty of better men; and I shall not miss it, because it has so much evil, and I shall have so much happiness."

Halyburton: "Though my body be sufficiently afflicted, yet my spirit is untouched. * * Free grace, free grace; not unto me."

Rev. Thomas Cartwright: "I have found unutterable comfort and happiness, and God has given me a glimpse of heaven. * * I have fought the good fight, I have finished my course, I have kept the faith. Henceforth there is laid up for me a crown which the Lord, the righteous Judge, shall give me at that day."

Hervey: "How thankful I am for death! It is the passage through which I get to the Lord and giver of eternal live. These light afflictions are but for a moment, and then comes an eternal weight of glory. O welcome, welcome death! Thou mayest well be reckoned among the treasures of the Christian. To live is Christ, to die is gain."

Robert Bruce: "Now God be with you, my children; I have breakfasted with you, and shall sup with my Lord Jesus Christ this night."

John Locke often exclaimed: "O the depth of the riches of the goodness and knowledge of God. * * I have lived long enough, and am thankful that I have enjoyed a happy life, but after all look upon this life as nothing better than vanity."

Bishop Burgess: "There must be something to bring every one to his journey's end. The days of our years are threescore years and ten; after which it is labour and sorrow. Why should I be taking so much care and pains, just as if I wished to live for ever, when, as you know (addressing a friend) I do not wish to live any longer than it pleases God." His last words were, "We have peace with God: and if we have peace with God, we have peace with all the world. Is it not so?"

Grimshaw: "I shall have my greatest grief and my greatest joy when I die—my greatest grief that I have done so *little* for Christ: my greatest joy that Christ has done so *much* for me."

Rev. James Harrington Evans: "In Jesus I stand: Jesus is a panacea. * * Beware of antinomianism. All *that religion* is a fallacy."

Toplady: "I believe God never gave such manifestations of his love to any creature, and suffered him to live."

Gilbert Tennent: "My assurance of salvation is built on the Scriptures, and is more sure than the sun and moon."

John Tennent: "Farewell my brethren, farewell father and mother, farewell world with all thy vain delights. Welcome God and Father—welcome sweet Lord Jesus! Welcome death—welcome eternity. Amen. Lord Jesus, come, Lord Jesus."

William Tennent: "Blessed be God, I have no wish to live, if it should be his will and pleasure to call me hence, unless it should be to see a happy issue to the severe and arduous controversy my country is engaged in; but even in this the will of the Lord be done."

Rev. Samuel Blair: "The Bridegroom is come, and we shall now have all things. My very soul thirsts for eternal rest."

Rev. Samuel Finley: "I see the eternal love and goodness of God. I see the love of Jesus. Oh to be dissolved, and to be with him! I long to be clothed with the complete righteousness of Christ."

Rev. Dr. Waddell: "Lord Jesus, receive my spirit."

John Newton: "More light, more love, more liberty. Hereafter I hope, when I shut my eyes on the things of time, to open them in a better world. What a thing it is to live under the shadow of the wings of the Almighty! I am going the way of all flesh. If the Lord were not gracious, how could I dare to stand before him?"

Rev. Henry Erskine said to his family: "I know that I am going to heaven, and if you follow my footsteps, you and I shall have a happy meeting there, ere long."

Rev. Ebenezer Erskine: "Though I die, the Lord liveth. I have known more of God since I came to this bed, than through all my life."

Ralph Erskine's last words were: "Victory, victory, victory!"

John Wesley: "The best of all is, God is with us."

Fletcher of Madely: "Head of the Church, be Head of my wife." To his physician, not a professed

Christian, he said, " O sir, you take much thought for my body, permit me to take thought for your soul." Gilpin says: " While he possessed the power of speech, he spoke as one whose lips had been touched with a *live coal from the altar.*"

Augustus Herman Franke: "I praise thee, dear Lord Jesus, for having washed me from all my sins, and made me a king and a priest in the presence of thy Father, and for having forgiven me the multitude of my sins. Blessed and praised be thou for having guided me during my whole life with maternal kindness, and for having spared me, according to thy great condescension, from much suffering. O forgive me, thou Saviour of my heart, if in this my painful disease, my human will, through weakness, has not been able to resign itself so joyfully to thy divine will as it ought; and govern me by thy Holy Spirit, and let thy divine power assist me to the end! O I know that thou art faithful and true! thou wilt never leave nor forsake me." His last words in reply to his wife, who asked whether his Saviour was near him, were, " Of that there is no doubt."

Dr. Thomas Scott, the commentator: "Christ is my all. He is my hope. O to realize the fulness of joy! O to have done with temptation! This is heaven begun! I have done with darkness for ever. Satan is vanquished. Nothing remains but salvation with eternal glory."

Dr. Heugh: "There are many testimonies in the gospel, but the outline of them all is just this, *Whosoever* believeth in Him shall not perish, but have everlasting life. This is the whole gospel. It's a terrible thing to overlook the gospel by *stinting* it. It's a terrible thing to *stint the gospel.* Men should neither be dividers, nor contractors of the gospel."

Andrew Fuller: "If I am saved, it will be by great and sovereign grace, BY GREAT AND SOVEREIGN GRACE. My mind is calm—no rapture, no despondency. *My hope is such that I am not afraid to plunge into eternity.*"

Rev. Dr. Richard Winter Hamilton: "It is my earnest desire that from this death-bed an impression may go forth, that may tell on those who lack the one thing needful."

Rev. George Burder's last prayer was for divine protection and spiritual blessings, closing with a petition that "our *poor, poor, poor* prayers might be accepted through the blessed Redeemer."

Legh Richmond: "It is only by coming to Christ as a little child, and as for the first time, that I can get peace."

Samuel Drew: "You may say with the greatest confidence that I am looking forward to a better country. Thank God, to-morrow I shall join the glorious company above." Again, "I trust I shall to-day be with the Lord Jesus."

Rev. Robert Housman: "Here I am, and here I shall remain, until it please the Lord to take me to himself; and then I shall sing of mercy and of judgment. Yea, unto thee, O Lord, will I sing for ever and ever."

John Frederic Oberlin: "Lord Jesus, take me speedily; nevertheless, *thy* will be done."

Felix Neff: "Adieu, adieu. I am departing to our Father in perfect peace. Victory, victory, victory! by Jesus Christ!"

Dr. Bogue: "I am looking to that compassionate Saviour, whose blood cleanseth from all sin."

Jeremiah Evarts: "We cannot understand—we cannot comprehend—wonderful glory! I will praise, I will praise him! Jesus reigns."

Summerfield: "Administer nothing, that will create a stupor, not even so much as a little porter and water, as I wish to be *perfectly collected*, so that I may have an *unclouded view*."

Dr. Payson: "Peace, peace; victory, victory." "I am going, but God will surely be with you." His last words were, "Faith and patience hold out."

Edward Bickersteth: "I have been thinking much of the precious promise, 'Let not your heart be troubled; ye believe in God, believe also in me.'"

Rev. Dr. Cornelius: "Elias Cornelius a spectacle to God, to angels, and to men! The Lord reigns, let the earth rejoice."

Robert Hall: "It is death—it is death—death! O the sufferings of this body." Mrs. Hall said, "But are you comfortable in your mind?" He promptly replied, "Very comfortable—very comfortable," and soon added, "Come, Lord Jesus, come"—and when his daughter added the word "quickly," he gave her a look expressive of the most complacent delight.

Dr. Nevins: "Death—Death—NOW COME, LORD JESUS—*Dear Saviour*."

John Heckewelder, during his last night on earth, repeated those favourite words:

> "The Saviour's blood and righteousness
> My beauty is and glorious dress;
> Thus well arrayed, I need not fear
> When in his presence I appear."

His last words were, "Golgotha, Gethsemane."

Wm. S. Graham: "I have passed through horrible

darkness, but it is past. Jesus will take me safely through the rest. My Saviour has conquered, my blessed, blessed Saviour! He can hold me up."

To Dr. Waugh one said, "You are now in the deep Jordan; have you any doubt that Christ will be with you?" He replied, "Certainly not! Who else? Who else?"

Rev. W. H. Hewitson: "The Lord has never forsaken me, and he never will—never. It is the best, the kindest, the most fatherly way. Faith receives it now; sight shall soon behold it."

Rev. Dr. John Stanford's last words, written about six hours before his death, were: "Composed in mind and meditation—looking to the mercy of the Lord Jesus."

Rev. Dr. Richard Furman: "O if such sinners as you and I ever get to heaven, redeeming grace shall be greatly magnified in our salvation." "I am a dying man, but my trust is in the Redeemer. I preach Christ to you dying, as I have attempted to do while living. I commend Christ and his salvation to you."

Rev. D. H. Gillette: "O that I had strength to shout. I feel so happy; I hope soon to be able." "O the precious Saviour; what is the world to me, with all its vanity? Give me Jesus." "Do not weep for me, I am going home."

Rev. Dr. Alexander Proudfit: "When will this lingering conflict end? Oh for a speedy and easy transition! Oh for deliverance from this corruptible body—this body of sin and death! Come, blessed Jesus, dear Saviour, come! come! I long to depart." His last words were that Jesus was present with him, and that he was not afraid to die.

James Brainerd Taylor: "Strive! Strive—to enter into the kingdom of heaven."

Rev. Dr. John H. Rice: "Mercy is triumphant."

Dr. Nettleton: "It is meet to trust in the Lord."

Bishop White of Pa., when dying, "fully expressed, with greater warmth and animation than it was believed his weakness would have allowed, and than was usual with him, his reliance upon the merits of the Redeemer alone for acceptance; and the comfort, the 'charming' gratification, of being enabled to trust in the divine goodness, and to realize the protecting care of God in life and in death."

Dr. Ashbel Green left the world, "blessing God for the comforts, which the gospel had imparted to him, and the ineffably glorious hopes it had inspired of sinless perfection beyond the grave."

Rev. Charles Simeon: "It is said, O death, where is thy sting? Do you see anything here?" "Does not this prove that my principles were not founded on fancies or enthusiasm, but that there is a *reality* in them? and I find them sufficient to support me in death."

Rev. Robert Anderson: "Peace! peace! How gracious God is in so making it all peace! I may say, with Lord Gambier, that although pain may distract my body, yet it cannot disturb my spirit." Turning to his wife he said, "Now is the time to claim God's promises. Never be afraid."

Bishop Moore of Va.: "I trust all things are arranged with me for both worlds." "I have nothing more to communicate but love for my dear children."

Dr. Thomas Arnold: "Thank God for giving me this pain: I have suffered so little pain in my life, that

I feel it is very good for me: now God has given it to me, and I do so thank him for it." "How thankful I am that my head is untouched."

Elisha Macurdy: "The Saviour is all my comfort." His last words were—"The water of life."

Thomas Cranfield: "A few more sighs, and then"—

Wilberforce Richmond: "The rest, which Christ gives, is sweet."

Dr. Bedell's last words were: "I thought I should have been at HOME before now." Then pointing to heaven he said, "There.'

CHAPTER XLI.

SAME SUBJECT—FEMALES—MISSIONARIES.

In these holy triumphs over death Christian females have been large sharers. Christ is gracious to the weaker vessels of mercy, no less than to the strong. Mrs. Savage, the sister of Matthew Henry, said: "I here leave the testimony of my experience that Christ's yoke is easy and his burden light."

Mrs. Hulton: "It is an awful thing for the best saint, who has his accounts most ready, to stand before the Judge of heaven and earth to hear his final doom. * * Here is nothing but confusion and emptiness, but it will not be so long."

Mrs. Isabella Graham: "I have no more doubt of going to my Saviour, than if I were already in his arms. My guilt is all transferred. He has cancelled all my debt; yet I would weep for my sins against so good a God. It seems to me there must be weeping even in heaven."

Mrs. Susan Huntington: "Glorious covenant! precious promises! I have given myself, soul and body, to Him, in whom they are yea and amen, and I do not fear. I desire him to do with me as shall please him."

Caroline Fry: "This is my bridal-day, the beginning of my life. O if this is dying, what a mercy! I have written a book to testify that God is Love. I now testify that he is Faithfulness and Truth. I never asked a petition of God that sooner or later I did not obtain."

Mrs. Elizabeth Fry: "O my dear Lord, keep and help thy servant." "This is a *strife*, but I am safe."

Sarah Martin of Yarmouth, the prisoner's friend, and a spirit kindred to Mrs. E. Fry said: "He never hides *his* face. It is *our sins*, which form the cloud between us and him. He is all love, *all light;* with him is no variableness, neither shadow of turning. My precious Saviour, my Beloved is always nigh. I can testify of his tender, supporting love. I have in health spoken of it to others, but till now I have never even experienced half its fulness."

Mrs. Hannah More: "Jesus is all in all. God of grace, God of light, God of love: whom have I in heaven but thee? It pleases God to afflict me not for his pleasure, but to do me good, to make me humble and thankful." "It is a glorious thing to die." Her last word was, "Joy!"

Mrs. Hawkes: "And now I cast self-righteousness all away—I cast myself on him. Take me as I am; make me as thou art; and if it may please thee, give me strength to endure."

Lady Colquhoun: "I hope to meet you all at the right hand of God."

Hannah Lindley Murray: "Glory to God on high, and on earth peace and good will to men! may thy name be glorified on the earth, O Lord God Almighty!"

Maria Fox: "I am thoroughly comfortable." "I know my Saviour loves me, and I am reposing in his love."

Miss Isabella Campbell: "O bear in mind that our

separation will be but short. Live unto God. Farewell."

Mrs. Margaret Breckinridge: "My hope is in the great Physician."

Mrs. Rumpff: "Now, Lord, give deliverance."

One asked Mary Lundie Duncan, "What is your hope?" Her prompt reply was, "THE CROSS."

To Mary Lyon, dying, her pastor said, "Christ precious." She raised both hands, clinched them, lifted her head from the pillow, and said audibly and with emphasis, "Yes." This was her last word.

Margaret Miller Davidson: "Mother, my own dear mother, do not grieve. Our parting will not be long. In life we were inseparable, and I feel that you cannot live without me. You will soon join me, and we shall part no more."

A dear young wife, whose husband now (1852) stands on one of the towers of Zion, recently left the world saying: "Farewell, dear husband! The Lord comfort you, and make you very useful It is sweet to die. Christ is precious."

Another bade farewell to a dear husband and five children, the youngest an infant, saying, "I shall soon see my Saviour as he is." In short, where is the Christian congregation, in which well authenticated traditions of the dying triumphs of God's people of both sexes do not abound?

One of the precious fruits of foreign missions has been the elevation of the piety of those, who remained at home, by the example of faith, patience, self-denial, happiness and triumphs of those, who left all to make known God's truth and grace to perishing men. To such God has always been good. In their last hours he has not left them alone. The Lord strengthened them upon the bed of languishing, and made all their bed in their sickness. The secret of the Lord was with them, and he showed them his covenant. A few of the dying words of such are here given to show how kind God is to his people at home and abroad, among friends and in the midst of strangers.

John Eliot said: "The evening clouds are passing away. The Lord Jesus, whom I have served, like Polycarp, for eighty years, forsakes me not. O come in glory. I have long waited for that coming; let no dark cloud rest on the work of the Indians. Let it live when I am dead." His very last words were, "Welcome! Joy!"

Christian Frederic Swartz: "Let my last conflict, O God, be full of peace and trust. Hitherto thou hast preserved me; hitherto thou hast brought me; benefits have been poured on me without ceasing. I deliver my spirit into thy hands—in mercy receive me; for thou hast redeemed me, thou faithful God." His last words were a request that his friends would sing the hymn beginning,

"Only to thee, Lord Jesus Christ."

David Brainerd: "I shall soon glorify God with the angels."

The last entry Henry Martyn made in his journal, reads thus: "I sat in the orchard, and thought with sweet comfort and peace of my God, in solitude my company, my friend and comforter."

Pliny Fisk, eagerly looking up, said: "Christ and his glory."

H. W. Fox: "I am very weak, can scarcely speak, but oh! happy! happy! happy!" "Jesus, Jesus must be first in the heart. He is first in mine, yes, he is."

Rev. Thomas Thomason: "This is a dark valley, but there is light at the end." "Thanks be unto God for his unspeakable gift." "Lord Jesus, receive my spirit." "Lord, give me patience." "I hope the Lord is coming quickly."

Mrs. Louisa Mundy: "The prospect is to me anything but gloomy."

Mrs. Harriet Winslow: "How good is the Lord!"

Rev. Wm. Carey, D. D.: "I cannot say I have any rapturous feelings; but I am confident in the promises of the Lord, and wish to leave my eternal interests in his hands—to place my hands in his, as a child would in his father's, to be led where and how he pleases."

Rev. Dr. Morrison: "We have a house not made with hands eternal in the heavens."

Rev. C. T. E. Rhenius: "We must have patience—patience."

Rev. Dr. Marshman: "Can you think of anything I am yet to do for the kingdom of Christ?"

Bishop Corrie: "From upwards of fifty years' experience of the world's insufficiency to afford happiness, and of the power of sin, unless God prevent, to work temporal and eternal ruin, *the grave begins to appear a refuge;* and I have *a deep conviction that they only are completely blessed who are in heaven.*"

Mrs. Jane Wilson: "I wish my friends to know that I never have regretted coming to Africa, although our mission among the Zoolahs has not yet seemed to effect any good."

Mrs. Anne Hasseltine Judson: "My husband is long in coming; the new missionaries are long in coming;

I must die alone, and leave my little one; but as it is the will of God, I acquiesce in his will. I am not afraid of death. Tell him the disease was most violent, and I could not write. Tell him how I suffered and died."

Mrs. Sarah B. Judson: "I ever love the Lord Jesus Christ." Mrs. Sarah L. Smith: "Lord Jesus, receive my spirit."

The last words in Dr. Abeel's journal are: "Death has no sting! Oh may the Conqueror continue with me till the close, and then! ! !"

Mrs. Mary E. Van Lennep's last words were: "Give my love, my very best love to father and mother: tell them I have a great many things to say to them, but I can't now. Tell them it will be very, very sweet, when all the redeemed meet together in heaven."

Indeed, in all the matchless dream of Bunyan, nothing is more admirable than the final passage of the pilgrims over Jordan. We should expect the great and strong ones to triumph, but the most feeble were not left comfortless. The last words uttered by Ready-to-halt were, "Welcome, life." The last words of Feeble-mind were, "Hold out, faith and patience." The last words of Despondency were, "Farewell, night! welcome, day!" Even his daughter Much-afraid "went through the river singing; but none could understand what she said." The secret of all these triumphs is declared by Mr. Standfast, when he says: "I see myself now at the end of my journey; my toilsome days are ended. I am going to see that head that was crowned with thorns, and that face that was spit upon for me.

"I have formerly lived by hearsay and faith; but now I go where I shall live by sight, and shall be with Him, in whose company I delight myself. I have loved to hear my Lord spoken of; and wherever I have seen the print of his shoe in the earth, there have I coveted to set my foot too.

"His name has been to me as a civet-box; yea, sweeter than all perfumes. His voice to me has been most sweet, and his countenance I have more desired than they that have most desired the light of the sun. His words I did use to gather for my food, and for antidotes against my faintings. He has held me, and kept me from mine iniquities; yea, my steps have been strengthened in his way."

Indeed it is the plan and purpose of God, through the death of his Son, to "destroy him that had the power of death, that is, the devil; and to deliver them, who through the fear of death, were all their life-time subject to bondage." We have seen how wondrously this is accomplished in the last days of many.

Some may ask, Is there no exception among believers? do all die such happy deaths? To answer in the affirmative would perhaps be going beyond what is written in God's word, or experienced by his people. Willison tells us of an eminently godly minister, who was very melancholy, and said to a friend, "What will you say of him, who is going out of the world, and can find no comfort?" His friend replied, "What will you say of our Saviour Christ, who, when he was going out of the world, found no comfort, but cried out, 'My God, my God! why hast thou forsaken me?'" Even if the child of God should not have a cloudless sky, or should leave the world in darkness, a great affliction it would be, but it would not take away his title to eternal joy. A man's *life*, not his death, must usually be the test of his real character, and the index to his future destiny. Besides, it is not our feelings, it is the *merit of Christ* that makes heaven sure to the penitent. Without any unfaithfulness, God in his inscrutable wisdom might permit one of his real friends to die in some distress of mind. If so, how sweet to such must be the rest and light of glory! They go from the hottest of the battle to the bosom of God, from spiritual distress to the fruition of Christ. Their sun, which goes down behind a cloud, rises in glory without obscurity for ever.

CHAPTER XLII.

THE IMMORTALITY OF THE SOUL.

SOME bold errorists have asserted that the immortality of the soul was not taught until after the time of Moses. They do not deny the immortality of the soul, not they. They only assert it is a modern notion. Let us examine their assertion. It is freely admitted that we have but scant records of the earliest ages. The whole history of the creation and of the world for the first two thousand years is contained in less than *eleven* chapters in Genesis. The five books of Moses, by far the greater part of which relates to the Jews, cover a period of *two thousand five hundred* and *fifty-three* years. In so brief a narrative no reasonable person will expect very full statements on matters not akin to the leading objects of the writer. Incidental notices of other matters are sufficient. The sacred writers often mention things as taken for granted, rather than formally state them. The lawgiver of the Jews had higher objects before him than to please the antiquarian. Yet he has cast more light on the early history of our race and of our world than all other writers united.

It is natural to inquire whether Adam knew anything about immortality. It is confessed he had an immortal soul. Did he know it? It is surprising, if he did not. He was formed "in the image, in the likeness" of God. It is agreed that he learned the use of language in less time than any other person ever did. Modern students of natural history, after all their researches, have not gained such knowledge of birds and beasts as he acquired. He gave names to all cattle, and to the fowls of the air, and to every beast of the field. Did he know so much of all God's works around him, and nothing of the grand work of the Almighty within him? Can it be believed that he did not know that he had a soul? or that his soul was immortal? When he saw an elephant tread on a worm and crush it, did he believe that he was no more immortal than that worm? God put Adam under a special trial. He forbade him to touch one particular fruit under a penalty thus expressed: "In the day thou eatest thereof thou shalt surely die," or "dying thou shalt die." Did Adam understand these words? Even natural religion teaches that God is good and will not deceive or beguile; that he will not threaten one penalty and inflict a heavier. To suspect him of that is to conceive blasphemy. That curse included the loss of God's favour, liability to his displeasure, to pain and disease; the dissolution of the body; the effacing of the moral image of God, forfeiture of communion with him, subjection to evil passions and tormenting fears, and misery for ever. All these things do follow that transgression. To say that Adam did not correctly understand the curse is mere assertion contradicted by natural religion. If he regarded the curse as including eternal death, then he understood that the human soul is immortal. If he knew the doctrine of the soul's immortality, why should he not teach it to his children, and they to theirs? Was "righteous Abel" ignorant of his own immortality? Had he no hope beyond this life? It requires far more credulity to believe this than the contrary.

Did not Enoch, the seventh from Adam, believe men's souls to be immortal? No man ever preached the doctrine of a future judgment more clearly than he. But if the soul is not immortal, but perishes with the body, then there can be no account given by any, who die before Christ's coming. Any fair statement of our accountability to God implies the doctrine of the immortality of the soul. The whole man that sinned, should be punished; the whole man that obeyed, should be rewarded. But "Enoch walked with God, and was not, for God took him." He was taken soul and body to heaven at the age of *three hundred* and *sixty-five* years, which was hardly the meridian of life in those days. Without separation his soul and body were glorified. Here is immortality beyond dispute. If in those days there were sceptics, here God demonstrated to them a future state, a blissful life beyond the present.

Moses forsook all the pleasures, wealth and power of Egypt, and welcomed toil, poverty and banishment. No man at *forty* years of age ever made a greater sacrifice. What sustained him? "He had respect unto the recompense of reward." And what was that? any thing earthly? a life in Midian? There was nothing there comparable to the crown of Egypt. Was he ambitious of being a leader and lawgiver of the Jews? It was nearly forty years, after he forsook the court of Pharaoh, before he was called to be the prophet of Israel, and when called, he was so reluctant to accept the office that finally "the anger of the

Lord was kindled against him." Exod. iv. 14. Nor was he permitted triumphantly to enter Canaan with his victorious legions, but died in the wilderness. What then was the reward which led him to forego his splendid earthly prospects? There is but one fair answer. He believed in an invisible world, in the immortality of the soul, in rewards beyond this life.

In the New Testament it is said Judas hanged himself and "went to his own place." In all the Scriptures there is not a more striking and solemn declaration of future existence and retribution. Is there nothing like it in the Pentateuch? There, speaking of six men, five of whom are known, and all of whom are believed to have been the true servants of God, it is said of each, that when he died he "was gathered unto his people." In Genesis this expression is applied to Ishmael, Isaac and Jacob. If there can be any doubt of the import of the phrase in these cases, let us take the remaining three, Abraham, Aaron and Moses. In them there is no room for doubt. The only way the expression, "*he was gathered unto his people,*" can fail to teach a future state is by supposing that it signifies that he "was buried with his people." This construction is inadmissible. "Then Abraham gave up the ghost, and died in a good old age, an old man and full of years; and *was gathered unto his people.*" Gen. xxv. 8. That he was not buried with his people we well know. His remote ancestors were buried in Chaldea. Terah, his father, was buried in Mesopotamia. Both these countries were hundreds of miles distant from Machpelah, in Canaan, where Abraham was buried. It is therefore not true that he was interred with his ancestors or people. Something else than burial therefore is taught by the phrase under consideration.

The second case cited to the purpose in hand, is found in Num. xx. 24. "*Aaron shall be gathered unto his people.*" From the subsequent context we learn that Aaron died in Mount Hor, in the wilderness, where none of his ancestors had ever been buried. Indeed it was far from any place, where they had resided. *He was not buried with his people.*

The third case is in Deut. xxxii. 49, 50 where God says to Moses, "Get thee up into this mountain * * * and die in the mount whither thou goest up, and *be gathered unto thy people;* as Aaron thy brother died in Mount Hor, and *was gathered unto his people.*" So Moses was not buried with his people, but in "Mount Nebo, in the land of Moab, which is over against Jericho, and no man knoweth of his sepulchre unto this day." We are thus shut up to the belief that this phrase means more than burial, and that it clearly teaches that *people* exist after death, and that the congregation of departed men receives accessions by the deaths of those whom they left behind.

If any demand further evidence that the Pentateuch teaches a future state, and especially one of bliss, here it is. God said to Moses, "I am the God of Abraham, the God of Isaac, and the God of Jacob." Christ himself urged this text in proof of a future state and said that "God is not the God of the dead, [the extinct] but of the living." This argument confounded and silenced the infidels of his day. But our modern infidels beat the Sadducees. It is not true that the Pentateuch is silent concerning immortality.

But some ask, does not Job himself express doubt

of the immortality of the soul? Does he not ask, "if a man die, shall he live again?" Job xiv. 14. The context clearly shows that all Job meant to assert was that death in man was total, and that the power of death over the body of man continued so as to prevent his return to this worldly life. Here is the whole passage: "There is hope of a tree, if it be cut down, that it will sprout again, and that the tender branch [or shoot] thereof will not cease. Though the root thereof wax old in the earth, and the stock thereof die in the ground; yet through the scent of water it will bud, and bring forth boughs like a plant. But man dieth and wasteth away: yea, man giveth up the ghost and where is he? As the waters fail from the sea, and as the flood decayeth and drieth up, so man lieth down and riseth not; till the heavens be no more, they shall not awake, nor be raised out of their sleep. O that thou wouldest hide me in the grave, that thou wouldest keep me secret, until thy wrath be past; that thou wouldest appoint me a set time, and remember me. If a man die, shall he live again?" The body of a tree may die, and it grow again, but if a man die, he will remain dead, "till the heavens be no more."

When we come to examine other parts of Scripture, the doctrine of the immortality of the soul shines out everywhere. Thus said David of his dead child, "Can I bring him back again? I shall go to him, but he shall not return to me." 2 Sam. xii. 23. So also when Christ says, "What is a man profited, if he shall gain the whole world, and lose his own soul?" the entire force of the question turns upon the reality of a future state of existence.

The word *immortal* is found but once in the Bible, 1 Tim. i. 17, and then it is applied to God, "the King eternal, immortal, invisible." The word *immortality*, however, is found five times. Once it refers to "the blessed and only potentate, the King of kings, and Lord of lords, who only hath immortality." 1 Tim. iv. 15, 16. In two cases (1 Cor. xv. 53, 54) it is applied to the resurrection body, "when this mortal shall have put on immortality." In the other cases it is applied to Christians, and clearly signifies not mere existence, but consummate glory and eternal blessedness in heaven. Thus when Paul (Rom. ii. 7) speaks of some, who "seek for glory, and honour, and immortality," he tells us they shall receive "eternal life." So when in 2 Tim. i. 10, he speaks of Christ as having "brought life and immortality to light through the Gospel," he does not mean that Jesus of Nazareth first taught the doctrine of an undying existence beyond the grave; but that by the Gospel he has shown us how to escape the second death, how to prevent our immortality from being a curse, how to attain to unfading and unending bliss in heaven. Jesus Christ has all the honour of a Saviour. To him is due the glory of making existence beyond this life a blessing to any of Adam's race. In all things he has the preeminence. All we have and all we hope for is through his grace.

CHAPTER XLIII.

THE HAPPY STATE OF GOD'S PEOPLE IMMEDIATELY AFTER DEATH.

THE Westminster Assembly taught that "the communion in glory with Christ, which the members of the invisible church enjoy immediately after death, is in that their souls are then made perfect in holiness, and received into the highest heavens, where they behold the face of God in light and glory, waiting for the full redemption of their bodies, which even in death continue united to Christ, and rest in their graves as in their beds, till at the last day they be again united to their souls." This statement refers to both the souls and the bodies of believers. First, the bodies of believers see corruption. They return to the dust. Dissolution follows the separation of the body from the soul. Death passes upon them as fully as upon the bodies of the wicked. The death of God's people is a reality. Secondly, death does not suspend, interrupt or impair the union which subsists between Christ and believers, either their souls or their bodies. As Christ is the Saviour of his people, at home and abroad, by day and by night, awake and asleep, so also in life and in death. The emphatic and beautiful language of Scripture is, that the bodies of the saints "sleep in Jesus." 1 Thess. iv. 14. Thirdly, so that there is nothing alarming or painful in the state of the bodies of the saints. If they sleep, they do well. They enter into peace. They rest in their beds. Isa. lvii. 2. Though their sleep may be long, it will not be too long. It is indeed profound, but it is sweet. It shall have an end; for, fourthly, they are "waiting for the adoption, *to wit*, the redemption of the body." Rom. viii. 23. This waiting is not irksome. The rest of the body is perfect, and the waiting here spoken of is a joyful expectation of the soul in glory. It looks for a reunion, and it shall surely take place. But on this point see the next chapter.

As to the souls of believers immediately after death, three things are asserted of them. First, they are made perfect in holiness. So the Scriptures assert that then the spirits of just men are made perfect, that we shall be like Christ, and the church be presented glorious, not having spot or wrinkle, or any such thing. Heb. xii. 23; 1 John iii. 2; Eph. v. 27. The second thing said of the souls of believers at death is, that they are received into the highest heavens. The Jews and others spoke of three heavens: first, the atmospheric heavens, the air; secondly, the starry heavens, where those bright orbs of light roll in silent grandeur, and shine to the glory of God; and thirdly, the blissful abode of angels and redeemed men, called by Paul the *third* heavens or paradise. 1 Cor xii. 2, 4. The third thing said of the righteous at death is that in heaven they behold the face of God in light and glory. "Blessed are the pure in heart, for they shall see God." Matt. v. 8. "As for me, I will behold thy face in righteousness." Psa. xvii. 15. To see God is to enjoy him. The Divinity, not incarnate, is not perceptible by any of our senses or faculties. God is the King eternal, immortal, and *invisible.* No man hath seen God at any time. No man can see him and live. But all the holy creatures above do see the face of God in the person of Jesus Christ. "We shall see him as he is." 1 John iii. 2. Now we see him "through a glass darkly, but then face to face." 1 Cor. xiii. 12. "And they shall see his face, and his name shall be in their foreheads." Rev. xxii. 4. The opinion that God's people are not at death admitted into the highest heavens, the abode of angels and of the glorified person of Jesus Christ, has long seemed to me heathenish, both in its origin and in its effects on the mind. The Scriptures clearly reveal that the person of our Lord is in heaven. "It came to pass, while he blessed them, he was parted from them, and carried *up into heaven*." Luke xxiv. 51. After his ascension the two angels said to his disciples, "Ye men of Galilee, why stand ye gazing *up into heaven?* This same Jesus which is taken up from you *into heaven*, shall so come in like manner as ye have seen him go *into heaven*." Acts i. 11. *The heavens* then have received "him until the times of restitution of all things." Acts iii. 21. Paul says our great "High-priest is passed *into the heavens*," (Heb. iv. 14;) that he "is set on the right hand of the majesty *in the heavens*," (Heb. viii. 1;) that Christ is entered "*into heaven itself*, now to appear in the presence of God for us." Heb. ix. 24. He "is gone *into heaven*, and is *on the right hand of God*." 1 Pet. iii. 22. From Revelation xxii. 1, we are clearly taught that "the throne of God and of the Lamb" is the same. Indeed John says expressly that "*in the midst of the throne*, and of the four beasts, and in the midst of the elders, stood a Lamb as it had been slain." Rev. v. 6. Christ's glorified person is therefore incontestably proved to be in the highest heavens. Now when Stephen saw the heavens opened, and Jesus standing on the right hand of God, and cried out, "Lord Jesus, receive my spirit," was his prayer not answered? Who dare say it was not? What humble Christian of a child-like spirit ever doubted it? If Christ did receive it, he but fulfilled his promise, I will "receive you unto myself, that where I am, there ye may be also." John xiv. 3. If he took Stephen to his bosom, he but fulfilled his own intercessory prayer: "Father, I will that they also whom thou hast given me be with me, that they may behold my glory which thou hast given me." John xvii. 20. It was the hope of being with his exalted Saviour that put Paul in such doubt: "I am in a strait betwixt two, having a desire to depart and to be with Christ, which is far better: nevertheless to abide in the flesh is more needful for you." Phil. i. 23, 24. Paul loved the work of serving the church. Pursued as he pursued it, it was heaven below, though stripes and bonds, and imprisonments awaited him in every city. God was with him, testifying of his mission. Christ was his salvation. The Spirit was his comforter. He was often refreshed by the love of the saints. He greatly rejoiced in the conversion of sinners, and in the growth of Christians. He says to some, "Now we live if ye stand fast." Yet to depart and be with Christ was far better than to exercise even an apostolical ministry. O blessed strait! O joyous perplexity! With Christ earth is like heaven. Without him heaven would be a world without a sun. There is none like him. There is no substitute for him. Blessed be God, we shall be with him. Paul's choice and strait lay between heaven and earth, celestial glory and earthly usefulness, not between earth and some other place unknown to God's people. In 2 Cor. v. 8, Paul says, "We are willing to be absent from the body and present with the Lord." Here he clearly teaches that the soul in its absence from the body is present with Christ, and does not wait till the resurrection before it enjoys that exalted privilege. He had just before said, "We know that if our earthly house of this tabernacle were dissolved, we have a building of God, a house not made with hands, eternal in the heavens. For in this we groan, earnestly desiring to be clothed upon with our house, which is from heaven." 2 Cor. v. 1, 2. Such language is wholly unmistakable.

So also to the penitent thief, Jesus Christ said, "This day shalt thou be with me in paradise." We have already seen how Paul uses the terms, paradise and the third heaven, interchangeably. Even Bellarmine admits that paradise and the third heaven are the same. The effort of some to make it appear that paradise is not the same as heaven, is as illogical as would be an attempt to show that hell and the lake of fire are two different places, whereas we know they are one and the same place. The Westminster Assembly having spoken of heaven and hell, say: "Besides these two places for souls separated from their bodies, the Scripture acknowledgeth none." Purgatory is an invention of a covetous priesthood. A paradise, different and remote from heaven, is a figment of dreamers, some of whom have written well on other subjects, but on this matter they have gotten their views rather from heathen poets than from inspired prophets and apostles. Dying believers often have no more doubt that they are going straightway into the blissful presence of Christ than they have of his existence. There is no "place of safe-keeping" for the souls of the saints but the bosom of God, the highest heavens.

In that blissful world, where Christ is, are the glorified bodies of Enoch and of Elijah, Heb. xi. 5, and 2 Kings ii. 11. Some also suppose that the saints, who arose after Christ's resurrection, and appeared to many in Jerusalem, did not return to their graves, but formed a part of his glorious retinue, as he returned to the bright mansions on high. There too are the spirits of just men made perfect. Lazarus was "afar off" from the rich man in hell. The former was in Abraham's bosom. The latter had his abode in what he called "this place of torment." The whole parable shows that these states were fixed, perpetual, unchangeable.

When we open God's word we are delighted with the abundance of promises of rest and bliss, all made in such a way as to create the hope of heavenly glory as soon as we, if believers, shall leave the world. Christ says to his persecuted disciples, "Rejoice and be exceeding glad; for great is your *reward in heaven*." Matt. v. 12. "Lay up for yourselves *treasures in heaven*," &c. Matt. vi. 20. "Whosoever shall confess me before men, him will I confess also *before my Father which is in heaven*." Matt. x. 32. "If thou wilt be perfect, go and sell that thou hast, and give to the poor; and thou shalt have *treasure in heaven*." Matt. xix. 21. Paul speaks to the Colossians of the "hope which is laid up for you *in heaven*." Coloss. i. 5. To the Hebrews he says, "Ye took joyfully the spoiling of your goods, knowing in yourselves that ye have *in heaven* a better and an enduring substance." Heb. x. 34. So he says that the suffering people of God "desire a better country, that is, a *heavenly*." Heb. xi. 16. So Peter says that his brethren had been begotten "to an inheritance incorruptible, and undefiled, and that fadeth not away, *reserved in heaven* for you." 1 Pet. i. 4. If these things were not so, how could the inspired preacher have "praised the dead which are already dead, more than the living, which are yet alive?" Ecc. iv. 2. No wise man could do that, unless he believed they were in heaven, which alone, according to Paul, is better than usefulness in the church on earth.

These views, drawn from God's word, have been very generally entertained by the Church of Christ in all ages. It is true some of the Fathers uttered very crude opinions on some things connected with this subject. Yet at times they speak very clearly. Take the following examples out of many. Tertullian says: "Hell is one thing, and Abraham's bosom another, as I suppose; neither is it to be believed that the bosom of Abraham, which is the habitation of a sacred kind of rest, was any part of hell" [*inferorum*]. "Neither could the rich man have lifted up his eyes, and that afar off, unless it had been unto places above him, and very far above him, by reason of the mighty distance between that height and that depth."

Ambrose: "Come into the bosom of Jacob; that, as poor Lazarus died in the bosom of Abraham, so thou also mayest rest in the tranquillity of the patriarch Jacob. For the bosom of the patriarch is a certain abode [*recessus*] of everlasting rest." "We shall go where holy Abraham openeth his bosom to receive the poor, as he did receive Lazarus; in which bosom they do rest, who in this world have endured grievous and sharp things." "Into paradise is an ascent, into hell a descent. Let them descend, saith he, quick into hell. And therefore poor Lazarus was by the angels lifted up into Abraham's bosom." "Behold that poor man abounding with all good things; whom the blessed rest of the holy patriarch did compass about." "Lazarus lying in Abraham's bosom enjoyed everlasting life."

Chrysostom: "Lazarus, who was worthy of heaven, and the kingdom that is there, being full of sores, was exposed to the tongues of dogs, and strove with perpetual hunger." "After famine, and sores, and lying in the porch, he enjoyed that refreshing which cannot be expressed by speech, even unspeakable good things."

Augustine: "I have not hitherto found, and I do yet inquire; neither do I remember that the canonical Scripture doth anywhere put hell in the good part. Now that the bosom of Abraham, and that rest, unto which the godly poor man was carried by the angels, should not be taken in the good part, I know not whether any good man can endure to hear; and therefore how we may believe it is in hell [*apud inferos*] I do not see." "I confess I have not yet found that it is called hell, where the souls of just men do rest." "How much more after this life may that bosom of Abraham be called paradise; where now there is no temptation, where is so great rest after all the griefs of this life! For neither is there wanting there a proper kind of light, and of its own kind [*sui generis*], and doubtless great; which that rich man out of the torments and darkness of hell, even from so remote a place, where a great gulf was fixed in the midst, did so behold, that he might there take notice of the poor man whom he had formerly despised." "The bosom of Abraham is the rest of the blessed poor, whose is the kingdom of heaven, in which after this life they are received."

Origen: "Thither will I go, where are the tabernacles of the righteous, where are the glories of the saints, where is the rest of the faithful, where is the consolation of the godly, where is the inheritance of the merciful, where is the bliss of the undefiled, where are the joys and consolation of such as love the truth. Thither will I go, where are light and life, where are glory and mirth, where are joy and exultation; whence grief and heaviness and groaning fly away, where they forget the former tribulations that they bare in the body upon earth. Thither will I go, where there is a putting off of tribulations, where there is a recompense of labours, where is the bosom of Abraham, where is the propriety of Isaac, where is the familiarity of Israel; where are the souls of the saints, the choir of angels, the voices of archangels, the illumination of the Holy Ghost, the kingdom of Christ, the endless glory and blessed presence [*conspectus*] of the eternal God the Father."

The happy conclusion at which we arrive, is that of the Westminster Assembly: "The souls of believers are, at their death, made perfect in holiness, and do immediately pass into glory;" or as the Church of Ireland expresses it: "After this life is ended, the souls of God's children will be presently received into heaven, there to enjoy unspeakable comforts."

CHAPTER XLIV.

THE RESURRECTION OF LIFE.

THE doctrine of the resurrection has always been offensive to the carnal mind. Infidels and ungodly men seem to manifest peculiar virulence against it. The cause of error on this subject is the same as in our Saviour's day. He said to the Sadducees, who denied it, "ye do err, not knowing the Scriptures, nor the power of God." The Scriptures teach the doctrine. The power of God is unlimited. "Why should it be thought a thing incredible with you, that God should raise the dead?" The history of the faith of God's people on this subject is briefly this. Without repeating what was said of Enoch in a former chapter, it may be stated that *eighteen hundred* and *seventy-two* years before Christ Abraham offered up Isaac. In Hebrews xi. 19, Paul says that the patriarch "accounted that God was able to raise him up, even from the dead, from whence also he received him in a figure." Abraham then believed this doctrine reasonable, and in offering up Isaac was sustained by it.

Job is thought to have lived about *sixteen hundred* and *fifty* years before Christ. His belief of this doctrine has never been disproved, though his statement on the subject has been much carped at and criticised. Yet it remains and shall ever remain firm and clear: "I know that my Redeemer liveth, and that he shall stand at the latter day upon the earth; and though after my skin worms destroy this body, yet in my flesh shall I see God; whom I shall see for myself, and mine eyes shall behold, and not another, though my reins be consumed within me." Job xix. 20—27. All human ingenuity is inadequate to the destruction of the glorious hopes here expressed. Fair and sober criticism rather strengthens than impairs the force of our translation.

About a *hundred* and *one* years later, and in his last sermon to the Israelites, Moses brings in God as saying: "I kill, and I make alive." Deut. xxxii. 39. For many centuries together Jewish writers held that this passage taught the doctrine of the resurrection. There is nothing forced in this construction. What is it to make alive, but to raise from the dead?

About *three hundred* and *ninety* years later, David foretold the resurrection of Christ, saying, "Thou wilt not suffer thy holy One to see corruption." Psa. xvi. 10. We have an inspired exposition of this passage given by the apostle Peter on the day of Pentecost. Acts ii. 27—32. We do therefore know that more than *eleven hundred* years before the Christian era, the resurrection of Christ was predicted.

Still later we find Ezekiel borrowing his splendid imagery from this doctrine, and crying out, "Can these bones live?" We also find Daniel plainly declaring it: "Many of them that sleep in the dust of the earth shall awake, some to everlasting life, and some to shame and everlasting contempt." Dan. xii. 2.

After the close of the canon of the Old Testament, we find the same doctrine held by the pious Jews, who suffered persecution under Antiochus. Hear some of the words of those seven brethren, whose fame as martyrs will probably last till time shall be no longer. One of them, just about to die, boldly says to the tyrant: "Thou, like a fury, takest us out of this present life, but the King of the world will raise us up, who have suffered for his laws, unto everlasting life." Another, stretching out his hands said: "These I had from heaven, and for His love I despise them, and from Him I hope to receive them again." Another in the awful hour of his sufferings said: "It is good, being put to death by men, to look for hope from God, to be raised up again by him."

That all the Jews, except those loose infidels, the Sadducees, believed this doctrine, none can doubt. When Christ said to the weeping Martha, "Thy brother shall rise again," she replied, "I know that he shall rise again at the last day." So Paul said, "I have hope toward God, which they themselves also allow, that there shall be a resurrection of the dead, both of the just and of the unjust." Acts xxiv. 15. In the 13th article of a creed of fundamental doctrines arranged by that learned Jew, Maimonides, more than a thousand years after Paul's time, are these words: "I believe with a perfect faith, that the dead shall be restored to life, when it shall seem fit to God the Creator." This creed was in general use among Israelites for centuries. Indeed Pocock tells us that in his day the Jews generally used these words at the graves of their friends: "Blessed be the Lord our God, who formed you with judgment, preserved you alive, delivered you up to death, who knows the number of you all, who will raise you up again, who will restore you with judgment. Blessed art thou, O Lord, who givest life to the dead: may the dead live, with my dead body may they rise again."

That the resurrection is a doctrine of the New Testament is very clear. Besides the texts already quoted take the following, uttered by Christ: "In the resurrection they neither marry, nor are given in marriage, but are as the angels of God in heaven." Matt. xxii. 30. "When thou makest a feast, call the poor, the maimed, the lame, the blind; and thou shalt be blessed; for they cannot recompense thee: for thou shalt be recompensed at the resurrection of the just." Luke xiv. 14. Again Christ speaks of "the children of the resurrection," who cannot "die any more." In many other places he says as much.

After the ascension of our Lord, his apostles continually bring up the same subject. One ground of offence to many was that they "preached through Jesus the resurrection from the dead." Acts iv. 2; xvii. 18, 32; xxiv. 21. It will not be denied that Lazarus was raised from the dead. See John xi. 43, 44; nor that several persons arose from the dead about the time of the resurrection of our Saviour. Matt. xxvii. 52, 53. That the resurrection of Christ was true all the apostles were witnesses. Acts i. 22. Indeed no man could be an apostle unless he had seen the Lord after his resurrection. Paul has summed up the whole doctrine in 1 Cor. xv. 12—23, and 35—49. "Now if Christ be preached that he rose from the dead, how say some among you that there is no resurrection of the dead? But if there be no resurrection of the dead, then is Christ not risen: and if Christ be not risen, then is our preaching vain, and your faith is also vain. Yea, and we are found false witnesses of God; because we have testified of God that he raised up Christ; whom he raised not up, if so be that the dead rise not. For if the dead rise not, then is not Christ raised: and if Christ be not raised, your faith is vain; ye are yet in your sins. Then they also which are fallen asleep in Christ are perished. If in this life only we have hope in Christ, we are of all men most miserable. But now is Christ risen from the dead, and become the first-fruits of them that slept. For since by man came death, by man came also the resurrection of the dead. For as in Adam all die, even so in Christ shall all be made alive. But every man in his own order; Christ the first-fruits; afterward they that are Christ's at his coming. * * But some man will say, How are the dead raised up? and with what body do they come? Thou fool, that which thou sowest is not quickened except it die: and that which thou sowest, thou sowest not that body that shall be, but bare grain; it may chance of wheat, or of some other grain: but God giveth it a body as it hath pleased him, and to every seed his own body. All flesh is not the same flesh; but there is one kind of flesh of men, another flesh of beasts, another of fishes, and another of birds. There are also celestial bodies, and bodies terrestrial; but the glory of the celestial is one, and the glory of the terrestrial is another. There is one glory of the sun, and another glory of the moon and another glory of the stars; for one star differeth from another star in glory. So also is the resurrection of the dead. It is sown in corruption, it is raised in incorruption: it is sown in dishonour, it is raised in glory: it is sown in weakness, it is raised in power: it is sown a natural body, it is raised a spiritual body. There is a natural body, and there is a spiritual body. And so it is written, the first man Adam was made a living soul, the last Adam was made a quickening spirit. Howbeit that was not first which is spiritual, but that which is natural, and afterward that which is spiritual. The first man is of the earth, earthy; the second man is the Lord from heaven. As is the earthy, such are they also that are earthy; and as is the heavenly, such are they also that are heavenly. And as we have borne the image of the earthy, we shall also bear the image of the heavenly." From this passage it is clear, 1. That the doctrine of the resurrection is fundamental. Without it preaching is idle and faith is vain. vs. 14, 17. 2. That the resurrection of Christ and that of his people are so connected that he who denies one subverts the other. vs. 12, 13. 3. That this doctrine is very consolatory to the suffering people of God, and nothing can compensate for the want of it. v. 14. 4. That the work of Christ as to his people would manifestly be imperfect if he did not raise them up. vs. 21, 22. 5. That hard questions concerning the resurrection are foolish and have not even the merit of originality. vs. 35, 36. 6. That nature affords us illustrations of many things quite as inexplicable as the resurrection of the dead, yet we do not deny the facts, as in the growth of grain. vs. 36, 37, 38. 7. That it does not at all impair the doctrine of the resurrection that the body we shall then have will be very different from the body we now have. vs. 39—41. 8. That some of the dead shall be raised in more glory than others. vs. 41. 42. 9. That the resurrection body shall be fashioned and formed by the Holy Ghost, and *so* shall be a *spiritual* body. v. 44. 10. The key to the right interpretation of the whole passage is found in the fact that Paul is writing to Christians, and is mainly treating of the *resurrection of the just*, and only incidentally of that of the *unjust*.

The doctrine of the resurrection is incorporated into every summary creed of the early orthodox Christians. The Apostles' Creed says: "I believe in the resurrection of the body." The Aquileian has it: "I believe in the resurrection of the flesh." That of Damascus says: "We believe we shall be raised with the same real members and flesh, in which we now live."

The Christian fathers are no less explicit: Jerome says: "The Catholic faith cannot be maintained, unless it be maintained that a body with flesh and bones, blood and members, be restored." In one place Tertullian calls the resurrection body *carnem angelificatam*—flesh made like that of angels. Elsewhere he says: "The body is the soul's sister and co-heir, and therefore shall share with it in its estate." In remarking on the 98th Psalm, Augustine clearly announces the same to be his belief. Even Origen, who held some crude opinions on the subject, says: "As we retain the same body from infancy to old age, though the characters appear to be much changed, so we ought to understand that the very same species will remain in the life to come, though changed very much for the better." Soon after he says: "The former species shall remain, though it be made more glorious." Again he says: "Is it not absurd, that the body, which bears the scars of wounds received for Christ's sake, and which as well as the soul endured cruel torments in persecutions, and suffered the penalties of bonds and imprisonments, should be deprived of the rewards due to it for so great sufferings? Does it not seem contrary to all reason, that the soul, which did not suffer alone, should be rewarded alone, and its vessel, the body, which served it with so great labour, should obtain no reward?"

We have seen how Jewish martyrs under Antiochus cleaved to this doctrine. Scarcely a *Christian* martyrdom is recorded at any length, which does not show that this doctrine was avowed by those faithful witnesses. About the year 177 the churches of Vienne and Lyons wrote a letter to the churches of Asia and Phrygia, describing their sufferings. This letter is still extant in Eusebius. In it they say, that their "persecutors would not suffer the bodies of the martyrs to be buried, but threw them to the dogs to be devoured, and burnt them to ashes, and then cast their ashes into the river; and this they did, as if they could overcome God, and hinder their resurrection, through belief of which they despised the greatest torments."

Yet this doctrine has always been opposed by wicked men. All the heathen philosophers rejected it. When Paul preached it at Athens, the seat of their most famous schools, "some mocked." Acts xvii. 32. In his Natural History, Pliny numbers it among impossibilities to recall the dead. Celsus calls the doctrine of the resurrection abominable, and insults the people of God as madmen, for believing it. Tertullian says every sect of the philosophers denied it. And Augustine says there was nothing in the Christian religion so vehemently opposed by them, as the doctrine of the resurrection. In every age men of the same mood and temper have hated it, and will do so to the end of time. Nevertheless, "it is a faithful saying, if we be dead with him, we shall also live with him." 2 Tim. ii. 11. By persuading men that there is no resurrection, errorists do but "overthrow their faith." 2 Tim. ii. 18. The real Christian is not to be spoiled through philosophy and vain deceit. He looks at this doctrine as a corner-stone, and knowing its truth he says with Paul, "O death, where is thy sting? O grave, where is thy victory." 1 Cor. xv. 55.

The Scriptures do not represent the resurrection of the wicked as a blessing, though they speak of it as certain. But the resurrection of the righteous is ever a theme of triumph. The resurrection of the wicked is "to shame and everlasting contempt." It is "the resurrection of the unjust." It is "the resurrection of damnation." John v. 29. On the other hand, through the grace of Christ the resurrection of the just is "a better resurrection." It is "the resurrection of life." John v. 29. It is the resurrection "to everlasting life." Dan. xii. 2. It is one of the inestimable blessings of Christ's mediation. To him alone is due all the glory of making a resurrection desirable. He said, "I am the resurrection and the life: he that believeth in me, though he were dead, yet shall he live." John v. 25. And as Jesus was "declared to be the Son of God with power, according to the Spirit of holiness, by the resurrection from the dead," Rom. i. 4; so "if we have been planted together in the likeness of his death, we shall be also in the likeness of his resurrection." Rom. vi. 5. How this doctrine is connected with Christ and with all that is precious in the hopes of believers, Paul declares: "Yea, doubtless, and I count all things but loss for the excellency of the knowledge of Christ Jesus my Lord: for whom I have suffered the loss of all things, and do count them but dung, that I may win Christ, and be found in him, not having mine own righteousness, which is of the law, but that which is through the faith of Christ, the righteousness, which is of God by faith; that I may know him, and the power of his resurrection, and the fellowship of his sufferings, being made conformable unto his death; if by any means I might attain unto the resurrection of the dead." Phil. iii. 8—11. Is it not enough that Jesus went before us, that he is risen from the dead, become the first-fruits of them that slept, and given us infallible assurance that "them that sleep in Jesus will God bring with him?" 1 Thess. iv. 14. So it is all, all through Christ, through Christ alone. Matchless One!!!

CHAPTER XLV.

THE FINAL JUDGMENT.

GOD has not concealed his intention of bringing every work into judgment, with every secret thing, whether it be good, or whether it be evil. From the earliest ages inspired men have freely and clearly spoken of the day of judgment. Enoch, who was the seventh from Adam, and all of whose life on earth, except the last twenty-two years, was cotemporaneous with that of Adam, prophesied, saying, "Behold, the Lord cometh with ten thousand of his saints, to execute judgment upon all, and to convince all that are ungodly among them of their ungodly deeds, which they have ungodly committed, and of all their hard speeches, which ungodly sinners have spoken against them." Three thousand years after Enoch, Jude found no fitter words, by which to warn daring sinners of their coming doom, than those just quoted from the antediluvian prophet. The doctrine of a judgment is a familiar theme among inspired writers of both testaments. It is taught in the law, in the prophets, in the psalms, in the gospels, and in the epistles. It was so well understood in the days of Christ and of Paul, that they simply call it "*that day*," thus designating it as the day of days, "the day for which all other days were made," and in comparison of which all other days are as nothing.

33

The day of judgment will be *the great day*. So inspired writers often and properly style it. It will exceed all other days for the brightness of its beginning. Other days had their dim twilight, but this will begin in ineffable effulgence. Their light was from the sun; the light of this shall be from Him who made all things. Other days dawn with general quiet, but this shall begin with great and unusual noises. "Our God shall come, and shall not keep silence; a fire shall devour before him, and it shall be very tempestuous round about him. He shall call to the heavens from above, and to the earth, that he may judge his people." Jesus shall come in like manner as he went up on high. "The Lord himself shall descend from heaven with a shout, with the voice of the archangel, and with the trump of God." On that day men will see sights, and hear sounds, unlike all that ever struck their senses before. The brightness of Immanuel's coming will extinguish the light of the heavenly bodies, and the sounds, which shall be heard, shall make the earth reel and stagger like a drunken man. This day will be crowded full of wonders. It will be begun, carried on, and closed with such displays of miracles as the world has never seen before. The results accomplished by it will be as wonderful as the progress of its events. Every way of God to man shall then be justified. All wickedness shall be put down. All cavil shall be for ever silenced. All judgment shall then be executed.

In speaking of the day of judgment and perdition of ungodly men, Peter says, "One day is with the Lord as a thousand years, and a thousand years as one day." From this some infer that the judgment-day will last a thousand years. This may be a mistaken conclusion, but that day will last long enough to answer all the purposes of a careful and universal scrutiny of human actions and characters. If this day be not a *long day*, it will be because God will, by his infinite perfections, make a few hours answer all the ends of a portion of duration equal to many generations. He can vindicate his ways, acquit the innocent, condemn the guilty, and show that he is just in saving sinners, without any of those slow processes to which human tribunals are subject. Yet there is a general impression that the day of judgment will commence at midnight, and last beyond what would be the limits of a day of our time. The word *day* in Scripture often designates a period much longer than *twenty-four* hours. The day of judgment will last long enough to answer all the ends of God in appointing it, and this is enough for us to *know*. The rest is open to conjecture.

The day of judgment is a day *fixed*. The time for it is set by God himself. "He hath *appointed* a day, in the which he will judge the world in righteousness, by that man whom he hath ordained." To God that day is known, to us it is unknown; to him it is certain, to us it is doubtful. "Of that day and hour knoweth no man, no, not the angels of heaven, but my Father only." It will come as a thief in the night, as the flood came on the old world, as the tempest of wrath came on the cities of the plain; yet it is unchangeably determined by God. Men may not be looking for it, but God sees it afar off. As nothing can hasten it, so that it shall come before God's purposes respecting the world are accomplished, so nothing can delay it one moment beyond the time fixed in God's eternal counsels for its coming.

Frequently the day of judgment is called "the day of the Lord." It will be the day when the Lord Christ shall appear in glory, display the wonders of his mediation and the perfection of his government, and will publicly be owned and crowned as Lord of all. There will be no disputes concerning the divinity of Christ, on or after the day of judgment, which will be *his* day. If the power that shall work, if the majesty that shall preside, if the knowledge that shall determine, if the justice that shall condemn, if the mercy that shall spare on that day be not divine, and convincingly so, it will be of no use to try to learn what is so. "The Father judgeth no man, but has committed all judgment to the Son." That day will be the day of the Lord Jesus.

The day of judgment will be above all others a *day of convocation*. The heavens and the earth shall furnish the assembly. The chariots of God, which are twenty thousand, shall roll down the skies, bearing in them ten thousand times ten thousand, an innumerable company of angels. Fallen angels too shall be there; and them that sleep in Jesus shall God bring with him. All that died in their sins shall be there; and all that are alive on the earth shall stand before God. Not one of all God's rational creatures shall be missing. Prophets, apostles, martyrs, confessors, saints, sinners, liars, hypocrites, infidels, blasphemers, haters of God, shall all be present. The assizes of the universe shall then be held. Millions on millions shall crowd this greatest of all congregations. "We must all appear before the judgment-seat of Christ." This will be the first and the last gathering of all the denizens of the universe.

The day of judgment will be one of *unparalleled excitement.* There will be no listless spectators of those scenes. Men have fallen asleep at a marriage, at a funeral, in the house of God, and in the chamber of the dying. But none will slumber when they shall see a world wrapped in flames, a universe convened for judgment, and the Judge on the great white throne. Every eye shall see, every ear shall attend to Him, who utters the words, "Come, ye blessed," "Depart, ye cursed." Every faculty of intelligence and of feeling will that day be roused to the highest exercises of which it is capable. Dreams, fancies, whims and wandering thoughts attend men in this life, but in that day all will be eagerness, thought, excitement.

The day of judgment will also be a day of *great surprise,* both to saints and sinners. So Christ expressly informs us: "Then shall the righteous answer him, saying, Lord, when saw we thee an hungered, and fed thee? or thirsty, and gave thee drink? When saw we thee a stranger, and took thee in? or naked, and clothed thee? Or, when saw we thee sick, or in prison, and came unto thee?" In like manner also shall the wicked say unto him, "Lord, when saw we thee an hungered, or athirst, or a stranger, or naked, or sick, or in prison, and did not minister unto thee?" If the sentences of the just and unjust were reversed at the day of judgment, the surprise would not be half so great. Jesus said: "Many will say unto me in that day, Lord, Lord, have we not prophesied in thy name? and in thy name have cast out devils? and in thy name done many wonderful works? And then will I profess unto them, I never knew you; depart from me, ye that work iniquity." Many will be saved, and many will be lost contrary to the judgments formed of them by their neighbours. But more will be saved, and more will be lost contrary to the opinions they had of themselves. Christians will wonder *that* they are saved, and *how* they are saved, and they will wonder that they should be commended for deeds full of imperfection. The wicked will be amazed *that* they are lost, and *how* they are lost, and especially that God puts no value upon their self-righteousness. The sons of God will receive more honour than they ever thought of claiming; while the wicked will find their hopes perishing one by one, and their lamp going out in obscure darkness. Christians will wonder why they *should* be saved. Sinners will wonder why they should *not* be saved. The latter will ask, "What have *we* done?" The former will say, "What have we *not* done?" The sinner says he does the best he can. The righteous says, "Behold, I am vile."

Many doubts, mysteries and perplexities will be fully and for ever removed in that great day. Things, which in this life were full of grievous darkness, will be then satisfactorily cleared up. God's providence, which is now accompanied by a thousand inexplicable things, will then be made plain. Now the wicked are exalted; then they shall be brought down to hell. Now the righteous are forsaken, afflicted, tormented; then the Lord will bring forth their righteousness as the light, and their judgment as the noonday. That day will wipe off all aspersions from the innocent, and fix guilt where it belongs, though never suspected before. God's truth, wisdom, holiness, justice, and mercy will shine brighter than the sun on that day. The slandered, injured and abused will then be vindicated; and the oppressed will rise up and clank the chains, with which tyrants had bound them, to the eternal confusion of wrong-doers. Many a righteous man, judicially murdered, will then face his corrupt judge with the suborned witnesses and perjured jurors who were at his trial. There will be a wonderful clearing up on that day.

It will also be a day of *exposure.* "Some men's sins are open beforehand, going before to judgment, and some they follow after." The fraud, cunning, hypocrisy, and deceit of wicked men will then appear. All those dark designs and plots, which meditated ruin to individuals, distress to families, perplexity to nations, or dishonour to God, shall be held up to reprobation. The light of that day will shine through and through the thickest web of iniquity, and show all its foul intricacies.

This will also be a day of *decision.* In this world appeals are often taken from lower to higher courts, from the judgment of cotemporaries to that of posterity, and from the judgment of man to that of God. But the tribunal of Christ is the court of the last resort. From his decision there lies no appeal. On that day, causes and destinies will not merely be inquired into; they will be *decided.* Thenceforward for ever, the law will be, "He that is unjust, let him be unjust still; and he which is filthy, let him be filthy still; and he that is righteous, let him be righteous still; and he that is holy, let him be holy still." Nothing can reverse, nor arrest the judgments of that day. Nothing can alter or vary the decree of the

Judge. It shall stand for ever. The judgment of the great day is called the "eternal judgment," because it will be irrevocable and everlasting in its effects. It will bind for ever.

The day of judgment will also be a day of *separations.* Here saints and sinners are strangely mixed together. There it will be very different. Christ says: "Let both tares and wheat grow together until the harvest; and in the time of harvest, I will say to the reapers, Gather ye together first the tares, and bind them in bundles to burn them; but gather the wheat into my barn." "When the Son of Man shall come in his glory, and all his holy angels with him, then shall he sit upon the throne of his glory: and before him shall be gathered all nations: and he shall separate them one from another, as a shepherd divideth his sheep from the goats; and he shall set the sheep on his right hand, but the goats on his left." This separation shall be final. The righteous and the wicked shall that day part to meet no more.

To Christ, his saints and angels, the day of judgment will be a day of *triumph.* The Lord will then make a show of his enemies openly. They that would not kiss the Son, shall be dashed in pieces like a potter's vessel. In his triumph, all his saints and angels shall share and glory.

To the wicked the same day will be full of *despair.* They will cry to the rocks and to the mountains: "Fall on us and cover us from the face of him that sitteth on the throne, and from the wrath of the Lamb; for the great day of his wrath is come, and who shall be able to stand?" Was more dreadful despair ever portrayed?

The day of judgment will be the *last day*. So Christ calls it. So inspired writers often teach. After it, "time shall be no longer." No more shall duration be measured by the alternations of day and night, or of the seasons; and there shall be no succession of seconds, minutes, hours, days, months, or years as now. All beyond the judgment-day is boundless, fathomless eternity. This last day will leave an ineffaceable impression on all minds. None will ever forget what they shall have seen, and heard, and felt on that day. The great days of earth may fade from the memories of saints and sinners, but this *last* great day shall never, never, never perish from the recollection of any.

It may well be doubted whether any man thinks as much as he should of the judgment-day. Justin Martyr said, "I seem always to be hearing these words: Awake ye dead and come to judgment." A modern writer speaking of the same day says: "It would seem as if Christ was always thinking of it. How frequently he speaks of it, and never but with the deepest solemnity." The apostles seem to have had everything associated with it.

"Seeing then that all these things shall be dissolved, what manner of persons ought ye to be in all holy conversation and godliness, looking for and hasting unto the coming of the day of God, wherein the heavens being on fire shall be dissolved, and the elements shall melt with fervent heat."

Reader, are you prepared for your last account? Have you made peace with God through our Lord Jesus Christ? Is all your hope in the precious blood and righteousness of Jesus Christ? Nothing of your own can save you in that day. It will burn as an oven. It will try your works and your hopes as by fire. If you have built on Christ, and on him only, then hold fast your confidence, which hath great recompense of reward.

But if you are yet in your sins, then be persuaded to "flee for refuge to the hope set before you in the gospel." "He that believeth on the Son hath everlasting life; and he that believeth not the Son shall not see life, but the wrath of God abideth on him." Nor can you be in too much haste, or too much in earnest, in this weighty matter. It is your life. "Behold, the Judge standeth before the door." And he says: "Behold, I come quickly, and my reward is with me, to give every man according to his work."

If you are out of Christ, you are unreconciled to God. There are three classes of controversy. The first is where neither party has done any wrong, but the whole contest has arisen from mistake. In this case, all that is required to settle the difficulty is light and explanation. This is not the nature of God's controversy with us. We may have, yea, we doubtless have often misapprehended his character, and will, and rights; but when we have understood them, we were more than ever averse to them. And God had never misunderstood us. He knows that we cordially hate him. Reconciliation by explanation is here impossible. A second kind of controversy is where both parties have done wrong, and of course both have suffered wrong. Here must be *mutual* acknowledgment, concession and reparation. But God has never wronged us. He has never demanded too much. He has never been a hard master. His precepts concerning all things are right, and every just man thinks so, and says so. We can never be reconciled in this way. The third kind of controversy is where all the fault and blame are on one side, the other party having been wholly innocent and fully right in every particular. This is the nature of God's controversy with us. We have sinned much, long, wantonly, stubbornly, heinously. We are all dead men, dead in trespasses and sins. If we wash ourselves with snow-water, and make us never so clean, yet he will plunge us in the ditch, and our own clothes shall abhor us. All our righteousnesses are as filthy rags. "God be merciful to me a sinner," is always an appropriate prayer.

Salvation by grace is every way suited to your case. You are a criminal. I have heard of one, who had broken the law. His soul was guilty. His fears went like iron into his soul. He was arrested and held "in strong prison." His case grew darker every day. No way of escape seemed possible. The day of trial came. The testimony was clear. There was no room for fair argument in his favour. The verdict was, "Guilty." The sentence followed. The day of execution came. He was led forth in chains. His spirit was crushed. Dry sorrow had drunk up his blood and spirits; not a tear did he shed. The green fields, the blue heavens, the hoary mountains, and the crystal streams had all faded from his mind. He thought as though he thought not. Some said he was hardened, some thought his mind wandered. All pitied him but himself. He said his sentence was just.

At that moment a cry was heard, "Open the way, and let the officer of the government pass." An avenue is cleared, and as soon closes. With quick step the new-comer ascends the scaffold, and hands the sheriff a paper duly signed and sealed. It is a pardon. In a proper way the sheriff reads to the guilty man his release from the penalty. His tears begin to flow, he utters a few broken sentences, his bosom heaves, it seems to him like a dream, he fears there is some mistake, he looks at the signature and seal. Surprise, gratitude, and abundant tears of joy mark the man who seemed just now to be past feeling. He is alive again. The sun shines in beauty, and nature seems to rejoice all around him.

But how came that pardon? It was obtained at the intercession of one whom he had always avoided and often contemned. Can he slight him again? No; he will search till he finds him, he will confess his past errors, he will express his thanks not once, but a thousand times. He will speak lightly of him no more. He will rise at midnight to serve him.

So is the case of the sinner saved by the blood, and righteousness, and intercession of Christ. He admires the Saviour. He calls him Lord. His heart melts whenever he thinks of his goodness towards him. His gratitude begets obedience, and he knows no Redeemer but one. He owns none else, he desires none else. Thus "the goodness of God leadeth to repentance."

There are some things of unparalleled interest in this final judgment. One is the glory which shall then be revealed in us. "In this life God treats and acknowledges us as his children, he clothes us with the righteousness of his Son, feeds us with his word, defends us from our spiritual enemies; but the most public declaration of his favour shall be in the next life, when all 'the children of the resurrection' shall be born in a day. Add further, although the souls of believers immediately upon their separation are received into heaven, and during the sleep of death enjoy admirable visions of glory; yet their blessedness is imperfect, in comparison of that excellent degree, which shall be enjoyed at the resurrection. As the Roman generals, after a complete conquest, first entered the city privately, and having obtained license of the Senate, made their triumphant entry with all the magnificence and splendour becoming the greatness of their victories: so after a faithful Christian 'hath fought the good fight,' and is come off 'more than a conqueror,' he enters privately the celestial city; but when the body is raised to immortality, he shall then, in the company and with the acclamations of the holy angels, have a glorious entry into it."

Another matter of interest in that day will be the display of mercy and grace then made. So Paul teaches: "The Lord give mercy unto the house of Onesiphorus; for he oft refreshed me, and was not ashamed of my chain; but, when he was in Rome, he sought me out very diligently, and found me. The Lord grant unto him that he may find mercy of the Lord IN THAT DAY." There will indeed be wonderful exhibitions of justice, terrible manifestations of wrath, but stupendous displays of mercy. Who of us will not then need mercy?

To some minds the greatest wonder of the last day will be the composure and calmness with which that day will be met by the righteous. John says, "Our love is made perfect, that we may have boldness in the day of judgment." I never should have thought of boldness at such a time, but that I find it in God's word. It is attained by love to Him, who on that day will be our advocate, the Lord our righteousness.

CHAPTER XLVI.

ETERNAL GLORY.

THE Judgment shall be immediately succeeded by amazing bliss and glory. In this heavenly happiness the entire persons of the saints shall partake. This is the hope, the desire and the inheritance of all true Christians. They are heirs of salvation, heirs according to the hope of eternal life, heirs according to the promise, heirs of righteousness by faith, heirs of the grace of life, heirs of the kingdom, heirs of God and joint-heirs with Jesus Christ. The indwelling of the Holy Ghost is "the earnest of our inheritance." Present sufferings for Christ's sake are sure pledges of our winning the kingdom. "If we suffer with him, we shall also reign with him." Our calling to be saints is a token of our share in coming glory. "God hath called us to his kingdom and glory." Our conformity to God is a sign that cannot be mistaken. "The Father hath made us meet to be partakers of the inheritance of the saints in light." Our justification proves the same. "They which receive abundance of grace and of the gift of righteousness, shall reign in life by Jesus Christ." The Lord Jesus has so ordained. "I appoint unto you a kingdom, even as my Father hath appointed unto me; that ye may eat and drink at my table in my kingdom." They inherit everlasting life, a kingdom prepared for them from the foundation of the world. "He that overcometh shall inherit all things, and I will make him my son."

There is a very pleasing variety in the modes of presenting heavenly things to our conceptions. At one time in view of the greatness of the way heaven is called a rest. Again it is styled a crown, a kingdom, an inheritance, glory, honour, immortality, eternal life, a house not made with hands, our Father's house, an heavenly temple, Mount Zion, the new heavens, the new Jerusalem. By selecting a great variety of the best and most excellent things known on earth, and yet showing no steadfast attachment to any one form of speech, the inspired writers leave us to infer that their clearest representations are but faint emblems of celestial bliss. Indeed they seem at a great loss for words to express their own conceptions on the subject. What two things are more unlike than gold and pure glass? One is transparent, the other opaque. One is colourless, the other yellow. One is brittle, the other may be hammered to the thinnest leaf. One is a human fabric, the other cannot be made by man. And yet John says, "The city was pure gold, like unto clear glass." Indeed, "eye hath not seen, nor ear heard, neither have entered into the heart of man, the things which God hath prepared for them that love him." Two persons admitted within the walls of the celestial city have returned to dwell on earth. One was Lazarus of Bethany, the brother of Mary and Martha. Whether he ever told his friends anything of what he had seen and heard in the invisible world, we have no means of knowing. Tradition says that after his return to life he never seemed deeply interested in worldly affairs, and ascribes this change in him to the visions of glory, which he had enjoyed. The other was Paul, who was caught up into Paradise, into the third heavens. Yet his account is short and chiefly negative: "I heard unspeakable words, which it is not lawful for a man to utter." This is his whole narrative. Angels have often visited our world, but even when they have assumed a human form and conversed with men, none of them ever attempted a description of the world of light, from which they came. Inspired men sometimes speak on the subject, but commonly in language highly figurative. Thus John tells us that the walls of the celestial city are fifteen hundred miles on each of its four sides, and as high as they are long. Is he giving us the exact dimensions of the great capital of God's dominions? or does he merely design to convey to our minds conceptions of vastness and magnificence quite beyond the scale of anything known on earth? John says expressly, "It doth not yet appear what we shall be." Paul also says: "We know in part, and we prophesy in part. But when that which is perfect is come, then that which is in part shall be done away. When I was a child I spake as a child, I understood as a child, I thought as a child; but when I became a man, I put away childish things. For now we see through a glass darkly; but then face to face; now I know in part; but then shall I know even as I am known." 1 Cor. xiii. 9—12. The saints in light probably in an hour gain more just and adequate and satisfying knowledge of that upper world, than the ablest divines have acquired in a long life-time of reading and meditation. As carnal men have very vague and erroneous conceptions of what it is to be born again, so the best men on earth know but little of what it is to be born intc glory.

To prepare for this eternal glory is the great business of life. Nothing is wiser than to make everything subordinate to the attainment of a crown of righteousness. To have the least fitness for heaven is an unspeakable blessing; and "to be rich in grace is the sure pledge that we shall be rich in glory." Indeed glory is grace completed, crowned, triumphant. There vast and accurate knowledge shall feed the immortal mind. "We shall know even as we are known." "The works and government of God will ever afford themes of inquiry, reflection and wonder." Under infallible guidance the mind of man can make hitherto unthought-of advances in knowledge.

The heavenly world is full of love, not of idle pretences and hollow professions, but of pure, holy affections. If in this world all men were as benevolent and condescending as some are, how happy men would be! Yet in the best of men on earth love is imperfect. Not so in heaven. There God, who is Love, reigns for ever. There Christ, who is full of divine compassion and gentleness, sits on the Mediatorial throne. There the love of the Spirit warms all hearts. The Seraphim are burning ones, because their natures are all on fire with pure, kind, grateful, complacential and benevolent affections. There the spirits of just men are made perfect in love. There is no lack of friendship in that exalted society. The company is select, being made up of God's elect. The whole body of the redeemed are there publicly married to Christ. The great attraction of heaven is the glorified person of Jesus Christ. "The Lamb is the light thereof."

"We shall be ever with the Lord." "He that sitteth on the throne shall dwell among them." Even in this world Christ is the delight of the sons of men. In viewing his character and love that great patriot and preacher, John Welch, exclaimed: "O love of love! O the height, and the depth, and the breadth, and the length of that love of thine, which passeth knowledge! O uncreated love! Beginning without beginning, and ending without end! Thou art my glory, my joy, my gain, my crown. Thou hast set me under thy shadow with great delight, and thy fruit is sweet to my taste. Thou hast brought me into thy banqueting-house, and placed me in thy orchard. Stay me with thy flagons, and comfort me with thine apples: for I am sick, and my soul is wounded with thy love." If such elevations of the affections can be attained here, what will not heavenly love be?

Heaven is also the abode of joy. "Well done, good and faithful servant, enter thou into the joy of thy Lord." It is called the joy of the Lord, because the Lord has prepared our bliss for us, and because he himself is the object chiefly enjoyed. "In thy presence is fulness of joy, and at thy right hand are pleasures for evermore." Here our greatest joys are short-lived, imperfect and unsatisfying. Nothing continues. All is unsettled and easily marred. There all is stable as eternity. Here ills in armies beset us. There sorrows cease, sickness, sadness and sighing flee away, bereavement never desolates, tears never flow, tempests never rage, temptations never vex, want, war, and death never enter, rust never corrupts, thieves never steal, days of weariness and nights of vanity are for ever unknown, sin never defiles, and peace reigns unbroken. There "the wicked cease from troubling, and the weary are at rest." "There is no darkness there; for the Lord God giveth them light, and the Lamb is the light thereof." The people that dwell there shall be forgiven their iniquity. They shall hunger no more, neither thirst any more. There are no discords, tumults, or enmities there. The employments never fatigue, never disgust, are never drivelling. Satiety is unknown. There is no dulness among the redeemed. The cruel mockings of earth shall be followed by kind congratulations and songs of deliverance. The eternal anthem is, "Unto him that loved us, and washed us from our sins in his own blood, and hath made us kings and priests unto God and his Father; to him be glory and dominion for ever and ever. Amen." If we are believers, heaven is just before us. "It is strange that a subject of grace should be so reluctant to become a subject of glory." Who would not wish to

> "Burst from the thraldom of encumbering clay,
> And spring to liberty, and light, and life?"

The most difficult part of salvation is at the first; but the most fruitful part of salvation is at the last. The choicest portion of every Christian's existence is before him. Nature is inferior to grace, and nature and grace are both inferior to glory. "The sons of God have much in hand and more in hope." The sights seen, the sounds heard, and the emotions felt in heaven are peculiar to that blessed abode; and all is durable as the throne of God. All flows from the bounty of an infinite God and Saviour. The grace of Christ in heaven displays its richest fruits to the rapturous gaze and boundless admiration of all holy creatures.

Could we but believe what God has spoken on this blessed theme, we might each say:

> "Farewell, vain world; my soul can bid adieu;
> My Saviour taught me to abandon you.
> Your charms may gratify a sensual mind,
> But cannot please a soul for God inclined.
> Forbear t' entice, cease then my soul to call:
> 'Tis fixed through grace; my God shall be my ALL.
> While he thus lets me heavenly glories view,
> Your beauties fade, my heart 's no room for you."

The alleluiahs of the hosts above are as the sound of many waters and of mighty thunderings. Their songs are of victory. They all have palms in their hands and are harping with their harps.

How near heaven may be none on earth can tell. The hill of Zion, the mount of God, the temple not made with hands, are often hard by, when we think them far distant. At all times we may say to God's people, "Now is your salvation nearer than when ye believed." Many of the saints daily arrive at their long sought home. The doves will all find their windows. "To be content to stay always in this world is above the obedience of angels." In all ages the saints have longed and fainted for an entrance into the upper sanctuary. Often have they cried, "O Lord, how long?" The prayer of one long since gathered to his people, well suits multitudes: "Lord, gather me with thy flock: they are fast a-gathering; the church's Head is gone; he has left the earth and entered into his glory; my brethren and friends many of them have arrived where he is; I am yet behind. O how great is the difference between my state and theirs. I am groaning out my complaint; they are singing God's praise; I sit in darkness and cannot see thy face, but they behold thee face to face. O should I be satisfied to stay behind, when my friends are gone? Shall I wander here in a hungry desert, when they are triumphing above, and dividing the spoils?" Let men think much of heavenly glory. Let them seek that city, which hath foundations, whose Maker and Builder is God. "He, who seldom thinks of heaven, is not likely to get there. The only sure way to hit the mark is to keep the eye steadily fixed upon it." Men go not to that blessed land without desiring it, intending it, forsaking all for it. If you love not to think of heaven, while you live, you will not love to be in heaven when you die. It is not wicked to long for the day when we shall enter into rest, provided there be no self-will or impatience indulged. How can it be sinful for us to wish to see the Lord?

Would you make sure of heaven? Make sure of an interest in Christ by faith. Would you be a partaker of his glory, then accept his grace. The celestial gates will be open to all such as are by God's Spirit fitted for the joys of paradise. None can be thus prepared but such as know Jesus Christ, and the power of his resurrection, who have made a covenant with him by sacrifice, and fled to him for refuge. JESUS CHRIST IS THE WAY, THE TRUTH, AND THE LIFE.

CHAPTER XLVII.

ALL HONOUR IS DUE TO CHRIST.

If these things be so, then we should study to magnify Christ, both in life and in death. He is *the* Saviour; and *such* a Saviour! He is mighty to redeem and strong to deliver. The law came by Moses, but grace and truth by Jesus Christ. He counted it not robbery to be equal with God, yet made himself of no reputation. It is therefore just that he should have a name above every name: that at the name of Jesus every knee should bow, of things in heaven, and things in earth, and things under the earth; and that every tongue should confess that Jesus Christ is Lord, to the glory of God the Father. He lays his hand upon both God and man. He has at once an almighty arm and a brother's heart. None is more exalted, yet none stoops so low. None is mightier, yet none is more tender. He shall not break the bruised reed, nor quench the smoking flax. He shall not fail, nor be discouraged, till he set judgment in the earth. He shall drink of the brook in the way; therefore shall he lift up the head. He is meek and lowly, merciful and mild; at the same time he is *the Son of God with power*. There is none like Jesus. Our Beloved is more than any other beloved. He alone can do sinners good. His blood atones. His obedience to the precept of the law is a perfect righteousness. His intercession is all prevalent and unspeakably glorious. This part of his work is still going on. It is a perpetual fruit of his love. We are deeply interested in it. Gurnall says: "Suppose a king's son should get out of a besieged city, and leave behind his wife and children, whom he loves as his own soul; would this prince, when arrived at his father's palace, delight himself with the splendour of the court, and forget his family in distress? No; he would come post to his father, and entreat him, as ever he loved him, that he would send all the force of his kingdom to raise the siege, and save his dear relations from perishing. Nor will Christ, though gone up from the world, and ascended into his glory, forget his children for a moment, that are left behind him." He ever liveth to make intercession for them. Him the Father heareth alway.

He is Prophet, Priest and King. He is made of God unto us wisdom, righteousness, sanctification and redemption. By his Spirit he enlightens, purifies and comforts the heart. His word cannot be broken. His power cannot be resisted. The law of heavenly kindness is in his heart. The covenant of his peace shall stand. Great is his faithfulness. He is both God and man. Some one has said: "A mere man, by himself alone, could as little redeem a world as he could create one; and though God by himself alone can doubtless create, uphold and govern the world; yet, in order to redeem it, the union of the two divided parts is necessary, and a voluntary satisfaction for sin is required, which he alone can make, who at the same time stands *above* the law and *under* the law." Who could see any fitness in a Saviour, who was not both God and man in one person for ever? Such an one is our Lord Jesus Christ. One of the ancients thought that he had been made solely for the purpose of admiring the sun. But, believing soul, thou hast been made a Christian, that thou mightest admire Christ. His name is Wonderful. I cannot tell thee in what he is most excellent. "I find no fault in him," in either of his offices, or in either of his natures, in his work, or in his sufferings, in his humiliation, or in his exaltation. In him dwell all excellencies, human and divine. He is full of grace and truth. His glory is that of the only-begotten of the Father. There is none like him, no, not one. He is the chiefest among ten thousand and altogether lovely. As the apple-tree among the trees of the wood, so is our Beloved among the sons of men. Wherever he is there is heaven. Redemption by his blood, salvation by his grace will justly be celebrated for ever. It should be highly and often spoken of in the church militant. This theme will be ever welcome to the holy, because it is infinite, and because it will ever be developing new wonders and glories. In the conduct of some of his professed people nothing is more incongruous, nothing awakens such doubts of their interest in his salvation, as their want of sentiments of glowing love to him and to his cause. By him alone can bond or free, Jew or Gentile, Greek or barbarian be saved. For such kindness as his it does not suffice that thankfulness be owned as a duty. If Christ had merely cherished some secret pity for us, and never expressed it, silence on our part would not be so bad. But he loved us openly. He loved us unto death. Never attempt to divide the honours which are due to him alone. Angels are indeed sent forth to minister to them, who shall be heirs of salvation, but they are not our saviours. The *instrument* of our salvation man may be, but God alone is its *Author*. Beware of sacrificing to your own net, and burning incense to your own drag. Left to yourself, you are neither wise, nor strong, nor prudent, nor holy, nor diligent, nor safe.

Praise and magnify the Lord Jesus Christ, for of him, and from him, and by him, and through him, and to him are all things. Praise him on the Sabbath, for since his resurrection it is "the Lord's day." Praise him the whole week, for his mercies flow down continually. Praise him at night, for his goodness runs through the day. Praise him in the morning, for those who seek him early shall find him. Praise him at midnight, for at that hour David gave thanks. Praise him seven times a-day, for every day he fills you with food and gladness. Praise him in sickness and in health, in joy and in sorrow, in life and in death. Crown him with songs, for he crowns the year with his goodness. Let his praise be continually in your mouth. Praise him the more when others maintain silence, or murmur against him, and blaspheme his holy name. Let their failure to do their duty arouse you to do yours. Whoever is found among the impious or profane, do you be numbered with the grateful. Would you make your burdens light? Extol the Son of God. That night cannot be very dark, in which he "giveth songs." Who would not magnify and honour such a Saviour? His works of creation praise him, and shall not his works of redemption bless him? His angels, his hosts, the sun and moon, the stars of light, the heaven of heavens, the water above the heavens, the dragons and all deeps, fire and hail, snowy vapours, stormy wind fulfilling his word, mountains and all hills, fruitful trees and all cedars, beasts and all cattle, creeping things and flying fowl, do praise him. Their voice is gone out to the ends of the world. Shall these all in their way praise him, and shall his people keep silence? Saints owe him a debt of gratitude for existence, for reason, for immortality; but for his grace they owe him a song that should never end. To say nothing against him at the best evinces a very low grade of virtue. To have a disposition to praise him and to suppress it is not enough. Let the feeling be indulged, let the song be sung, let the shout be uttered. Let all the saints cry, Hosanna to the Son of David, let them laud him saying, Alleluiah. He that hath a praising heart hath a continual feast. Praise him in the highest.

If saved, this shall be our work when the sun and moon shall be gone for ever. In the temple above they sing a new song, saying, Thou art worthy: for thou wast slain, and hast redeemed us to God by thy blood out of every kindred, and tongue, and people, and nation; and hast made us unto our God kings and priests. "And I beheld," says one who saw, "and I heard the voice of many angels round about the throne, and the beasts, and the elders; and the number of them was ten thousand times ten thousand, and thousands of thousands: saying with a loud voice, Worthy is the Lamb that was slain to receive power, and riches, and wisdom, and strength, and honour, and glory, and blessing. And every creature, which is in heaven, and on the earth, and under the earth, and such as are in the sea, and all that are in them, heard I saying, Blessing, and honour, and glory, and power, be unto him that sitteth upon the throne, and unto the Lamb for ever and ever. And the four beasts said, Amen. And the four and twenty elders fell down and worshipped him that liveth for ever and ever." Who, who would not join this grandest chorus of the universe? If creation praises its Maker, shall not the new creation magnify its Author? He is the Alpha and the Omega, the First and the Last, the Author and Finisher of our faith. He is Christ the Lord. Jehovah says: "Whoso offereth praise glorifieth me." Often does he bind us by the most solemn commands to do this duty. Hear his words: "Give unto the Lord, ye kindreds of the people, give unto the Lord glory and strength." "Give unto the Lord the glory due unto his name: come before him, worship the Lord in the beauty of holiness." "Ye that fear the Lord praise him; all the seed of Jacob glorify him." These are but samples of his authoritative teachings. In accordance with them let us ever say, "Not unto us, O Lord, not unto us, but unto thy name give glory, for thy mercy and for thy truth's sake." "Unto him be glory in the Church by Jesus Christ, throughout all ages, world without end." "To God only wise be glory, through Jesus Christ, for ever. Amen." Let us not be offended at doxologies to Christ. None but his enemies dislike to hear him praised by hosannas in the highest. "When the chief-priests and scribes saw the wonderful things that he did, and the children crying in the temple, saying, Hosanna to the Son of David, they were sore displeased." Matt. xxi. 11, 15. Be not like these surly old hypocrites, but like those little children out of whose mouths he perfected praise. Do as Pliny says the early Christians did, and "sing a hymn to Jesus Christ as God," as your Saviour and your eternal portion.

CHAPTER XLVIII.

CHRISTIANS LONG TO SEE CHRIST.

SINNERS, saved by the grace of our Lord Jesus Christ, greatly love his person, and long to see him, and to be filled with his fulness. He that has seen the Son, has seen the Father. He is the brightness of the Father's glory, and the express image of his person. Yet his divinity is so veiled by his flesh that we fear not to come near him. Formerly many denied the proper humanity of Christ, but now the attack is against his divinity. Both are fundamental. If he is not the true God, he is not eternal life. His humanity makes him most approachable.

> Till God in human flesh I see,
> My thoughts no comfort find;
> The holy, just and sacred Three
> Are terrors to my mind.

Jesus is the source of all hope, and joy, and peace, and life, and comfort to the pious. Therefore they love him, and long to be with him, that they may behold his glory, which he had with the Father before the world was.

In this life the saints look to the Saviour by faith; in the next they behold him by immediate vision. Here they see him through a glass darkly; there they see him face to face. The stronger their faith, the clearer the view they here have of him. Sometimes a sight of him even through a glass, is wonderful, and makes the soul like the chariots of Amminadib. Such a sight has often made God's people welcome whips, and chains, and dungeons, and death. But the vision of him in the next world will transcend all human conceptions. There he is not only glorious as on the mount of transfiguration; but he is as gentle, as kind, as tender as when he wept at the grave of Lazarus, gave eyes to the blind, and feet to the lame, or granted mercy to a wretch hanging by his side. True, he weeps no more, but his present kindness soothes every sorrow in the hearts of his "hidden ones." Yea, his hand wipes all tears from their faces. Even the old disciple who groaned out his sixty years on earth, and the little infant redeemed by his blood, though it wept out its week of life, shall sigh no more for ever. His glory and his tenderness expel all sadness, bar all sorrows.

Here his people behold him in their closets. While they sit alone and keep silence, he speaks comfortably to them, he puts in his hand by the hole of the door. Jesus reveals himself to those who love secret devotion. He visits where his flocks rest at noon. Would you have clear views of Jesus? Lay aside your worldliness, enter into your chamber, and shut your door about you. If you but mingle with the crowd, you may look in vain for soul-transforming views of the Redeemer. Blessed Saviour, why is my heart so slow to seek thee in solitude? "While the King sitteth at his table, my spikenard sendeth forth the smell thereof." I must seek him more. I will hearken unto him, and walk in his ways; then he will soon subdue my enemies, then shall he feed me with the finest of the wheat, and with honey out of the rock shall he satisfy me. Lord, increase my faith.

It is also well to ascend the mount of ordinances, that we may see him in his beauty and glory. There he is held in his galleries. There he often manifests himself in the breaking of bread. In the songs of Zion, in public prayers, in gospel preaching, how gloriously does Christ often come and make his abode with his people, and fill their hearts with joy and peace! "Blessed are they that dwell in thy house; they will be still praising thee. * * A day in thy courts is better than a thousand. I had rather be a door-keeper in the house of my God, than to dwell in the tents of wickedness." Often do his saints go down from his house, satisfied as with marrow and fatness, when some word in season, borne to their hearts by the blessed Spirit, has been spoken by the servant of Christ.

Many get pleasant views of Christ in the valley of humiliation, which flows with wholesome waters, abounds with precious fruits, and is the constant resort of our souls' Beloved. Some of the sights there seen, such as the evil of sin and the wickedness of our own hearts, are not pleasant; but these make a sight of Jesus the more ravishing. Every child of God finds great treasure in this valley. Some have thought it better than the mount of transfiguration, and would gladly abide there all their days; for there they see Jesus as they never see him anywhere else. The place suits them well.

We often get a blessed view of our Saviour, when we are in the furnace of affliction. Sometimes its heat is intense; but the hotter, the better, if Jesus be with us, and our faith fail not. When the furnace of

Nebuchadnezzar was made seven times hotter than usual, and the three faithful Hebrews were cast into it, there was one seen walking with them, and "his form was like unto the Son of God." Many Christians declare that they never saw happier days than when adversity pressed hard upon them. This is just what Jesus promised: "I will not leave you comfortless: I will come to you." John xiv. 12.

But the brightest vision of Christ will be when "we shall see him as he is." The sight of husband, wife, child, parent, friend, or lover, never was so gladsome as the sight of the Saviour shall be. Blessed vision! The righteous long for it. To be with Christ, and like Christ, and to behold his glory, will constitute the heaven for which they hope. Though I should never see another pleasant sight in this world, may I at last behold that blessed face, which was buffeted for me. Once his visage was so marred more than any man, and his form more than the sons of men. But when Paul saw him on the way to Damascus, he shined with a light, "above the brightness of the sun." And when John saw him, he fell at his feet as dead; but he laid his hand upon him, saying, "Fear not; I am the first, and the last; I am he that liveth, and was dead, and behold I am alive for evermore, Amen; and have the keys of hell and of death." Rev. i. 17, 18. Lord Jesus, help me, intercede for me, comfort me, forsake me not, but bring me to behold thy face in righteousness.

All these blessed visions are by *the grace of our Lord Jesus Christ.* He is our *Lord*, our Governor, our King. "One is your Master, even Christ." "Ye call me Master and Lord, and ye say well; for so I am." "Other lords have had dominion over us; but by thee only will we make mention of thy name." Like Thomas let us ever say, "My Lord and my God!" If we really feel that he is our Master, and we his disciples; our Lord, and we his servants; we shall walk as he walked, we shall delight in his authority over us, we shall be happy in doing and suffering his holy will.

He is also *Jesus*, which is the proper name of our Saviour. No name was ever more appropriate. Joshua was a saviour, and so were many others; but they were so only as *instruments*, while he is the *author* of salvation. Their deliverances were temporal and political. His salvation is spiritual and everlasting.

Our Lord Jesus is *Christ*. The Hebrew word, *Messiah*, and the Greek word, *Christ*, both signify *anointed*. Christ was the Lord's anointed in the highest sense. He had the oil of gladness poured upon him above all his fellows. Thus we read in that beautiful narrative in Luke iv. 14—22: "And Jesus returned in the power of the Spirit into Galilee; and there went out a fame of him through all the region round about. And he taught in their synagogues, being glorified of all. And he came to Nazareth, where he had been brought up; and, as his custom was, he went into the synagogue on the Sabbath-day, and stood up for to read. And there was given him the book of the prophet Esaias. And when he had opened the book, he found the place, where it was written, The Spirit of the Lord God is upon me, because he hath anointed me to preach the gospel to the poor; he hath sent me to heal the broken-hearted, to preach deliverance to the captives, and recovering of sight to the blind, to set at liberty them that are bruised, to preach the acceptable year of the Lord. And he closed the book, and he gave it again to the minister, and sat down. And the eyes of all them that were in the synagogue were fastened on him. And he began to say unto them, This day is this Scripture fulfilled in your ears. And all bare him witness, and wondered at the gracious words which proceeded out of his mouth." This settles the fact, and points out the manner of his anointing. God the Father poured upon our Lord Jesus the Holy Ghost, and thus he became the Christ of God. Well might Peter say at the Council at Jerusalem, "We believe that through the grace of our Lord Jesus Christ, we shall be saved even as they." "The grace of our Lord Jesus Christ" is a phrase that occurs in the New Testament more than a dozen times, and always in a manner well suited to affect our hearts. Ten times it occurs in the form of a benediction: "The grace of our Lord Jesus Christ be with you," or "with your spirit," or "with you all." The text where it is mentioned most at length is found in 2 Cor. viii. 9: "Ye know the grace of our Lord Jesus Christ, that though he was rich, yet for your sakes he became poor, that ye through his poverty might be rich." There is the whole Gospel in epitome. The rich became poor, that the poor might become rich. Who would not wish to see this blessed Lord Jesus Christ?

When the celebrated Lord Duplessis of France was dying, he said: "Away, away with all merit; I call for nothing but mercy, free mercy." When secretly praying, he was heard to say, "I fly, I fly to heaven. Let the angels carry me to the bosom of my Saviour." Again he said, "I know that my Redeemer liveth, and I shall see him with these eyes," and so he went to the Saviour.

When near his end, Payson said: "I have done nothing myself. I have not fought, but Christ has fought for me; I have not run, but Christ has carried me; I have not worked, but Christ has wrought in me. Christ has done all." Who would not wish to see such a friend, such a Saviour!

CHAPTER XLIX.

THE DANGER OF REJECTING SALVATION.

ONE of the most solemn appeals ever made is that of Paul: "How shall we escape, if we neglect so great salvation?" The peril of despising the grace of our Lord Jesus Christ is extreme and awful. Some commit this sin secretly, others openly, some through ignorance, others knowingly, some with daring blasphemy, others with trembling; but all through unbelief. A late writer holds this language: "A meaning far different from the historical definition of divines is currently given to the word *salvation;* a word, however, which, after every softening, is not sincerely congenial with the highest religion of the time. Its direct opposition to *damnation* is very much lost, and instead of denoting mere rescue from a penal doom, it is accepted as an expression for *personal union with God*, *spiritual perfectness* of character: or without reference to any penal alternative, the *simple attainment of a blessed and immortal state.*" More error and misrepresentation are seldom found in so short a sentence. For what church ever taught that *salvation* is "mere rescue from a penal doom?" God's people are, indeed, "saved from wrath," and a great deliverance is thus vouchsafed to them. By the grace of Christ they do "escape the damnation of hell." But he, who rescues them from a just and fiery indignation, also clothes them with righteousness, makes them partakers of the divine nature, restores to them the lost image of God, fits them for the companionship of angels, and receives them to glory. "The attainment of a blessed and immortal state" is no less a part of the salvation secured by Jesus Christ, than is "rescue from a penal doom."

But still it seems "the word *salvation*, after every softening, is not sincerely congenial" with what this writer is pleased to call "the highest religion of the time." The highest religion! Is there any religion higher than that, which had its origin in heaven, "which at the first began to be spoken by the Lord, and was confirmed unto us by them that heard him: God also bearing them witness, both with signs and wonders, and with divers miracles, and gifts of the Holy Ghost, according to his own will?" Is there any religion above that, at the birth of whose author "a multitude of the heavenly host praised God, saying, Glory to God in the highest, and on earth peace, good will toward men?" What religion excels that, which takes poor, vile, ignorant, guilty, helpless sinners, and raises them to sonship with God, and makes them partakers of his holiness? If this writer means to say that there is a system of religion more elevated than that revealed in the Bible, then he is an infidel, and should be treated as such. That is, he ought to be instructed in the evidences of Christianity. In the Scriptures there is no "softening" of the words *save*, *saved*, and *salvation*. They occur in some hundreds of texts, and although they are not always, yet they are often used in the highest religious sense, both in the Old and New Testaments. Here are a few cases.

"SAVE thy people, and bless thine inheritance; feed them also, and lift them up for ever." Psa. xxviii. 9. "Thou shalt call his name JESUS; for he shall SAVE his people from their sins." Matt. i. 21. "The Son of man is come to seek and to SAVE that which was lost." Luke xix. 10. "It is a faithful saying, and worthy of all acceptation, that Christ Jesus came into the world to SAVE sinners, of whom I am chief." 1 Tim. i. 15. "He is able also to SAVE them to the uttermost, that come unto God by him." Heb. vii. 25. "Israel shall be SAVED in the Lord with an everlasting SALVATION." Isa. xlv. 17. "Believe in the Lord Jesus Christ and thou shalt be SAVED." Acts xiv. 31. "Thou art the God of my SALVATION." Psa. xxv. 5. "God hath chosen you to SALVATION." 2 Thess. ii. 13. Many other texts might be added, but these are sufficient. Inspired writers and converted men are not shy of these words. They love them. They glory in them. Meantime what a confession does our author make for himself and for a class, whom he represents. Their religion does not accord with even the *terms* of the Bible. With the Romanist and Romanizer baptism is regeneration. With some, sin is a misfortune, not a crime; wrath is a fiction, hell a chimĕra, damnation a fancy, and even SALVATION a dream. How slow are men in learning that spiritual things are spiritually discerned, and that the kingdom of heaven can be entered by none but little children! "The state of the heart has the chief influence, in the search after truth. Humility, contrition, simplicity, sanctity—these are the handmaids of the understanding in the investigation of religion." The pride of science, the flippancy of self-conceit, the arrogance of spiritual ignorance are great foes to learning the simple truth. To all who are wise in their own eyes, even "the word *salvation* is not sincerely congenial."

Its "direct opposition to damnation" is clearly taught in Scripture, as in Mark xvi. 16. "He that believeth and is baptized, shall be saved; but he that believeth not shall be damned." To the humble such words are not offensive. They love the truth. But that such sounds are exceedingly unwelcome to the ears of the unregenerate, every preacher of righteousness painfully knows. It seems to be impossible for some men to *endure sound doctrine.* They have no congeniality with it, no taste for it, yet they do not all, like this writer, attack both the doctrines and the very words of the Holy Ghost. Let such remember who it is that has said, "He that believeth on him, is not condemned; but he that believeth not, is condemned already, because he hath not believed in the name of the only begotten Son of God." "He that believeth on the Son hath everlasting life: and he that believeth not the Son, shall not see life; but the wrath of God abideth on him." John iii. 18, 36. Nay, so clear is the evidence of the truth of God's word, that men who refuse to receive it shall still be judged by it. Christ says expressly, "He that rejecteth me, and receiveth not my words, hath one that judgeth him: the words that I have spoken, the same shall judge him in the last day." John xii. 48.

If the word *salvation* is distasteful, how is the thing itself? Do men of this school have any sense of their lost condition? Admitting human innocence, the offer of salvation is worse than idle; but before a man can rest in the persuasion that he is without sin, and not under wrath, he must renounce God's word, sear his own conscience, and be fearfully left to himself. No man more needs the pity and prayers of his neighbours, or the compassion of his Maker, than he who thinks he is without sin, and has no need of a Saviour. Yet there certainly is a class of men, who dislike not only damnation, but salvation, not only wrath, but grace, not only the divine severity, but also the goodness of God. A conversion, more than the death of a sinner, a revival of religion more than a pestilence, seem to arouse the enmity of the carnal mind. The practical view of fallen human nature presented by such persons as this writer is appalling proof of the blindness and wickedness of men. When a starving man is too proud to receive bread, when a man bleeding to death rejects the aid of a surgeon, when a drowning man refuses the rope, that is thrown him, there is in each case folly and wilfulness; but there is no such madness, no such perverseness, as when a sinner rejects mercy, grace, salvation. "Ye will not come to me, that ye might have life;" "how can ye believe, which receive honour one of another, and seek not the honour that cometh from God only?" are among the kind and solemn teachings of Christ to those who refuse his grace.

Converted men feel very differently about *salvation*. To them there is no sweeter word, unless it is the name of Jesus, which means Saviour. A young Hindoo convert when dying, said to his attendant: "Sing, brother, sing." His friend said: "Of what shall I sing?" He replied; "O sing of salvation, sing of salvation." Thousands have substantially said the same thing. They were not ashamed of the testi mony of our Lord, who saved them and called them with a holy calling, not according to their works, but according to his own purpose and grace, which was given them in Christ Jesus before the world began. Every redeemed sinner loves salvation, loves to sing of it and to publish it abroad. Where is the Christian that does not unite in this song?

Salvation, O salvation!
The joyful sound proclaim,
Till earth's remotest nation
Has learned Messiah's name.

If you love not salvation, you love not our Lord Jesus Christ and will be accursed when he cometh. He, that hates salvation, loves death. If you despise grace, you despise your own mercies. Prophets, apostles, martyrs, and people of God of every age have not ceased to proclaim, and upon divine authority too, that Christ is our Life. "Neither is there salvation in any other: for there is none other name under heaven, given among men, whereby we must be saved." Acts iv. 12. And how dreadful it will be to perish with the offer of mercy pressed upon us by the Lord! We shall die without remedy because we shall then have sinned against the only remedy. Inspired writers seem to be filled with horror, whenever they contemplate sinners rejecting salvation. Hear Paul: "He that despised Moses' law, died without mercy under two or three witnesses: of how much sorer punishment, suppose ye, shall he be thought worthy, who hath trodden under foot the Son of God, and hath counted the blood of the covenant, wherewith he was sanctified, an unholy thing, and hath done despite to the Spirit of grace? For we know him that hath said, Vengeance belongeth unto me, I will recompense, saith the Lord. And again, The Lord shall judge his people. It is a fearful thing to fall into the hands of the living God." Heb. x. 28—31.

CHAPTER L.

THE WONDERS OF GRACE WILL NEVER CEASE.

THE elder President Edwards has written an admirable work, called "The History of Redemption." He, who shall read it, will be well rewarded. But in *no* sense will the history of redemption be complete till the last of the elect shall be called, justified, sanctified and glorified. And in the *highest* sense that history will never be finished, for redemption will for ever be evolving new objects of admiration and thanksgiving. It may well be doubted whether all the books extant, which record the wonders of God's love in the application of redemption to the souls of men, possess interest and variety equal to the rich storehouse of spiritual knowledge, which would be opened to us, if the religious experience of all living Christians were perfectly delineated. Indeed the inward life of every child of God is the history of the application of redemption in epitome. What heights and depths of religious experience belong to every generation of the people of God! The thief on the cross was, doubtless, not the last dying culprit, who sought and found mercy. Saul of Tarsus was not the last blasphemer and persecutor, to whom the Lord sent salvation. Manasseh was not the last gray-headed sinner that repented and turned to the Lord, who "was entreated of him, and heard his supplication." Scores of such are living in every Christian nation, proving that a man can be born again when he is old.. There are now living and may be seen thousands of people, who well illustrate the patience of the saints, who are patterns of meekness, who love tenderly and strongly, who constantly lament the sins of their times, who have learned in whatsoever state they are therewith to be content, who rejoice in tribulation, who bear all things, believe all things, hope all things, endure all things, and yet count not themselves to have attained, neither are they already perfect, but they are striving after higher attainments, and pressing forward towards the mark for the prize of their high calling in Christ Jesus. It is great kindness in God to give to the world, in the persons of his people of every generation, bright examples of virtuous, happy poverty, of cheerful submission in affliction, of a noble spirit of self-sacrifice, of great gentleness of heart, of tenderness of conscience, and of the true fear of God, so undeniable that even men of the world see and reverence the power of divine grace. God also from age to age deals with much patience and gentleness towards timid, feeble-minded, humble souls. Out of the mouths of babes and sucklings he ordains strength. In times of vengeance he spares his people "as a man spareth his own son that serveth him;" he comforts them as a mother comforteth her own child; he is to them a sun and a shield, a rock of defence and a high tower, a refuge and a present help in time of trouble; from them he withholds no good thing; he gives them peace in believing; he is merciful to their unrighteousness; he blots out their sins; he loves them freely; he accepts them graciously; in them he shows what his grace can still do; to them he fulfils all the exceeding great and precious promises of the covenant. The worm Jacob threshes the mountains. God evinces every day that the race is not to the swift, nor the battle to the strong. By his grace the feeble among the saints are yet as David, and the house of David as the angel of God. All these things occur from age to age in a manner so striking as to arrest the attention of all, who have spiritual discernment. In every generation the God of patience grants to his servants with one mind, and one mouth to glorify God, even the Father of our Lord Jesus Christ. The oath of the covenant, the blood of Jesus, his intercession in heaven, and the power of his Spirit achieve these wonders. God is unchangeable. Jesus Christ is the same yesterday, to-day, and for ever. The covenant is perpetual. A promise made to a believer three thousand years ago is good and true in the case of all believers. "Whatsoever things were written aforetime, were written for our learning, that we through patience and comfort of the Scriptures might have hope."

One of the most remarkable chapters in the history of God's church has been furnished by modern missions to the heathen. Wherever the gospel is preached and takes effect, it produces marvellous results. A Hindoo woman applied for baptism. The servant of Christ told her, as in candor he was bound to do, what she must suffer, the loss of caste, the displeasure of her husband, and many persecutions. She replied: "I know all this; I considered about that before I came to you. I am ready and willing to bear it all. I am ready to sacrifice all to my Lord. Surely, sir, I cannot endure anything in comparison to what he suffered for me."

On his death-bed John Brown of Haddington said: "Here is a wonder—a sinner saved by the blood of God's Son! There are wonders in heaven, and wonders in the earth; but the least part of redemption's work is more wonderful than they all."

CHAPTER LI

THE OFFERS OF FREE GRACE ARE TO ALL INDISCRIMINATELY.

It is always right and obligatory to point men to Christ. Eternal life by the Son of God is to be pressed upon their acceptance. No man has any commission to preach the gospel except one that bids him offer mercy "to every creature." "Whosoever will" is scriptural language. This method of proclaiming salvation suits all classes of men. The strong believer and the timid penitent alike draw life and hope from Christ freely offered. "Weak souls are to be comforted with Christ, not with their own faith." Even a young believer may look to Christ until his heart burns within him, and he shouts for joy; but let any man look steadfastly at his own weakness, vileness, guilt, and misery, and not get a glimpse of Christ crucified, and hope will die within him. God never mocks any of his creatures. And while it is true that Jesus Christ died with the intention of saving his people, and none others, as he himself says, "I lay down my life for the sheep;" yet it is no less true that there is an infinite storehouse of merit in Jesus Christ. It is also certain that by God's authority, a full and free salvation is indiscriminately offered to sinners. The final ruin of incorrigible transgressors will be brought about by their unbelief, not by the scantiness of the provisions of the gospel; by their enmity, not by any want of merit in Christ; by their hardness of heart, not by any lack of sincerity in the offers of salvation; by their wilful rejection of blood-bought mercy, not by the insufficiency of the work and sufferings of Jesus Christ. It is no part of sound doctrine that the merit of our Saviour will be exhausted in the salvation of those whom the Father gave to the Son, in the covenant of redemption. No branch of the church of Christ holds that Christ's humiliation and sufferings would have been less if the number of his elect had been less; nor that his humiliation and sufferings would have been greater if his chosen had been more numerous. The merit of Christ is in its very nature boundless. It possesses infinite, inexhaustible worth. The offer of life is to be made indiscriminately because God so commands, because finite men can make it in no other way, and because the provisions of the gospel are as well suited to the wants of one man as to those of another. The call to men to believe the gospel should be earnest and urgent, because God so makes it, because the matter is of infinite moment, because men are very sottish in their sins, and so greatly need to be aroused from their guilty slumbers, and because their damnation slumbereth not. The offer of salvation is sincere, for God says so. It is consistent, because God never denies himself. It is kind, because it is sent in love, and cost more than we shall ever be able to repay. This has been and is the doctrine of all pure churches.

The words of the Synod of Dort are express: "The death of the Son of God is the only and most perfect sacrifice and satisfaction for sins, of infinite price and value, abundantly sufficient to expiate the sins of the whole world." Again: "The promise of the gospel is, that whosoever believeth in Christ crucified, shall not perish, but have everlasting life. Which promise ought to be announced and proposed, promiscuously and indiscriminately, to all nations and men, to whom God in his good pleasure hath sent the gospel, with the command to repent and believe."

The London Baptists' Confession says: "The preaching of the gospel to the conversion of sinners, is absolutely free; no way requiring, as absolutely necessary, any qualifications, preparations, or terrors of the law, or preceding ministry of the law, but only and alone the naked soul, a sinner and ungodly, to receive Christ crucified, dead and buried, and risen again; who is made a Prince and a Saviour for such sinners as through the gospel shall be brought to believe on him."

Calvin says: "We know the promises to be effectual to us only when we receive them by faith: on the contrary, the annihilation of faith is the abolition of the promises. If this is their nature, we may perceive that there is no discordance between these two things: God's having appointed from eternity on whom he will bestow his favour and exercise his wrath, and his proclaiming salvation to all. Indeed, I maintain that there is the most perfect harmony between them." In the Synod of Dort we have an example of the very staunchest Calvinists who have met in modern times; in Calvin we have the very ablest expounder of the doctrines of grace since the days of Augustine, if not since the days of Paul, yet they would have salvation offered to all.

Few men have written on the death of Christ with

more force than John Owen. His matured sentiments on this subject have been precious to the people of God for two full centuries. He says that "it was the intention and purpose of God that his Son should offer a sacrifice of infinite worth, value, and dignity, sufficient in itself for the redeeming of all and every man, if it had pleased the Lord to employ it to that purpose; yea, and of other worlds also, if the Lord should freely make them, and would redeem them. Sufficient, we say then, was the sacrifice of Christ for the redemption of the whole world, and for the expiation of all the sins of all and every man in the world. This sufficiency of his sacrifice hath a two-fold rise. First, the dignity of the person that did offer and was offered. Secondly, the greatness of the pain he endured, by which he was able to bear, and did undergo the whole curse of the law of God due to sin; *and this sets out the innate, real, true worth of the blood-shedding of Jesus Christ.*" If any man has a more blessed gospel than this to preach, he has not yet told the world what it is.

Flavel says: "It is confessed, there is sufficiency of virtue in the sacrifice of Christ to redeem the whole world."

Manton says: "For these six thousand years, God has been multiplying pardons, and yet free grace is not tired. Christ undertook to satisfy, and he hath money enough to pay. It were folly to think that an emperor's revenue will not pay a beggar's debt. Mercy is an ocean, ever flowing, yet ever full."

The Rev. Thomas Boston says, that "there was virtue and efficacy enough in Christ's oblation to satisfy offended justice for the sins of the whole world, yea, and of millions of worlds more; for his blood hath infinite value, because of the excellency and dignity of his person."

John Brown of Haddington: "Such is the infinite dignity of Christ's person, that his fulfilment of the broken law is sufficient to balance all the debt of all the elect, nay, of millions of guilty worlds." In proof, he refers to Col. ii. 9; Isa. vii. 14, and ix. 6; Jer. xxiii. 6; Zech. xiii. 7; Titus ii. 13, 14, and Acts xx. 28. Again he says, that "In respect of its intrinsic worth as the obedience and sufferings of a divine person, Christ's satisfaction is sufficient for the ransom of all mankind, and being fulfilled in human nature, is equally suited to all their necessities." No surer, broader foundation for a sincere, consistent, general offer of mercy and grace could be desired, than is here admitted to exist in the finished work of the Mediator.

Dr. Witherspoon lays down three propositions on this subject, which can hardly be questioned. 1. "The obedience and death of Christ are of value sufficient to expiate the guilt of all the sins of every individual that ever lived, or ever shall live on earth. This cannot be denied, since the subjects to be redeemed are finite, the price paid for their redemption infinite." 2. "Notwithstanding this, every individual of the human race is not in fact partaker of this purchase, but many die in their sins, and perish for ever." 3. "There is in the death of Christ a sufficient foundation laid for the preaching of the gospel indefinitely to all without exception. It is the command of God that this should be done. Mark xvi. 15: 'And he said unto them, Go ye into all the world, and preach the gospel to every creature.' The effect of this is, that the misery of the unbelieving and impenitent shall be entirely at their own door; and they shall not only die in their own sins, but shall suffer to eternity for the most heinous of all sins, despising the remedy and refusing to hear the Son of God."

It may not be generally known how much the urgent and indiscriminate offer of salvation by grace has been opposed. The great Secession from the Church of Scotland, under Erskine and others, was in part because of the wrong done to this blessed truth by the loose men who were the dominant party of that day. At least the Moderates then greatly impugned the doctrine of free offers of life to sinners. It may well be doubted whether a scene partaking more of the moral sublime has occurred in the last hundred and fifty years, than when Ebenezer Erskine arose in the Synod of Fife and said: "Moderator, our Lord Jesus says of himself, 'My Father giveth you the true bread from heaven.' This he uttered to a promiscuous multitude; and let me see the man who dare say he said wrong." The heavenly sweetness and solemnity of the speaker for the time hushed every controvertist.

Dr. Bellamy says: "Christ's merits are sufficient for all the world, and the door of mercy is opened wide enough for all the world; and God the supreme Governor has proclaimed himself reconcilable to all the world, if they will believe and repent." Let all sinners know that if they perish, it will not be because Christ has not died, nor because his merits are not sufficient to meet all the demands of law and justice against them, if they will but obey the gospel call.

Matthew Henry says: "The eleven apostles must send *others* to those places, where they could not *go themselves*, and, in short, make it the business of their lives to send the glad tidings of the gospel *up ana down the world*, with all possible fidelity and care, not as an amusement or entertainment, but as a solemn message from God to men, and an appointed means of making men happy. 'Tell as many as you can, and bid them tell others, it is a message of universal concern, and *therefore* ought to *have* a universal welcome, because it *gives* a universal welcome.'"

Dr. Doddridge: "The commission Christ gave his apostles, though it *began at Jerusalem*, did not end there; nor was it confined within the narrow limits of Judea; but they were appointed to *go into all the world, and preach the gospel to every creature.*"

Dr. Scott says that the apostles and their co-labourers "did testify to their fellow sinners everywhere, that 'the Father had sent the Son to be the Saviour of the world,' and to confer pardon, grace, and eternal life, on all men, in every place, who sought them from the Father, through the propitiation of the Son, by living faith in his name."

Dr. Hodge says: "The doctrine of the atonement produces in us its proper effects, when it leads us to see that God is just; that he is infinitely gracious; that we are deprived of all ground of boasting; that the way of salvation, which is open for us, is open for all men; and that the motives to all duty, instead of being weakened, are enforced and multiplied."

Haldane says that Christ's "sacrifice could not have been sufficient for any, if it had not been sufficient for all. An atonement of infinite value was necessary for every individual that shall be saved, and more could not be necessary for all the world. The intrinsic sufficiency of Christ's sacrifice was doubtless in view in the divine appointment concerning it. God made provision of such a sacrifice as was not only sufficient effectually to take away the sins of all the elect; but also sufficient to be laid before all mankind, in the dispensation of the gospel. In the gospel it was to be declared to all mankind that, in their nature, the Son of God had made an atonement of infinite value, and brought in everlasting righteousness, which shall be upon all that believe. This atonement, then, being all-sufficient in itself, is proclaimed to all who hear the gospel. All are invited to rely upon it for pardon and acceptance, as freely and fully as if they knew that God designed it for them from all eternity, and all who thus rely upon it shall experience the blessing of its efficacy and infinite value."

Let not perishing men, therefore, stand at a distance and say, There is no way of escape, no door of mercy open, no salvation offered to us, and we must die in our sins. The calls of the gospel are as sincere on the part of God to men, who refuse salvation, as to those who accept it. That is, God is infinitely sincere in all he says and does.

CHAPTER LII.

THE DOCTRINE OF FREE GRACE IS SAFE AND REFORMS SINNERS

If any doctrine can turn a serpent into a dove, or a lion into a lamb, it is the glorious doctrine of salvation by the grace of Christ. The reason why Paul was not ashamed of the Gospel was not because it was full of eloquence, or tragical scenes, or a pleasing philosophy, but because it was "the power of God unto salvation to every one that believeth." That system of truth, which reforms the vicious, puts the profane to praying, makes God-fearing men of drunkards, subdues the passionate, establishes every where the law of kindness, binds together the discordant elements of society by the golden chain of charity, and brings to those, who receive it, all the blessings of salvation, cannot have had its original from earth or hell. So Paul thought. Hence his zeal for the precious truth. "God forbid that I should glory save in the cross of our Lord Jesus Christ, by whom the world is crucified unto me, and I unto the world." "What things were gain to me those I counted loss for Christ. Yea doubtless, and I count all things but loss for the excellency of the knowledge of Christ Jesus my Lord." "We preach Christ crucified." "Other foundation can no man lay than that is laid, which is Jesus Christ." "We are fools for Christ, we are weak, we are despised. Even to this hour we both suffer hunger, and thirst, and are naked, and are buffeted, and have no certain dwelling-place, and labour, working with our own hands, being reviled, persecuted, defamed, we are made the filth of the world, and are the offscouring of all things unto this day." Men, who would joyfully bear such things, prove the power of the truth in their daily triumphs. Long before Paul's day, David celebrated the power of the truth: "The law of the Lord is perfect, converting the soul: the testimony of the Lord is sure, making wise the simple." One entire New Testament church consisted of those, who had been "darkness." Eph. v. 8. Another consisted in part of those, who had been fornicators, idolaters, adulterers, effeminate, abusers of themselves with mankind, thieves, covetous, drunkards, revilers and extortioners. But when the Gospel reached them in power, soon they were washed, sanctified, and justified in the name of the Lord Jesus, and by the Spirit of our God. 1 Cor. vi. 9—11.

The transforming power of the Gospel has always been celebrated by its friends. Lactantius says: "Give me a man of a passionate, abusive, headstrong disposition: with a few only of the words of God, I will make him gentle as a lamb. Give me a greedy, avaricious, tenacious wretch, and I will teach him to distribute his riches with a liberal and unsparing hand. Give me a cruel and blood-thirsty monster; and all his rage shall be changed into true benignity. Give me a man addicted to injustice, full of ignorance, and immersed in wickedness; he shall soon become just, prudent and innocent." Many writers, both ancient and modern, bear a similar testimony. When the missionaries first went to Greenland, for a long time, the savages mocked them, mimicked their reading, singing and praying, attempted to drown all devotion by hideous howlings, and the beating of drums, ridiculed them with the keenest sarcasms, upbraided them with their ignorance because they had to learn the language of their country, pelted them with stones, climbed on their shoulders, seized many of their goods and shattered them to pieces, and even attempted to destroy the little boat, which was essential to the procuring of their subsistence. In short they even meditated and attempted to murder them. They said: "Show us the God you describe, then will we believe in him and serve him." "We have prayed to him when we were sick, or had nothing to eat, but he heard us not." "We need nothing but a sound body and enough to eat." "Your heaven and your spiritual pleasures may be good enough for you, but they would be tiresome to us." Having for five years endured all obloquy, peril, suffering and derision, these humble missionaries were at length able to preach to the people and translate portions of Scripture for their use. At length one of them spoke of the redemption of sinners by Jesus Christ. "He was enabled to describe the sufferings and death of the Redeemer with more than ordinary force and energy; and he, at the same time, read to them from the New Testament the history of his agony and of his bloody sweat in the garden. Upon this one of their number, named Kaiarnak, stepped up to the table, and in an earnest affecting manner exclaimed. 'How was that? Tell me it once more; for I also would fain be saved.'" These words aroused the missionary to new life and energy and thus began that wonderful change, which has made Greenland so famous in the annals of Christianity. The history of Kaiarnak in subsequent life was not unlike that of the fierce, bloody Africaner after his conversion.

David Brainerd also tells us that the doctrines of grace were above all others blessed to the reformation of his poor Indians. "It is worthy of remark that numbers of these people are brought to a strict compliance with the rules of *morality* and *sobriety*, and to a conscientious performance of the *external duties* of Christianity by the *internal* power and influence of divine truths—the peculiar doctrines of grace—upon their minds; without their having these *moral duties* frequently repeated and inculcated upon them, and the contrary vices particularly exposed and spoken against." And he states quite at length how the truth operated upon them, curing their strongest evil propensities, and completely reforming their lives. The strong man armed may long keep his goods in peace, but when a stronger than he cometh, he taketh away his goods. It must be so. It is God's eternal plan and unchangeable purpose that Christ should destroy the works of the devil. How could it be otherwise? For Davenant well says that "by the death of Christ we are greatly stirred up, both to a caution against, and a detestation of sin: for that must needs be deadly, which could be healed in no other way than by the death of Christ." And Glascock says that "the sufferings and obedience of Christ afford the highest motives to dissuade from sin and press to holiness, and lay a man under an infinite obligation in point of gratitude to live unto God. That very grace, which enables him to believe in Christ, equally inclines him to love God." It always must be so. "If God's people at any time fall into sin," says Miller, "it is not while they are eyeing the perfection of Christ's righteousness, but when they lose sight of it." A heart moved by the love of Christ will love to make sacrifices of all it has for his glory. Augustine beautifully says: "How sweet it is to deny all sinful sweets! how pleasant it is to forego these sinful pleasures for the sake of Christ!"

Berridge says: "Morality can never thrive unless grounded wholly upon grace. The heathen, for want of this foundation could do nothing; they spoke some noble truths, but spoke to men with withered limbs and loathing appetites; they were like way-posts, which show a road, but cannot help a cripple forwards." "God has shown us in his word how little human wit and strength can do to compass reformation. Reason has explored the moral path, planted it with roses, and fenced it round with motives, but all in vain. Nature still recoils; no motives drawn from Plato's works, nor yet from the Gospel of Christ, will of themselves suffice; no cords will bind the heart to God and duty, but the cords of grace."

The prophet Zechariah (chapters xii. and xiii.) well describes the process of turning to God through Jesus Christ: "I will pour upon the house of David, and upon the inhabitants of Jerusalem, the spirit of grace, and of supplications: and they shall look upon me whom they have pierced, and they shall mourn for him, as one mourneth for his only son, and shall be in bitterness for him as one that is in bitterness for his firstborn. In that day shall there be a great mourning in

Jerusalem as the mourning of Hadadrimmon in the valley of Megiddon. And the land shall mourn, every family apart; the family of the house of David apart, and their wives apart; the family of the house of Nathan apart, and their wives apart; the family of the house of Levi apart, and their wives apart; the family of the house of Shimei apart, and their wives apart; all the families that remain, every family apart, and their wives apart. In that day there shall be a fountain opened to the house of David and to the inhabitants of Jerusalem for sin and for uncleanness. And it shall come to pass in that day, saith the Lord of hosts, that I will cut off the names of the idols out of the land, and they shall no more be remembered; and also I will cause the [false] prophets and the unclean spirit to pass out of the land." Here we are informed 1. that God's Spirit is necessary to bring men to true repentance; 2. that the Holy Spirit takes of the things of Christ and shows them to men for their salvation; 3. that Gospel truth when rightly understood affects all classes alike, even David, the king, Nathan, the prophet, Levi, the priest, Shimei, one of the lowest of the people, men and their wives; 4. that true repentance inclines people to go alone and weep; 5. that such weeping will lead the soul to the blood of Christ; 6. and then idolatry and error, sin and heresy will be driven from among the people. Such weeping for sin will weep away all love of iniquity. One believing view of Christ does more to mortify sin than all the terrors of the Lord. The late Dr. Matthews of New Albany said: "In my opinion the sun is not more evidently intended, nor better calculated to warm, and enlighten the earth;

the eye is not more evidently fitted for the purposes of vision, than are these doctrines to enlighten and purify the mind, to make us, and keep us sincere, humble, devout, intelligent and useful Christians." Such testimonies ought to have weight.

The powerlessness of mere principles of morality, and the mighty energy of Gospel truths are strikingly illustrated in the ministry of Dr. Chalmers at Kilmany. When about to leave that parish in 1815, he delivered an address to the inhabitants, in which he said: "I cannot but record the effect of an actual, though undesigned experiment, which I prosecuted for upward of twelve years among you. For the greater part of that time I could expatiate on the meanness of dishonesty, on the villainy of falsehood, on the despicable arts of calumny; in a word upon all those deformities of character, which awaken the natural indignation of the human heart against the pests and disturbers of human society. Now, could I, upon the strength of these warm expostulations, have got the thief to give up his stealing, and the evil speaker his censoriousness, and the liar his deviations from truth, I should have felt all the repose of one who had gotten his ultimate object. It never occurred to me that all this might have been done, and yet the soul of every hearer have remained in full alienation from God: and that even could I have established in the bosom of one, who stole, such a principle of abhorrence at the meanness of dishonesty, that he was prevailed upon to steal no more, he might still have retained a heart as completely unturned to God, as totally unpossessed of a principle of love to him as before. In a word, though I might have made him a more upright and honourable man, I might have left him as destitute of religious principle as ever. But the interesting fact is that during the whole of that period, in which I made no attempt against the natural enmity of the mind to God, while I was inattentive to the way, in which this enmity is dissolved, even by the free offer on the one hand, and the believing acceptance on the other, of the Gospel salvation, while Christ, through whose blood the sinner, who by nature stands afar off, is brought near to the heavenly Lawgiver whom he has offended, was ever scarcely spoken of, or spoken of in such a way as stripped Him of all the importance of his character and his offices, even at this time I certainly did press the reformation of honour, and truth, and integrity among my people; but I never once heard of any such reformation having been effected among them. I am not sensible that all the vehemence with which I urged the virtues and the proprieties of social life, had the weight of a feather on the moral habits of my parishioners. And it was not till I got impressed by the utter alienation of the heart in all its desires and affections from God; it was not till reconciliation to him became the distinct and prominent object of my ministerial exertions; it was not till I took the scriptural way of laying the method of reconciliation before them; it was not till the free offer of forgiveness through the blood of Christ was urged upon their acceptance, and the Holy Spirit given through the channel of Christ's mediatorship to all who ask him, was set before them as the unceasing object of their dependence and their prayers; in one word, it was not till the contemplations of my people were turned to these great and essential elements in the business of a soul providing for its interests with God and the concerns of eternity, that I ever heard of any of those subordinate reformations, which I aforetime made the earnest and the zealous, but I am afraid at the same time, the ultimate object of my earlier ministrations. Ye servants, whose scrupulous fidelity has now attracted the notice, and drawn forth in my hearing a delightful testimony from your masters, what mischief you would have done, had your zeal for doctrines and sacraments been accompanied by the sloth and remissness, and what, in the prevailing tone of relaxation, is accounted the allowable purloining of your earlier days! But a sense of your Heavenly Master's eye has brought another influence to bear upon you; and while you are thus striving to adorn the doctrine of God your Saviour in all things, you may, poor as you are, reclaim the great ones of the land to the acknowledgment of the faith. You have at least taught me, that to preach Christ is the only effective way of preaching morality in all its branches."

CHAPTER LIII.

THE CONCLUSION.—AN OFFER OF LIFE MADE TO THE PERISHING.

THE end of ploughing and sowing is the harvest. The end of trial is reward. The end of this discussion should be salvation. Respected reader, will you not flee from the wrath to come, and lay hold on eternal life? Do you need assurance of a cordial reception from Christ? The Scriptures give it in every variety of form. They utter no uncertain sound. Listen to their voice. By Moses God says: "Oh that they were wise, that they understood this, that they would consider their latter end." Deut. xxxii. 29. Moses was hardly dead when by Joshua God called again: "Fear the Lord and serve him in sincerity and in truth." Josh. xxiv. 14. By that great prophet Elijah he expostulates thus: "How long halt ye between two opinions? If the LORD be God follow him, but if Baal, then follow him." 1 Kings xviii. 21. By David he calls us saying: "Kiss the Son, lest he be angry, and ye perish from the way, when his wrath is kindled but a little. Blessed are all they that put their trust in him." Psa. ii. 12. By David's son, Solomon, God again promises his love, saying: "Wisdom crieth without; she uttereth her voice in the streets: she crieth in the chief-places of concourse, in the openings of the gates; in the city she uttereth her words, saying,

How long, ye simple ones, will ye love simplicity, and the scorners delight in scorning, and fools hate knowledge? Turn you at my reproof: behold, I will pour out my Spirit unto you, I will make known my words unto you." Prov. i. 20—23. By Isaiah, animated with the brightest hopes and the most cheering truths, he says: "Ho, every one that thirsteth, come ye to the waters, and he that hath no money; come ye, buy and eat; yea come, buy wine and milk without money and without price. Wherefore do ye spend money for that which is not bread, and your labour for that which satisfieth not? Hearken diligently unto me, and eat ye that which is good, and let your soul delight itself in fatness. Incline your ear, and come unto me: hear and your soul shall live; and I will make an everlasting covenant with you, even the sure mercies of David." Isa. lv. 1—3. By the tender-hearted, weeping Jeremiah God says: "I will yet plead with you, and with your children's children will I plead." "Wilt thou not from this time cry unto me, My Father, thou art the guide of my youth?" Jer. ii. 9, and iii. 4. By the majestic and vehement Ezekiel, Jehovah swears: "As I live, saith the LORD God, I have no pleasure in the death of the wicked, but that the wicked turn from his wicked way and live; turn ye, turn ye from your evil ways; for why will ye die, O house of Israel?" Ezek. xxxiii. 11. By Hosea God lovingly says: "I will betroth thee unto me for ever; yea, I will betroth thee unto me in righteousness, and in judgment, and in loving-kindness, and in mercies. I will even betroth thee unto me in faithfulness. * * * O Israel, thou hast destroyed thyself, but in me is thy help." Hos. ii. 19, 20, and xiii. 9. By Zechariah God proclaims his grace, saying, "Turn you to the strong hold, ye prisoners of hope: even to-day do I declare that I will render double unto thee." Zech. ix. 12.

When Jesus Christ came he cried; "Come unto me, all ye that labour and are heavy laden, and I will give you rest. Take my yoke upon you, and learn of me: for I am meek and lowly in heart; and ye shall find rest unto your souls. For my yoke is easy and my burden is light." "Him that cometh unto me I will in no wise cast out." "In the last day, that great day of the feast, Jesus stood and cried saying, If any man thirst, let him come unto me and drink." Matt. xi. 28—30, John vi. 37, and vii. 37. And blessed Paul says, that "God was in Christ reconciling the world unto himself, not imputing their trespasses unto them; and hath committed unto us the word of reconciliation. Now then we are ambassadors for Christ, as though God did beseech you by us, we pray you in Christ's stead be ye reconciled to God." 2 Cor. v. 19, 20. And as if all these forms of speech were not enough, our Lord after his ascension to heaven spake words of the kindest invitation, which are recorded in the very last book of Scripture. Hear them: "Behold, I stand at the door and knock: if any man hear my voice and open the door, I will come in to him, and will sup with him, and he with me." "I Jesus have sent mine angel to testify unto you these things in the churches. The Spirit and the bride say, Come. And let him that heareth say, Come. And let him that is athirst come. And whosoever will, let him take the water of life freely." Rev. iii. 20, 22, xvi. 17. Indeed the whole tenor of the Saviour's call is, "Repent ye and believe the gospel." Mark i. 15. "This is his commandment: That we should believe on the name of his Son Jesus Christ." 1 John iii. 23. "He that believeth on the Son hath everlasting life: and he that believeth not the Son, shall not see life; but the wrath of God abideth on him." John iii. 36.

These divine sentences are presented in one unbroken connection that you may see how rich is the variety of forms, in which perishing sinners are called to light and life. They are commanded, invited, besought, warned, threatened, wooed by promises, allured by kindnesses, and pointed to the coming wrath, and all for the purpose of bringing them to Christ.

There has been much said about the warrant for believing in Christ. But sinners need no warrant for their faith beyond what God's word has given. Traill says: "This is the call of the gospel, he that dares trust Christ with his soul upon the warrant of the gospel shall be saved for ever. The Lord tries people this way. We have no more to do but to take pen in hand, and say, Amen, O Lord: it is a good bargain and a true word, and I will trust my soul on it." No man requires any other authority than that of his Maker for doing anything. What was Abraham's authority for offering up Isaac? The command of God and nothing else. We have the same command for believing in the Lord Jesus. What warrant has any man for going to an entertainment? If he has the invitation of him, who makes the feast, that is enough. It is folly to seek any other. Well, God says, "Come, for all things are now ready." When a wife beseeches her husband not to herd with the worthless and drunken, can he be at any loss to know what conduct will please her? When a government connects the heaviest penalties with a course of behaviour, do we need any other helps to know its will? Now God has heaped offer upon offer. He has pledged his word before the universe. He has bound himself by his oath. He is the God of truth and cannot lie. Yea, he spared not his own Son, but delivered him up for us all. That Son has suffered all and done all, that was necessary for our complete restoration; and the Spirit of Christ has gone forth calling men to repentance. Messengers, who themselves were once condemned and afterwards obtained mercy without any merit of their own, have been sent abroad all over the earth, and commanded to make an urgent and indiscriminate offer of grace to all the rebellious, who will throw down their arms, and receive a pardon bought with blood. Many millions of our race have sought and found salvation. Indeed from the days of our first parents to this hour, there has been a long line of sinners redeemed and saved by the blood of Jesus and the grace of God. Each one of these is a monument of the rich, free, saving mercy of Jehovah. Each one testifies how freely Jesus will forgive. Does any one wish to know how God will treat returning, penitent sinners? Let him behold the loving-kindness of the Lord to the thousands and ten thousands of his murderers in Jerusalem, who soon after his ascension to glory sought and obtained full pardon. Not one of all our race has ever been recovered from the ruins of the apostacy, who does not stand to tell how rich are the drops of atoning blood, how ample is the robe of Christ's righteousness, how kind is the Father of mercies, how loving is the Holy Spirit, how free and abundant is the grace of God. Authority for laying hold of salvation is found in every call, command and exhortation to turn and live. Come, come to Jesus Christ. Come all. Come now. With John Brown of Whitburn we boldly say that "the vilest of men have just the same right to Christ and his merits, as the best of men; a right founded not in their awakened desires, nor on anything in themselves, but purely, solely, entirely on the free grace of the Saviour. We are all sinners, though in a greater or less degree; and we all flee to Christ, not as deserving, but as guilty creatures." The Lord justifieth *the ungodly*, who believe in Jesus. O come to Christ before it is too late, lest like the Emperor Adrian when dying you should exclaim: "O my poor wandering soul! alas! whither art thou going? where must thou lodge this night? Thou shalt never jest any more, never be merry any more." Will you believe? Will you be saved by Jesus Christ? WILL YOU?

Now the God of peace that brought again from the dead our Lord Jesus Christ, that great Shepherd of the sheep, through the blood of the everlasting covenant, make you perfect in every good work to do his will, working in you that which is well-pleasing in his sight, through Jesus Christ; to whom be glory for ever and ever. Amen.

THE END.